D1387164

C++ in the Lab

Lab Manual to Accompany
C++ *How To Program, Fourth Edition*

**Deitel™ Books, Cyber Classrooms, Complete Tra
published by ●**

HOW TO PROGRAM **Series**

Advanced Java™ 2 Platform How to Program

C How to Program, 3/E

C++ How to Program, 4/E

C# How to Program

e-Business and e-Commerce How to Program

Internet and World Wide Web How to Program, 2/E

Java™ How to Program, 4/E

Perl How to Program

Python How to Program

Visual Basic® 6 How to Program

Visual Basic® .NET How to Program, 2/E

Visual C++® .NET How to Program (Fall 2002)

Wireless Internet & Mobile Business How to Program

XML How to Program

DEITEL™ Developer **Series**

Java™ Web Services for Experienced
  Programmers
Web Services A Technical Introduction
Java 2 Micro Edition for Experienced
  Programmers (Spring 2003)
Java 2 Enterprise Edition for Experienced
  Programmers (Spring 2003)
ASP .NET and Web Services with Visual
  Basic® .NET for Experienced
  Programmers (Spring 2003)
ASP .NET and Web Services with C# for
  Experienced Programmers (Spring
  2003)
.NET A Technical Introduction (2003)

For Managers Series

e-Business and e-Commerce for Managers

.NET How to Program **Series**

C# How to Program
Visual Basic® .NET How to Program, 2/E
Visual C++ .NET How to Program (Fall
  2002)

Visual Studio® **Series**

C# How to Program
Visual Basic® .NET How to Program, 2/E
Visual C++ .NET How to Program (Fall
  2002)
Getting Started with Microsoft® Visual
  C++® 6 with an Introduction to MFC
Visual Basic® 6 How to Program

Coming Soon

e-books and e-whitepapers
Premium CourseCompass, WebCT and
  Blackboard Multimedia Cyber
  Classroom versions

ining Courses and Web-Based Training Courses
Prentice Hall

●

Multimedia Cyber Classroom and Web-Based Training Series

(For information regarding DEITEL™ Web-based training visit **www.ptgtraining.com**)

C++ Multimedia Cyber Classroom, 4/E

C# Multimedia Cyber Classroom

e-Business and e-Commerce Multimedia Cyber Classroom

Internet and World Wide Web Multimedia Cyber Classroom, 2/E

Java™ 2 Multimedia Cyber Classroom, 4/E

Perl Multimedia Cyber Classroom

Python Multimedia Cyber Classroom

Visual Basic® 6 Multimedia Cyber Classroom

Visual Basic® .NET Multimedia Cyber Classroom, 2/E

Wireless Internet & Mobile Business Programming Multimedia Cyber Classroom

XML Multimedia Cyber Classroom

The Complete Training Course Series

The Complete C++ Training Course, 4/E

The Complete C# Training Course

The Complete e-Business and e-Commerce Programming Training Course

The Complete Internet and World Wide Web Programming Training Course, 2/E

The Complete Java™ 2 Training Course, 4/E

The Complete Perl Training Course

The Complete Python Training Course

The Complete Visual Basic® 6 Training Course

The Complete Visual Basic® .NET Training Course, 2/E

The Complete Wireless Internet & Mobile Business Programming Training Course

The Complete XML Programming

●

To follow the Deitel publishing program, please register at

www.deitel.com/newsletter/subscribe.html

for the *DEITEL*™ *BUZZ ONLINE* e-mail newsletter.

To communicate with the authors, send e-mail to:

deitel@deitel.com

For information on corporate on-site seminars offered by Deitel & Associates, Inc. worldwide, visit:

www.deitel.com

For continuing updates on Prentice Hall and Deitel publications visit:

●

www.deitel.com,
www.prenhall.com/deitel or
www.InformIT.com/deitel

C++ in the Lab
Lab Manual to Accompany
C++ How to Program, Fourth Edition

H. M. Deitel
Deitel & Associates, Inc.

P. J. Deitel
Deitel & Associates, Inc.

T. R. Nieto
Deitel & Associates, Inc.

Prentice
Hall

PRENTICE HALL, Upper Saddle River, New Jersey 07458

Library of Congress Cataloging-in-Publication Data

On file

Vice President and Editorial Director: *Marcia Horton*
Acquisitions Editor: *Petra J. Recter*
Associate Editor: *Jennifer Cappello*
Vice President and Director of Production and Manufacturing, ESM: *David W. Riccardi*
Executive Managing Editor: *Vince O'Brien*
Managing Editor: *Tom Manshreck*
Formatter: *John F. Lovell*
Director of Creative Services: *Paul Belfanti*
Senior Manager, Artworks: *Patricia Burns*
Audio-Visual Editor: *Xiaohong Zhu*
Creative Director: *Carole Anson*
Design Technical Support: *John Christiana*
Cover Illustration: *Dr. Harvey Deitel, Tamara L. Newnam and Laura Treibick*
Manufacturing Manager: *Trudy Pisciotti*
Manufacturing Buyer: *Ilene Kahn*

 © 2003 by Prentice-Hall, Inc.
Upper Saddle River, New Jersey 07458

The authors and publisher of this book have used their best efforts in preparing this book. These efforts include the development, research, and testing of the theories and programs to determine their effectiveness. The authors and publisher make no warranty of any kind, expressed or implied, with regard to these programs or to the documentation contained in this book. The authors and publisher shall not be liable in any event for incidental or consequential damages in connection with, or arising out of, the furnishing, performance, or use of these programs.

Many of the designations used by manufacturers and sellers to distinguish their products are claimed as trademarks and registered trademarks. Where those designations appear in this book, and Prentice Hall and the authors were aware of a trademark claim, the designations have been printed in initial caps or all caps. All product names mentioned remain trademarks or registered trademarks of their respective owners.

All rights reserved. No part of this book may be reproduced, in any form or by any means, without permission in writing from the publisher.

Printed in the United States of America

10 9 8 7 6 5 4 3 2 1

ISBN 0-13-038478-X

Prentice-Hall International (UK) Limited, *London*
Prentice-Hall of Australia Pty. Limited, *Sydney*
Prentice-Hall Canada Inc., *Toronto*
Prentice-Hall Hispanoamericana, S.A., *Mexico*
Prentice-Hall of India Private Limited, *New Delhi*
Prentice-Hall of Japan, Inc., *Tokyo*
Pearson Education Asia Pte. Ltd., *Singapore*
Editora Prentice-Hall do Brasil, Ltda., *Rio de Janeiro*

Trademarks

DEITEL, DIVE INTO, and LIVE CODE are trademarks of Deitel and Associates, Inc.

Contents

Preface

Many colleges conduct programming classes in laboratory environments. This lab manual complements our introductory/intermediate textbook, *C++ How to Program, Fourth Edition,* and the optional *C++ Multimedia Cyber Classroom, Fourth Edition,* by providing a series of hands-on lab assignments designed to reinforce students' understanding of lecture material. For continuing updates on this lab manual and all Deitel & Associates, Inc. publications and services, please register at **www.deitel.com/newsletter/subscribe.html** to receive the *The DEITEL™ BUZZ ONLINE* e-mail newsletter.

Closed Laboratories

There are two types of Computer Science laboratory classes—*closed laboratories* and *open laboratories*. Closed laboratories are scheduled classes supervised by an instructor. Closed laboratories provide an excellent learning environment because students can apply concepts presented in class to carefully designed lab problems. Additionally, instructors are better able to gauge the students' understanding of the material by monitoring the students' progress in lab. This lab manual is designed for closed laboratory sessions of approximately two hours each. Open laboratories do not have specified meeting times and students do not work on the lab assignments under an instructor's supervision; this lab manual also can be used effectively for open laboratories and self-study.

About C++ in the Lab

This lab manual focuses on Chapters 1–14 and 17 of *C++ How to Program, Fourth Edition.*[1] Each chapter in this lab manual corresponds to its equivalent chapter in *C++ How to Program, Fourth Edition,* and is divided into three major sections: *Prelab Activities*, *Lab Exercises* and *Postlab Activities*.[2] Each chapter contains the following pedagogic features:

Objectives Section

The Objectives section formally introduces a chapter's lab by highlighting the key topics to be covered. After completing the lab, students can confirm their mastery of the material by reviewing the objectives.

---

1. These chapters are appropriate for introductory/intermediate-level Computer Science courses. Professors desiring labs for higher-numbered chapters or additional laboratory materials for Chapters 1–14 and 17 should contact the authors at **deitel@deitel.com** We will respond promptly. Please provide us with your specific requirements and as much advance notice as possible.
2. We expect few introductory classes to advance beyond Chapter 10 of this lab manual. For this reason, the labs in Chapters 11–14 and 17 do not contain the extensive sets of activities available in the previous chapters. Nevertheless, instructors will be able to conduct effective labs using the exercises we have included on these topics.

Assignment Checklist

Each chapter contains an assignment checklist, which allows students to mark which exercises the instructor assigns. Each page in the lab manual is perforated, so students can submit their answers (if required) by tearing out the pages.

Prelab Activities

Prelab Activities are intended to be completed by students after studying each chapter in *C++ How to Program, Fourth Edition*. *Prelab Activities* test students' understanding of the material presented in *C++ How to Program, Fourth Edition* and in lecture, and prepare students for the programming exercises presented in the lab session. (These activities may be finished before or during lab, at the instructor's discretion.) The exercises focus on important terminology and programming concepts and make excellent self-review problems for students. This lab manual contains the following types of *Prelab Activities*:

140 Matching Exercises (count includes separate parts)

Matching exercises present students with a column of important programming terms and a column of descriptions of those terms. Students must match the terms to the corresponding definitions. These exercises help ensure that students understand important terminology.

134 Fill-in-the-Blank Exercises

Fill-in-the-blank exercises present students with sentences missing key words; students must provide the missing word(s). Like the matching exercises, these exercises ensure that students understand important terminology.

68 Short-Answer Questions

Short-answer questions ask focused questions to test students' understanding of C++ concepts. Students are expected to provide a brief answer for each question.

55 Programming-Output Exercises

Reading code is as important as writing code. The programming-output exercises provide students with short code segments and ask the students to determine what each segment does, without the student actually running the program. These exercises reinforce students' understanding of program control and programming concepts.

71 Correct-the-Code Exercises

Error detection and debugging are some of the most important and most difficult skills to master in computer programming. The correct-the-code exercises provide students with code segments that contain one or more errors. Students are asked to identify and fix all errors. These exercises are intended to be completed without the aid of a compiler.

Lab Exercises

The most important section in each chapter is the *Lab Exercises* section. These exercises are designed to teach students how to apply the material learned in *C++ How to Program, Fourth Edition* and to prepare them for writing C++ programs. Each lab contains one or more lab exercises and a debugging problem. The *Lab Exercises* contain the following:

148 Lab Objectives

The lab objectives highlight specific concepts from the corresponding chapter in *C++ How to Program, Fourth Edition* on which the lab exercise focuses. The objectives give students the opportunity, after reading the chapter, to determine whether they have met the intended goals. The objectives serve as confidence builders and as a source of positive reinforcement.

30 Problem Descriptions

These descriptions contain detailed explanations of the programs and how the programs should be written. Many of these problems are taken from the exercise sets of *C++ How to Program, Fourth Edition*. These problems have been carefully tested in our corporate seminars and by the hundreds of colleges and universities worldwide that use *C++ How to Program*.

56 Sample Outputs

One or more sample outputs are provided for every lab exercise. The sample outputs illustrate the desired program behavior. The information depicted in the outputs further clarifies the problem descriptions and aids the students with writing programs. Students also use the outputs to confirm that their programs are working properly.

31 Program Templates

Program templates are C++ programs in which one or more key lines of code have been removed and replaced with comments that provide information about the missing code. These templates offer students a starting point from which to begin programming and provide insights into how a problem can be solved. Program templates are available at **www.deitel.com/books/downloads.html#cppHTP4** and **www.prenhall.com/deitel**.

118 Problem-Solving Tips

The problem-solving tips are suggestions and hints that students should use during the labs. These tips highlight key issues that students will need to consider when solving the lab exercises.

98 Follow-Up Questions and Activities

These questions often ask students to make modifications to template solutions. These exercises are designed to further students' understanding of C++, to demonstrate how a similar program may be solved or to implement an alternative solution. Students also are asked to interpret their solutions to ensure that they understand the crucial programming concepts.

13 Debugging Problems

The challenging debugging exercises alert students to the types of errors they are likely to encounter while programming. Each problem consists of a block of code that contains syntax errors and/or logic errors. These programs are intended to be compiled and executed during the laboratory sessions. Source-code files for the debugging exercises are available at **www.deitel.com/books/downloads.html#cppHTP4** and **www.prenhall.com/deitel**.

Postlab Activities

Postlab Activities are intended to be completed by students after their lab sessions. Students find these activities useful for self-study, especially students who complete the lab sessions quickly. Professors may assign these activities to reinforce key concepts or to provide students with more programming experience. The activities test the students' understanding of the material they learned in the labs. Two types of programming activities are provided: coding exercises and programming challenges.

92 Coding Exercises

Coding exercises are short and serve as review after the *Prelab Activities* and *Lab Exercises* have been completed. These exercises require students to write programs or program segments to illustrate specific concepts from the textbook.

31 Programming Challenges

Programming challenges allow students to apply the knowledge they have gained in class to substantial programming exercises. Hints, sample outputs and/or pseudocode are provided to aid students with these problems. If students successfully complete the programming challenges for a chapter, they have mastered the chapter material. Most programming challenges are taken from the *C++ How to Program, Fourth Edition* exercise sets.[3]

Instructor's Manual for C++ in the Lab

An *Instructor's Manual* contains the solutions to the *Prelab Activities*, *Lab Exercises* and *Postlab Activities*. [*NOTE*: **Please do not write to us requesting the instructor's manual. Distribution of this material is strictly limited to college professors teaching from the book. Instructors may obtain the instructor's manual only from their Prentice Hall representatives. We regret that we cannot provide the solutions to professionals.**]

Ancillary Package for C++ How to Program, Fourth Edition

C++ How to Program, Fourth Edition has extensive ancillary materials available to instructors teaching from the book. The *Instructor's Manual CD* contains solutions to the vast majority of the end-of-chapter exercises. A *Test Item File* is available for creating quizzes or exams. In addition, we provide *PowerPoint® Lecture Notes* (**www.prenhall.com/deitel**) containing all the code and figures in the text. Instructors are encouraged to customize these slides to meet their own classroom needs; students may download these slides as well. Prentice Hall provides a *Companion Web Site* (**www.prenhall.com/deitel**) that includes additional resources for instructors and students. For instructors, the Web site includes a *Syllabus Manager* for course planning and links to the *PowerPoint® Lecture Notes*. For students, the Web site provides chapter objectives, true/false self-review exercises and answers, chapter highlights and reference materials.

C++ Multimedia Cyber Classroom, Fourth Edition and The Complete C++ Training Course, Fourth Edition

We have prepared an optional interactive, CD-ROM-based, software version of *C++ How to Program, Fourth Edition* called the *C++ Multimedia Cyber Classroom, Fourth Edition*. This Windows® resource is loaded with features for learning and reference.

The CD provides an introduction in which the authors overview the *Cyber Classroom*'s features. The textbook's LIVE-CODE™ example programs truly "come alive" in the *Cyber Classroom*. If you are viewing a program and want to execute it, you simply click the lightning-bolt icon, and the program will run. You immediately will see the program's outputs. If you want to modify a program and see the effects of your changes, simply click the floppy-disk icon, causing the source code to be "lifted off" the CD and "dropped into" one of your own directories so you can edit the text, recompile the program and try out your new version. Click the audio icon, and one of the authors will discuss the program and "walk you through" the code.

The *Cyber Classroom* also provides navigational aids, including extensive hyperlinking. The *Cyber Classroom* is browser based, so it remembers sections that you have visited recently and allows you to move forward or backward among them. The thousands of index entries are hyperlinked to their text occurrences. Furthermore, when you key in a term using the "find" feature, the *Cyber Classroom* will locate occurrences of that term throughout the text. The Table of Contents entries are "hot," so clicking a chapter name or section name takes you immediately to that chapter or section. Professors tell us that their students enjoy using the *Cyber Classroom*, spend more time on their courses and master more of the material than in textbook-only courses.

The *Cyber Classroom* is wrapped with the textbook at a discount in *The Complete C++ Training Course, Fourth Edition*. If you have the book already and would like to purchase the *C++ Multimedia Cyber Classroom, Fourth Edition* (ISBN: 0-13-100253-8) separately, visit **www.InformIT.com/cyberclassrooms**.

---

3. *C++ How to Program, Fourth Edition* contains a rich set of exercises for each chapter. Solutions are available for all the programming challenges on **www.deitel.com/books/downloads.html#cppHTP4** and **www.-prenhall.com/deitel**. Instructors who want to assign *Postlab* programming challenges for which students are not provided with the answers should visit **www.deitel.com/books/downloads.html**. A PDF document is provided that lists the *C++ How to Program, Fourth Edition* exercise solutions that are provided on the *C++ Multimedia Cyber Classroom, Fourth Edition*.

Acknowledgments

We would like to thank several of the participants in our Deitel & Associates, Inc. College Internship Program[4] who helped develop this lab manual.

- Mike Dos'Santos, a senior majoring in computer science at Northeastern University, helped certify the technical accuracy of every chapter. Mike also made significant contributions to the Instructor's manual.

- Jason Rosenfeld, a graduate of Northwestern University with a degree in computer science, devoted long hours to the development of the previous edition.

- Jeffrey C. Hamm, a junior majoring in computer science at Northeastern University, contributed to every chapter in the previous edition.

We are fortunate to have been able to work on this project with the dedicated team of publishing professionals at Prentice Hall. We especially appreciate the extraordinary efforts of our computer science editor, Petra Recter, assistant-editor Sarah Burrows and their boss—our mentor in publishing—Marcia Horton, Editorial Director of Prentice Hall's Engineering and Computer Science Division. Vince O'Brien did a marvelous job managing the production of this lab manual. We would also like to thank Rose Sullivan for helping to develop the formatting styles used in this lab manual.

We sincerely appreciate the efforts of our reviewers:

- Richard Albright (University of Delaware)
- J. Browning (Browning Tech Systems)
- John Conley (Devry Institute Arizona)
- Ray Desrosiers (Texas Tech University)
- Howard Francis (Pikeville College)
- Cindy Fry (Baylor University)
- Judy Jernigan (Tyler Junior College)
- Harold Kollmeier (Wentworth Institute of Technology)
- Ed Korntved (Northwest Nazarene University)
- Marty Kwestel (New Jersey Institute of Technology)
- Bob McMorrow (Southeastern Louisiana University)
- Wayne Morris (Wabash Valley College)
- David Nguyen (California State Polytechnic University-Pomona)
- Wolfgang Pelz (The University of Akron)
- Ron Schwartz (Florida Atlantic University)
- An Wang (LaSalle College)

Under a tight time schedule, these reviewers scrutinized every aspect of the lab manual and made many suggestions for improving the accuracy and completeness of the presentation.

---

4. The *Deitel & Associates, Inc. College Internship Program* offers a limited number of salaried positions to Boston-area college students majoring in Computer Science, Information Technology, Marketing, Management and English. Students work at our corporate headquarters in Maynard, Massachusetts full-time in the summers and, for those attending college in the Boston area, part-time during the academic year. We also offer full-time internship positions for students interested in taking a semester off from school to gain industry experience. Regular full-time positions are available to college graduates. For more information about this competitive program, please contact the president of Deitel & Associates, Inc., Abbey Deitel, at **deitel@deitel.com** and visit our Web site, **www.deitel.com**.

We would sincerely appreciate your comments, criticisms, corrections and suggestions for improving this lab manual. Please address all correspondence to

deitel@deitel.com

We will respond promptly. Well, that's it for now. Good luck!

Dr. Harvey M. Deitel
Paul J. Deitel
Tem R. Nieto

About the Authors

Dr. Harvey M. Deitel, Chairman and Chief Strategy Officer (CSO) of Deitel & Associates, Inc., has 41 years experience in the computing field, including extensive industry and academic experience. Dr. Deitel earned B.S. and M.S. degrees from the Massachusetts Institute of Technology and a Ph.D. from Boston University. He worked on the pioneering virtual-memory operating-systems projects at IBM and MIT that developed techniques now widely implemented in systems such as UNIX, Linux and Windows XP. He has 20 years of college teaching experience, including earning tenure and serving as the Chairman of the Computer Science Department at Boston College before founding Deitel & Associates, Inc., with his son, Paul J. Deitel. He and Paul are the co-authors of several dozen books and multimedia packages and they are writing many more. With translations published in Japanese, Russian, Spanish, Traditional Chinese, Simplified Chinese, Korean, French, Polish, Italian, Portuguese, Greek, Urdu and Turkish, the Deitels' texts have earned international recognition. Dr. Deitel has delivered professional seminars to major corporations, government organizations and various branches of the military.

Paul J. Deitel, CEO and Chief Technical Officer of Deitel & Associates, Inc., is a graduate of the Massachusetts Institute of Technology's Sloan School of Management, where he studied Information Technology. Through Deitel & Associates, Inc., he has delivered C, C++, Java, Internet and World Wide Web courses to industry clients, including Compaq, Sun Microsystems, White Sands Missile Range, Rogue Wave Software, Boeing, Dell, Stratus, Fidelity, Cambridge Technology Partners, Open Environment Corporation, One Wave, Hyperion Software, Lucent Technologies, Adra Systems, Entergy, CableData Systems, NASA at the Kennedy Space Center, the National Severe Storm Laboratory, IBM and many other organizations. He has lectured on C++ and Java for the Boston Chapter of the Association for Computing Machinery and has taught satellite-based Java courses through a cooperative venture of Deitel & Associates, Prentice Hall and the Technology Education Network. He and his father, Dr. Harvey M. Deitel, are the world's best-selling Computer Science textbook authors.

Tem R. Nieto, Director of Product Development of Deitel & Associates, Inc., is a graduate of the Massachusetts Institute of Technology. Through Deitel & Associates, Inc., he has delivered courses for industry clients including Sun Microsystems, Compaq, EMC, Stratus, Fidelity, NASDAQ, Art Technology, Progress Software, Toys "R" Us, Operational Support Facility of the National Oceanographic and Atmospheric Administration, Jet Propulsion Laboratory, Nynex, Motorola, Federal Reserve Bank of Chicago, Banyan, Schlumberger, University of Notre Dame, NASA, various military installations and many others. He has co-authored numerous books and multimedia packages with the Deitels and has contributed to virtually every Deitel & Associates, Inc., publication.

About Deitel & Associates, Inc.

Deitel & Associates, Inc., is an internationally recognized corporate training and content-creation organization specializing in programming languages education, Internet/World Wide Web software technology, e-business/e-commerce software technology and object technology. The company provides courses on Internet and World Wide Web programming, wireless Internet programming, object technology, and major programming languages and platforms, such as C++, Visual C++® .NET, Visual Basic® .NET, C#, Java™, advanced Java, C, XML, Perl, Python and more. The founders of Deitel & Associates, Inc., are Dr. Harvey M. Deitel and Paul J. Deitel. The company's clients include many of the world's largest computer companies, government agencies, branches of the military and business organizations. Through its 25-year publishing partnership with Prentice Hall, Deitel & Associates, Inc., publishes leading-edge programming textbooks, professional books, interactive CD-ROM-based multimedia *Cyber Classrooms*, *Complete Training Courses*, e-books, e-matter, Web-based training courses, and e-content for course-management systems and learning management systems. Deitel & Associates, Inc., and the authors can be reached via e-mail at

deitel@deitel.com

To learn more about Deitel & Associates, Inc., its publications and its worldwide corporate on-site curriculum, see the last few pages of *C++ How to Program, Fourth Edition* or visit

www.deitel.com

Individuals wishing to purchase Deitel books, *Cyber Classrooms*, *Complete Training Courses* and Web-based training courses can do so through

```
www.deitel.com
www.prenhall.com
www.Informit.com
www.InformIT.com/cyberclassrooms
```

Bulk orders by corporations and academic institutions should be placed directly with Prentice Hall. See the last few pages of *C++ How to Program, Fourth Edition* for worldwide-ordering details.

1

Introduction to Computers and C++ Programming

Objectives

- To write simple computer programs in C++. This lab steps you through the creation of your first C++ programs.
- To use simple input and output statements in C++. This lab introduces **cout** statements to output both text and variables and **cin** statements to input data from the user.
- To become familiar with fundamental data types. After completing this lab, you should be able to declare and use variables that contain both integer values and floating-point values.
- To use arithmetic operators. This lab demonstrates how to use the standard arithmetic operators in C++ programs.
- To understand the precedence of arithmetic operators. C++ enforces a strict precedence on the arithmetic operators; forgetting this precedence can result in logic errors in your programs.
- To write simple decision-making statements. Chapter 1 of *C++ How to Program: Fourth Edition* introduces **if** statements. This lab gives you practice using them to control the actions of a computer program.

Assignment Checklist

Name: _____   **Date:** _____

Section: _____

Exercises	Assigned: Circle assignments	Date Due
Prelab Activities		
Matching	YES NO	
Fill in the Blank	11, 12, 13, 14, 15, 16, 17, 18, 19, 20, 21	
Short Answer	22, 23, 24, 25, 26, 27, 28	
Programming Output	29, 30, 31, 32, 33	
Correct the Code	34, 35, 36, 37, 38, 39, 40	
Lab Exercises		
Exercise 1 — Sum, Average, Max and Min	YES NO	
Follow-Up Questions	1, 2, 3	
Exercise 2 — Multiples	YES NO	
Follow-Up Questions	1, 2, 3, 4	
Exercise 3 — Separating Digits	YES NO	
Follow-Up Questions	1, 2, 3	
Debugging	YES NO	
Labs Provided by Instructor		
1.		
2.		
3.		
Postlab Activities		
Coding Exercises	1, 2, 3, 4, 5, 6, 7, 8	
Programming Challenges	9, 10, 11	

Assignment Checklist

Name:

Prelab Activities

Matching

Name: _____   **Date:**_____

Section: _____

After reading Chapter 1 of *C++ How to Program: Fourth Edition*, answer the given questions. These questions are intended to test and reinforce your understanding of key concepts and may be done either before the lab or during the lab.

For each term in the column on the left, write the corresponding letter for the description that best matches it from the column on the right.

Term	Description
____ 1. Hardware	a) Device capable of performing computations and making logical decisions at speeds millions and even billions of times faster than a human being.
____ 2. Stream extraction operator	b) "Administrative" section of a computer.
____ 3. ALU	c) Programming language, like C and C++, in which simple statements accomplish substantial tasks.
____ 4. Portable	d) Devices such as the screen, keyboard, CD-ROM, memory and processing unit.
____ 5. Computer	e) Disciplined approach to writing programs that are clear, easy to test and debug, and easy to modify.
____ 6. Objects	f) Reusable software components.
____ 7. Stream insertion operator	g) Property of carefully designed programs which allows them to run on different computers.
____ 8. Structured programming	h) `>>`.
____ 9. CPU	i) "Manufacturing" section of a computer. Performs calculations.
____ 10. High-level language	j) `<<`.

Prelab Activities

Name:

Matching

Prelab Activities   Name:

Fill in the Blank

Name: _____   **Date:**_____

Section: _____

Fill in the blank for each of the following statements:

11. Compilers translate high-level language programs into _____.

12. _____ programs directly execute high-level language programs without the need for compiling them into machine language.

13. C++ programs typically go through six phases of development: edit, preprocess, _____, link, load and execute.

14. Divide-by-zero is generally a(n) _____ error—the program terminates immediately.

15. _____ represents the standard input stream.

16. _____ represents the standard output stream.

17. Single-line comments begin with _____.

18. _____ is the first function executed in a C++ program.

19. All variables in a C++ program must be _____ before they are used.

20. The _____ statement allows a program to make a decision.

21. _____ operators and _____ operators can be used in **if** conditions.

Prelab Activities

Name: _____

Fill in the Blank

Prelab Activities   Name:

Short Answer

Name: _____   **Date:**_____

Section: _____

In the space provided, answer each of the given questions. Your answers should be as concise as possible; aim for two or three sentences.

22. What is object-oriented programming?

23. What is a syntax error? Give an example.

24. What is a logic error? Give an example.

Prelab Activities   Name: _____

Short Answer

25. What are redundant parentheses? When might a programmer use them?

26. What are standard library functions? Why is it better to use them rather than writing your own?

27. Write an example of a preprocessor directive.

28. Describe any two logical units of a computer.

Prelab Activities   Name:

Programming Output

Name: _____   **Date:** _____

Section: _____

For each of the given program segments, read the code and write the output in the space provided below each program. [*Note*: Do not execute these programs on a computer.]

29. What is the output of the following program?

```
1   #include <iostream>
2
3   using std::cout;
4   using std::endl;
5
6   int main()
7   {
8      int x;
9      int y;
10
11     x = 30;
12     y = 2;
13     cout << x * y + 9 / 3 << endl;
14
15     return 0;
16
17  } // end main
```

Your answer:

30. What is output by the following line of code?

```
1   cout << ( 8 * 4 * 2 + 6 ) / 2 + 4;
```

Your answer:

Prelab Activities   Name:

Programming Output

31. What is output by the following program? Assume that the user enters **5** for **input**.

```cpp
1   #include <iostream>
2
3   using std::cout;
4   using std::cin;
5   using std::endl;
6
7   int main()
8   {
9      int input;
10
11     cout << "Please enter an integer: ";
12     cin >> input;
13
14     if ( input != 7 )
15        cout << "Hello" << endl;
16
17     if ( input == 7 )
18        cout << "Goodbye" << endl;
19
20     return 0;
21
22  } // end main
```

Your answer:

Prelab Activities   Name:

Programming Output

32. What is output by the following program? Assume the user enters **2** for **input**.

```cpp
1   #include <iostream>
2
3   using std::cout;
4   using std::cin;
5   using std::endl;
6
7   int main()
8   {
9      int input;
10
11     cout << "Please enter an integer: ";
12     cin >> input;
13
14     if ( input >= 0 )
15         cout << "Hello" << endl;
16
17     cout << "Goodbye" << endl;
18
19     return 0;
20
21  } // end main
```

Your answer:

Prelab Activities   Name:

Programming Output

33. What is output by the following program?

```
1   #include <iostream>
2
3   using std::cout;
4   using std::cin;
5   using std::endl;
6
7   int main()
8   {
9      int x = 3;
10     int y = 9;
11     int z = 77;
12
13     if ( x == ( y / 3 ) )
14        cout << "H";
15
16     if ( z != 77 )
17        cout << "q";
18
19     if ( z == 77 )
20        cout << "e";
21
22     if ( z * y + x < 0 )
23        cout << "g";
24
25     if ( y == ( x * x ) )
26        cout << "11";
27
28     cout << "o!" << endl;
29
30     return 0;
31
32  } // end main
```

Your answer:

Prelab Activities

Name: _____

Correct the Code

Name: _____   **Date:**_____

Section: _____

For each of the given program segments, determine if there is an error in the code. If there is an error, specify whether it is a logic error or a syntax error, circle the error in the program and write the corrected code in the space provided after each problem. If the code does not contain an error, write "no error." [*Note*: It is possible that a program segment may contain multiple errors.]

34. The following program should print an integer to the screen:

```
1   #include <iostream>;
2
3   using std::cout;
4   using std::endl;
5
6   int main()
7   {
8       int x = 30;
9       int y = 2;
10
11      cout << x * y + 9 / 3 << endl;
12
13      return 0;
14
15  } // end main
```

Your answer:

35. The following segment of code should declare an integer variable and assign it the value **6**.

```
1   int 1stPlace = 6
2   1stPlace = 6;
```

Your answer:

Prelab Activities   Name:

Correct the Code

36. The following code should determine if variable **x** is less than or equal to **9**. Assume **using std::cout;** has been provided.

```
1   int x = 9;
2
3   if ( x < = 9 )
4      cout << "Less than or equal to.";
```

Your answer:

37. The following code should test if **q** is equivalent to **0**. Assume **using std::cout;** has been provided.

```
1   int q = 0;
2
3   cout << "q is: " << q;
4
5   if ( q = 0 )
6      cout << "q is equal to 0";
```

Your answer:

38. The following code segment should determine if an integer variable's value is greater than zero. Assume that **using std::cout;** has been provided.

```
1   int x = 9;
2
3   if ( x > 0 );
4      cout << "Greater than zero";
```

Your answer:

Prelab Activities

Name:

Correct the Code

39. The following program should print **302** to the screen:

```
1   #include <iostream>
2
3   using std::cout;
4   using std::end;
5
6   int ma in()
7   {
8       int x = 30;
9       int y = 2;
10
11      cout << y << x << endl;
12
13      return 0;
14
15  } // end main
```

Your answer:

40. The following code should compare two integers for inequality. Assume **using std::cout;** has been
    provided.

```
1   int x = 9;
2   int y = 3;
3
4   if ( x =! y )
5       cout << "Not equal";
```

Your answer:

Prelab Activities   Name:

Correct the Code

Lab Exercises

Lab Exercise 1 — Sum, Average, Max and Min

Name: _____   Date:_____

Section: _____

This problem is intended to be solved in a closed-lab session with a teaching assistant or instructor present. The problem is divided into six parts:

1. Lab Objectives

2. Description of the Problem

3. Sample Output

4. Program Template (Fig. L 1.1)

5. Problem-Solving Tips

6. Follow-Up Questions and Activities

The program template represents a complete working C++ program, with one or more key lines of code replaced with comments. Read the problem description and examine the sample output; then study the template code. Using the problem-solving tips as a guide, replace the /* */ comments with C++ code. Compile and execute the program. Compare your output with the sample output provided. Then answer the follow-up questions. The source code for the template is available at **www.deitel.com** and **www.prenhall.com./deitel**.

Lab Objectives

This lab was designed to reinforce programming concepts from Chapter 1 of *C++ How To Program: Fourth Edition*. In this lab, you will practice:

- Using **cout** to output text and variables.

- Using **cin** to input data from the user.

- Using **if** statements to make decisions based on the truth or falsity of a condition.

- Using the arithmetic operators to perform mathematical operations.

The follow-up questions and activities also will give you practice:

- Comparing **<** to **<=**.

- Declaring and using variables.

- Using integer division.

Description of the Problem

Write a program that inputs three integers from the keyboard, and prints the sum, average, product, smallest and largest of these numbers. The screen dialogue should appear as follows: [*Note:* **13**, **27** and **14** are input by the user.]

Lab Exercises   Name:

Lab Exercise 1 — Sum, Average, Max and Min

Sample Output

```
Input three different integers: 13 27 14
Sum is 54
Average is 18
Product is 4914
Smallest is 13
Largest is 27
```

Template

```cpp
 1   // Chapter 1 of C++ How to Program
 2   // numbercompare.cpp
 3
 4   #include <iostream>
 5
 6   using std::cout;
 7   using std::cin;
 8   using std::endl;
 9
10   int main()
11   {
12      int number1;
13      int number2;
14      int number3;
15      int smallest;
16      int largest;
17
18      cout << "Input three different integers: ";  // prompt
19      /* Write a statement to read in values for number1, number2 and
20         number3 using a single cin statement */
21
22      largest = num1;  // assume first number is largest
23
24      /* Write a statement to determine if number2 is greater than
25         largest. If so assign number2 to largest */
26
27      /* Write a statement to determine if number3 is greater than
28         largest. If so assign number3 to largest */
29
30      smallest = num1;  // assume first number is smallest
31
32      /* Write a statement to determine if number2 is less than
33         smallest. If so assign number2 to smallest */
34
35      /* Write a statement to determine if number3 is less than
36         smallest. If so assign number3 to smallest */
37
38      /* Write an output statement that prints the sum, average,
39         product, largest and smallest */
40
41      return 0;
42
43   } // end main
```

Fig. L 1.1   numbercompare.cpp.

Lab Exercises   Name:

Lab Exercise 1 — Sum, Average, Max and Min

Problem-Solving Tips

1. The input data consists of three integer values, so you will need to declare three **int** variables to represent them.

2. Prompt for three integer values. You will use one **cin** statement to read each input into a variable. Declare a variable named **largest** that stores the largest value and a variable **smallest** that stores the smallest value.

3. You can pick any one of the variables (except **smallest**) and assign it to **largest**. It does not matter which variable you choose, because you are going to test **largest** against the other two variables.

4. Using an **if** statement, compare **largest** against one of the other variables. If the content of **largest** is smaller, then store the variable's content in **largest**.

5. Using an **if** statement, compare **largest** against the remaining variable. If the content of **largest** is smaller, then store the variable's content in **largest**. At this point you are guaranteed to have the largest value stored in **largest**.

6. You can pick any one of the variables (except **largest**) and assign it to **smallest**. It does not matter which variable you choose, because you are going to test **smallest** against the other two variables.

7. Using an **if** statement, compare **smallest** against one of the other variables. If the contents of **smallest** is greater, then store the variable's contents in **smallest**.

8. Using an **if** statement, compare **smallest** against the remaining variable. If the content of **smallest** is larger, then store the variable's content in **smallest**. At this point you are guaranteed to have the smallest value stored in **smallest**.

9. Write a **cout** statement that outputs the sum, average, product (i.e., multiplication), largest and smallest values.

10. Be sure to follow the spacing and indentation conventions mentioned in the text. Before and after each control structure place a line of vertical space to make the control structure "stand out." Indent all of the body statements of **main**. Indent all of the body statements of each control structure.

11. If you have any questions as you proceed, ask your lab instructor for assistance.

Follow-Up Questions and Activities

1. Modify your solution to use three separate **cin** statements rather than one. Write a separate prompt for each **cin**.

2. Does it matter whether **<** or **<=** is used when making comparisons to determine the smallest integer? Which did you use and why?

Lab Exercises   Name:

Lab Exercise 1 — Sum, Average, Max and Min

3. In the program you probably noticed that an **average** variable was not used. Create an integer variable **average** and store the average in it. Then print the value stored in **average**. Is the output different from what you observed previously?

Lab Exercises   Name: _____

Lab Exercise 2 — Multiples

Name: _____   Date: _____

Section: _____

This problem is intended to be solved in a closed-lab session with a teaching assistant or instructor present. The problem is divided into six parts:

1. Lab Objectives
2. Description of the Problem
3. Sample Output
4. Program Template (Fig. L 1.2)
5. Problem-Solving Tips
6. Follow-Up Questions and Activities

The program template represents a complete working C++ program, with one or more key lines of code replaced with comments. Read the problem description and examine the sample output; then study the template code. Using the problem-solving tips as a guide, replace the **/* */** comments with C++ code. Compile and execute the program. Compare your output with the sample output provided. Then answer the follow-up questions. The source code for the template is available at **www.deitel.com** and **www.prenhall.com./deitel**.

Lab Objectives

This lab was designed to reinforce programming concepts from Chapter 1 of *C++ How To Program: Fourth Edition*. In this lab, you will practice:

- Using **cout** to output text and values.

- Using **cin** to input data from the user.

- Using **if** statements to make decisions based on the truth or falsity of a condition.

- Using the modulus operator (**%**) to determine the remainder of a division operation.

The follow-up questions and activities also will give you practice:

- Recognizing common mistakes with the **if** statement.

- Including compound statements inside an **if** clause.

- Adapting a program to solve a similar problem.

Description of the Problem

Write a program that reads in two integers and determines and prints if the first is a multiple of the second. [*Hint*: Use the modulus operator.]

Lab Exercises   Name:

Lab Exercise 2 — Multiples

Sample Output

```
Enter two integers: 22 8
22 is not a multiple of 8
```

Template

```cpp
1   // Chapter 1 of C++ How to Program
2   // multiples.cpp
3   #include <iostream>
4
5   using std::cout;
6   using std::cin;
7   using std::endl;
8
9   int main()
10  {
11      /* Write variable declarations here */
12
13      cout << "Enter two integers: ";
14      /* Write a cin statement to read data into variables here */
15
16      if ( /* Write a condition that tests if number1 is a multiple of
17             number2 */ )
18          cout << number1 << " is a multiple of " << number2 << endl;
19
20      if ( /* Write a condition that tests if num1 is not a multiple
21             of num2 */ )
22          cout << number1 << " is not a multiple of " << number2 << endl;
23
24      return 0;
25
26  } // end main
```

Fig. L 1.2   `multiples.cpp`.

Problem-Solving Tips

1. The input data consists of two integers, so you will use **int** to represent them.

2. Prompt the user for two integer values and use **cin** to read them into their respective variables.

3. Use an **if** statement to determine if the first number input is a multiple of the second number input. To accomplish this, you will need to use the modulus operator, **%**. If one number divides into another evenly, the modulus operation results in **0**. If the result is zero, output the fact that the first number is a multiple of the second number.

4. Use an **if** statement to determine if the first number input is not a multiple of the second number input. To accomplish this, you will need to use the modulus operator, **%**. If one number does not divide into another evenly, the modulus operation results in a non-zero value. If non-zero, output the fact that the first number is not a multiple of the second.

Lab Exercises   Name: _____

Lab Exercise 2 — Multiples

5. Be sure to follow the spacing and indentation conventions mentioned in the text. Before and after each control structure place a line of vertical space to make the control structure "stand out." Indent all of the body statements of **main**. Indent all of the body statements of each control structure.

6. If you have any questions as you proceed, ask your lab instructor for assistance.

Follow-Up Questions and Activities

1. Can the modulus operator be used with non-integer operands? Can it be used with negative numbers? Assume that the user entered the following sets of numbers. For each set, what does the expression in the third column output? If there is an error, explain why.

Integer 1	Integer 2	Expression	Output
73	22	`cout << 73 % 22;`	_____
0	100	`cout << 0 % 100;`	_____
100	0	`cout << 100 % 0;`	_____
−3	3	`cout << -3 % 3;`	_____
9	4.5	`cout << 9 % 4.5;`	_____
16	2	`cout << 16 % 2;`	_____

2. Place a semicolon at the end of the **if** statement in your solution that corresponds to the **if** statement on lines 16–17 in the template. What happens? Explain.

3. Rewrite the **cout** statement in your solution that corresponds to the **cout** statement on line 18 in the template. This statement should now look as follows:

```
cout << number1;
cout << " is a multiple of ";
cout << number2 << endl;
```

Rerun the program. Observe the differences. Why is the output different?

Lab Exercises   Name:

Lab Exercise 2 — Multiples

4. Modify the program to determine whether a number entered is even or odd. [*Note:* Now, the user needs to enter only one number.]

Lab Exercises   Name:

Lab Exercise 3 — Separating Digits

Name: _____   **Date:**_____

Section: _____

This problem is intended to be solved in a closed-lab session with a teaching assistant or instructor present. The problem is divided into six parts:

1. Lab Objectives
2. Description of the Problem
3. Sample Output
4. Program Template (Fig. L 1.3)
5. Problem-Solving Tips
6. Follow-Up Questions and Activities

The program template represents a complete working C++ program, with one or more key lines of code replaced with comments. Read the problem description and examine the sample output; then study the template code. Using the problem-solving tips as a guide, replace the **/* */** comments with C++ code. Compile and execute the program. Compare your output with the sample output provided. Then answer the follow-up questions. The source code for the template is available at **www.deitel.com** and **www.prenhall.com./deitel**.

Lab Objectives

This lab was designed to reinforce programming concepts from Chapter 1 of *C++ How To Program: Fourth Edition*. In this lab, you will practice:

- Using the modulus operator (**%**) to determine the remainder of a division operation.

- Integer division, which differs from arithmetic division because the decimal portion of the result is eliminated.

The follow-up questions and activities also will give you practice:

- Examining what happens during program execution when the user enters input which is invalid.

- Using type **double** to declare floating-point variables.

- Adapting a program to solve a similar problem.

Problem Description

Write a program that inputs a five-digit number, separates the number into its individual digits and prints the digits separated from one another by three spaces each. [*Hint*: Use integer division and the modulus operator.] For example, if the user inputs **42339**, the program should print what is shown in the sample output.

Lab Exercises   Name:

Lab Exercise 3 — Separating Digits

Sample Output

```
4    2    3    3    9
```

Template

```cpp
1    // Chapter 1 of C++ How to Program
2    // digits.cpp
3    #include <iostream>
4
5    using std::cout;
6    using std::cin;
7    using std::endl;
8
9    int main()
10   {
11      int number;
12
13      cout << "Enter a five-digit number: ";
14      cin >> number;
15
16      /* Write a statement to print the left-most digit of the
17         5-digit number */
18      /* Write a statement that changes number from 5-digits
19         to 4-digits */
20      /* Write a statement to print the left-most digit of the
21         4-digit number */
22      /* Write a statement that changes number from 4-digits
23         to 3-digits */
24      /* Write a statement to print the left-most digit of the
25         3-digit number */
26      /* Write a statement that changes number from 3-digits
27         to 2-digits */
28      /* Write a statement to print the left-most digit of the
29         2-digit number */
30      /* Write a statement that changes number from 2-digits
31         to 1-digit */
32      cout << number << endl;
33
34      return 0;
35
36   } // end main
```

Fig. L 1.3   **digits.cpp**.

Problem-Solving Tips

1. The input data consists of one integer, so you will use **int** to represent it. Note that the description indicates that one five-digit number is to be input—not five separate digits.

Lab Exercises   Name:

Lab Exercise 3 — Separating Digits

2. You will use a series of statements to "break-down" the number into its individual digits using combinations of modulus, **%** and division, **/**.

3. After the number has been input using **cin**, divide the number by **10000** to get the first digit. Why does this work? Because the number input is five digits long, it is divided by **10000** to obtain the left-most digit. In C++, dividing an integer by an integer results in an integer. For example, **42339 / 10000** evaluates to **4** because **10000** divides evenly into **42339** exactly **4** times. The remainder is truncated.

4. Change the number to a 4-digit number using the modulus operator. The number modulus **10000** evaluates to the integer remainder. In this case, the right-most four digits. For example, **42339 % 10000** results in **2339**. Assign the results of this modulus operation to the variable that stores the five-digit number input.

5. This pattern of division and modulus repeats itself—each time the number used in the divide/modulus calculation is reduced by a factor of **10**. The first digit is obtained by dividing the five-digit number by **10000**. The five-digit number is then assigned the result of the five-digit number modulus **10000**. After the number is changed to a four-digit number, divide/modulus by **1000**. After the number is changed to a three-digit number, divide/modulus by **100**. And so on.

6. Be sure to follow the spacing and indentation conventions mentioned in the text. Before and after each control structure place a line of vertical space to make the control structure "stand out." Indent all of the body statements of **main**. Indent all of the body statements of each control structure.

7. If you have any questions as you proceed, ask your lab instructor for assistance.

Follow-Up Questions and Activities

1. What are the results of the following expressions?

   24 / 5 = _____

   18 % 3 = _____

   13 % 9 = _____

   13 / 2 % 2 = _____

2. What happens when the user inputs a number which has fewer than five digits? Why? What is the output when **1763** is entered?

Lab Exercises   Name:

Lab Exercise 3 — Separating Digits

3. The program you completed in this lab exercise inputs a number with multiple digits and separates the digits. Write the inverse program, a program which asks the user for three one-digit numbers and combines them into a single three-digit number. [*Hint:* Model your answer after Problem-Solving Tips 3, 4 and 5 in the previous section.]

Lab Exercises   Name: _____

Debugging

Name: _____   Date: _____

Section: _____

The program in this section does not run properly. Fix all the syntax errors so that the program will compile success-fully. Once the program compiles, compare the output with the sample output, and eliminate any logic errors that may exist. The sample output demonstrates what the program's output should be once the program's code has been corrected. **debugging01.cpp** (Fig. L 1.4) is available at **www.deitel.com** and at **www.prenhall.com/ deitel**.

Sample Output

```
Enter two integer values: 5 2
The value of z is: 3
```

```
Enter two integer values: 2 7
The value of z is: 5
```

```
Enter two integer values: 4 4
The value of z is: 8
```

Broken Code

```
1    // Chapter 1 of C++ How To Program
2    // Debugging problem
3
4    int main()
5    {
6       int x;
7       int y;
8       int z;
9
10      cout << "Enter two integer values: ";
11      cin << x, y;
12
13      if ( x > y )
14         z == x - y;
15
16      if ( x < y )
17         z == y - x
18
```

Fig. L 1.4   debugging01.cpp. (Part 1 of 2.)

Lab Exercises   Name:

Debugging

```
19      if ( x == y );
20          z == x + y;
21
22      cout << "The value of z is: " << z;
23
24  } // end main
```

Fig. L 1.4   debugging01.cpp. (Part 2 of 2.)

Postlab Activities

Coding Exercises

Name: _____   **Date:**_____

Section: _____

These coding exercises reinforce the lessons learned in the lab and provide additional programming experience outside the classroom and laboratory environment. They serve as a review after you have completed the Prelab Activities and Lab Exercises successfully.

For each of the following problems, write a program or a program segment that performs the specified action.

1. Write the statement which includes the **iostream** file in a program. Also write the appropriate **using** statements to allow input, output and **endl**.

2. Declare three integer variables.

3. Write a line of code that prints all three integer values from Coding Exercise 2 separated by hyphens, **-**.

4. Write a single line of code that reads values into the three integer variables from Coding Exercise 2.

5. Modify your solution to Coding Exercise 4 to write a C++ program that determines which variable's value is the largest. Use variable **largest** to store the largest value.

Postlab Activities   Name:

Coding Exercises

6. Modify your solution to Coding Exercise 5 to write a C++ program that determines which integer variable's value is the smallest. Use variable **smallest** to store the smallest value.

Postlab Activities   Name:

Coding Exercises

7. Modify your solution from Coding Exercise 6 to write a C++ program that determines which variable contains the middle integer of three inputs. Use variable **middle** to store the middle value. Assume that all three integers are different. [*Hint*: Find the largest and smallest values first.]

Postlab Activities   Name:

Coding Exercises

8. Write statements that test if any of the variable's values are equal and if so print that they are equal. For example, if two variables have the same value, **5**, print "**5 and 5 are equal**."

Postlab Activities   Name: _____

Programming Challenges

Name: _____   Date:_____

Section: _____

The Programming Challenges are more involved than the Coding Exercises and may require a significant amount of time to complete. Write a C++ program for each of the problems in this section. The answers to these problems are available at **www.deitel.com**, **www.prenhall.com/deitel** and on the *C++ Multimedia Cyber Classroom: Fourth Edition*. Pseudocode, hints and/or sample outputs are provided to aid you in your programming.

9. Write a program that prints the numbers 1 to 4 on the same line with each pair of adjacent numbers separated by one space. Write the program using the following methods:

    a) Using one output statement with one stream-insertion operator.

    b) Using one output statement with four stream-insertion operators.

    c) Using four output statements.

Hints:

  • Use **//** to separate your program into three clearly marked sections, one for each part (i.e., a–c) of the problem.

  • For Part a) the entire output should be contained within one string.

  • Use either **endl** or **"\n"** after each part to separate their output.

  • Your output should look like:

```
1 2 3 4
1 2 3 4
1 2 3 4
```

10. Write a program that asks the user to enter two integers, obtains the numbers from the user, then prints the larger number followed by the words "**is larger**." If the numbers are equal, print the message "**These numbers are equal**."

Hints:

  • A typical run of your program might look as follows:

```
Enter two integers: 5 3
5 is larger.
```

Postlab Activities   Name:

Programming Challenges

- The user should input both integers at once, i.e., **cin >> x >> y;**
- Remember to print spaces after printing integers to the screen.

11. Write a program that reads in five integers and determines and prints the largest and the smallest integers in the group. Use only the programming techniques you learned in Chapter 1 of *C++ How to Program: Fourth Edition*.

Hints:

- This program requires seven variables: five for user input and two to store the largest and the smallest, respectively.
- As soon as the user inputs the values, assign the **largest** and **smallest** variables the value of the first input. If instead, **largest** was initially assigned to zero, this would be a logic error because negative numbers could be input by the user.
- Ten separate **if** statements are required to compare each input to **largest** and **smallest**.

Control Structures

Objectives

- To understand basic problem-solving techniques.
- To be able to develop algorithms through the process of top-down stepwise refinement.
- To be able to use the **if**, **if/else** and **switch** selection structures to choose among alternative actions.
- To be able to use the **while**, **do/while** and **for** repetition structures to execute statements in a program repeatedly.
- To understand counter-controlled repetition and sentinel-controlled repetition.
- To be able to use the increment, decrement, assignment and logical operators.
- To be able to use **break** and **continue** program control statements.

Assignment Checklist

Name: _____   **Date:**_____

Section: _____

Exercises	*Assigned:* Circle assignments	Date Due
Prelab Activities		
Matching	YES NO	
Fill in the Blank	13, 14, 15, 16, 17	
Short Answer	18, 19, 20, 21, 22, 23, 24	
Programming Output	25, 26, 27, 28, 29, 30	
Correct the Code	31, 32, 33, 34, 35, 36, 37, 38, 39, 40	
Lab Exercises		
Lab Exercise 1 — Department Store	YES NO	
Follow-Up Questions and Activities	1, 2, 3, 4	
Lab Exercise 2 — Payroll	YES NO	
Follow-Up Questions and Activities	1, 2, 3	
Lab Exercise 3 — Pythagorean Triples	YES NO	
Follow-Up Questions and Activities	1, 2, 3, 4	
Debugging	YES NO	
Labs Provided by Instructor		
1.		
2.		
3.		
Postlab Activities		
Coding Exercises	1, 2, 3, 4, 5, 6, 7, 8, 9, 10, 11	
Programming Challenges	12, 13, 14, 15	

Assignment Checklist

Name:

Prelab Activities

Matching

Name: _____   Date:_____

Section: _____

After reading Chapter 2 of *C++ How to Program: Fourth Edition*, answer the given questions. These questions are intended to test and reinforce your understanding of key concepts and may be done either before the lab or during the lab.

For each term in the column on the left, write the corresponding letter for the description that best matches it from the column on the right.

Term	Description
____ 1. ==	a) Assignment operator.
____ 2. Pseudocode	b) Used to choose among alternative courses of action.
____ 3. Algorithm	c) Addition assignment operator.
____ 4. =	d) Conditional operator.
____ 5. Selection structure	e) Allows programmers to specify an action to be repeated while some condition is true.
____ 6. Sentinel	f) Logical AND.
____ 7. ++	g) Logical OR.
____ 8. &&	h) Increment operator.
____ 9. ||	i) Special value which indicates the end of data entry.
____ 10. +=	j) Procedure for solving problems in terms of actions and order.
____ 11. ?:	k) Artificial and informal language.
____ 12. Repetition structure	l) Equality operator.

Prelab Activities   Name:

Matching

Prelab Activities   Name:

Fill in the Blank

Name: _____   **Date:**_____

Section: _____

Fill in the blank for each of the following statements:

13. A(n) _____ error causes a program to fail and terminate prematurely.

14. The _____ selection structure performs an indicated action only when its condition is **true**; otherwise, the action is skipped.

15. When using _____-controlled repetition, the number of repetitions is not known before the loop begins executing.

16. The unary cast operator _____ creates a temporary copy of its operand.

17. The _____ and _____ statements are used with control structures to alter the flow of control.

Prelab Activities

Name:

Fill in the Blank

Prelab Activities   Name:

Short Answer

Name: _____   **Date:**_____

Section: _____

In the space provided, answer each of the given questions. Your answers should be as concise as possible; aim for two or three sentences.

18. Explain the difference between a **while** statement and a **do/while** statement. Draw an activity diagram for each.

19. List the three types of selection structures and the three types of repetition structures.

Prelab Activities

Name:

Short Answer

20. Fill in the third column in the following tables:

expression1	expression2	expression1 || expression2
false	*false*	_____
false	*true*	_____
true	*false*	_____
true	*true*	_____

expression1	expression2	expression1 && expression2
false	*false*	_____
false	*true*	_____
true	*false*	_____
true	*true*	_____

21. What is the difference between the preincrement and postincrement operators (i.e., **++x** and **x++**; respectively)?

22. Define and discuss the difference between a logic error and a syntax error.

Prelab Activities   Name:

Short Answer

23. Define and discuss the difference between unary, binary and ternary operators. Give an example of each.

24. When must you use curly braces ({}) in conjunction with a selection or repetition structure?

Prelab Activities

Name:

Short Answer

Prelab Activities   Name: _____

Programming Output

Name: _____   Date: _____

Section: _____

For each of the given program segments, read the code and write the output in the space provided below each program. [*Note*: Do not execute these programs on a computer.]

25. What is output by the following program segment?

```
1   int x = 1;
2
3   while ( x <= 5 ) {
4       x++;
5       cout << "The value of x is: " << x << endl;
6   }
7
8   cout << "The final value of x is: " << x << endl;
```

Your answer:

26. What is output by the following **for** loop?

```
1   for ( int i = 0; i < 5; i++ )
2       cout << i << " ";
```

Your answer:

Prelab Activities   Name:

Programming Output

27. What is output by the following program segment?

```
1   int grade1 = 65;
2   int grade2 = 55;
3
4   cout << "The student with a grade of " << grade1 << " "
5        << ( grade1 >= 60 ? "Passed\n" : "Failed\n" );
6
7   cout << "The student with a grade of " << grade2 << " "
8        << ( grade2 >= 60 ? "Passed\n" : "Failed\n" );
```

Your answer:

28. What is output by the following program segment?

```
1   for ( int i = 1; i <= 10; i++ ) {
2
3      switch ( i ) {
4
5         case 1:
6            cout << "The value of x is 1\n";
7            break;
8
9         case 4:
10           cout << "The value of x is 4\n";
11
12        case 6:
13           cout << "The value of x is 6\n";
14           break;
15
16        default:
17           cout << "The value of x is neither 1, 4 nor 6\n";
18     }
19  }
```

Your answer:

Prelab Activities

Name:

Programming Output

29.   What is output by the following program segment?

```
1   int x;
2
3   for ( x = 1; x <= 10; x++ ) {
4
5      if ( x == 7 )
6         break;
7
8      if ( x == 3 )
9         continue;
10
11     cout << x << " ";
12  }
13
14  cout << endl << "The final value of x is: " << x << endl;
```

Your answer:

30.   In C++, it is possible to omit any of the statements in the header of a **for** loop. Doing so makes the loop more difficult to read, but does not produce a syntax error. Empty statements are represented by a semicolon (**;**). What is the output of the following program segment?

```
1   int x = 1;
2
3   for ( ; x <= 10; x++ );
4      cout << "The value of x is: " << x << endl;
```

Your answer:

Prelab Activities

Name:

Programming Output

Prelab Activities   Name:

Correct the Code

Name: _____   Date: _____

Section: _____

For each of the given program segments, determine if there is an error in the code. If there is an error, specify whether it is a logic error or a syntax error, circle the error in the program and write the corrected code in the space provided after each problem. If the code does not contain an error, write "no error." [*Note*: It is possible that a program segment may contain multiple errors.]

31. This program segment should calculate if a student has a passing grade. If so, **Passed.** should be printed. Otherwise, both **Failed.** and **You must take this course again.** should be printed.

```
1   if ( grade >= 60 )
2       cout << "Passed.\n"
3   else
4       cout << "Failed.\n"
5       cout << "You must take this course again.\n"
```

Your answer:

32. This program segment should calculate the product of all the integers between **1** and **5**, inclusive.

```
1   for ( int i = 1; i < 5; i++ ) {
2       int product = 1;
3
4       product *= i;
5   }
```

Your answer:

Prelab Activities   Name:

Correct the Code

33. This **for** loop should divide **i** by **i − 1**, using integer division, and print the result.

```
1   while ( int i = 1; i <= 5; i++ )
2       cout << i / ( i - 1 ) << " ";
```

Your answer:

34. In C++, it is possible to omit any of the statements in the header of a **for** loop. Doing so, makes the loop more difficult to read, but does not produce a syntax error. Empty statements are represented by a semicolon (**;**). This **for** loop should print all the integers between **5** and **1000**, inclusive, that are evenly divisible by **5**.

```
1   int i = 5;
2
3   for ( ; ; i += 5 ) {
4       cout << i << " ";
5
6       if ( i = 1000 )
7           break;
8   }
```

Your answer:

35. This **while** loop should compute the product of all integers between **1** and **5**, inclusive.

```
1   int i = 1;
2   int product = 1;
3
4   while ( i <= 5 );
5       product *= i;
```

Your answer:

Prelab Activities   Name:

Correct the Code

36. This **switch** structure should print either **x is 5**, **x is 10** or **x is neither 5 nor 10**.

```
 1   switch ( x ) {
 1
 2      case: 5
 3         cout << "x is 5\n";
 4
 5      case: 10
 6         cout << "x is 10\n";
 7
 8      case default:
 9         cout << "x is neither 5 nor 10\n";
10   }
```

Your answer:

37. In C++, it is possible to have multiple statements placed in a **for** loop header. Multiple statements are composed of comma-separated lists and logical operators. This program segment should print the sum of consecutive odd and even integers between **1** and **10**, inclusive. The expected output is shown below the code segment.

```
 1   for ( int i = 1, j = 2; i <= 10 && j <= 10; i++, j++ )
 2      cout << i << " + " << j << " = " << i + j << endl;
```

```
1 + 2 = 3
3 + 4 = 7
5 + 6 = 11
7 + 8 = 15
9 + 10 = 19
```

Your answer:

Prelab Activities

Name:

Correct the Code

38. This **for** loop should compute the product of **i** times **2**, plus **1**. For example, if the counter is **4**, the program should print **4 * 2 + 1 = 9**. It should loop from **1** to **10**.

```
1   for ( int i = 1, i = 10, i++ )
2       cout << i << " * 2 + 1 = " << ++( i * 2 ) << endl;
```

Your answer:

39. The following program segment should print the value of **x * y** until either **x** reaches **5** or **y** reaches **5**:

```
1   int x = 1;
2
3   for ( int y = 2; x == 5 && y == 5; y++ ) {
4       cout << x * y << endl;
5       x++;
6   }
```

Your answer:

40. The following program segment should print all the even integers between **0** and **100**, inclusive:

```
1   for ( int x = 0; x % 2 != 1; x += 2 ) {
2       cout << x << " ";
3
4       if ( x >= 100 )
5           break;
6   }
```

Your answer:

Lab Exercises

Lab Exercise 1—Department Store

Name: _____   **Date:**_____

Section: _____

This problem is intended to be solved in a closed-lab session with a teaching assistant or instructor present. The problem is divided into six parts:

1. Lab Objectives

2. Description of the Problem

3. Sample Output

4. Program Template (Fig. L 2.1)

5. Problem-Solving Tips

6. Follow-Up Questions and Activities

The program template represents a complete working C++ program, with one or more key lines of code replaced with comments. Read the problem description and examine the sample output; then study the template code. Using the problem-solving tips as a guide, replace the **/* */** comments with C++ code. Compile and execute the program. Compare your output with the sample output provided. Then answer the follow-up questions. The source code for the template is available at **www.deitel.com** and **www.prenhall.com./deitel**.

Lab Objectives

This lab was designed to reinforce programming concepts from Chapter 2 of *C++ How To Program: Fourth Edition*. In this lab, you will practice:

- writing pseudocode.

- using sentinel-controlled repetition.

- using selection structures.

The follow-up questions and activities also will give you practice:

- recognizing invalid user input.

- using counter-controlled repetition.

- differentiating between **while** and **do/while** loops.

Lab Exercises

Lab Exercise 1—Department Store

Lab Exercises   Name: _____

Lab Exercise 1 — Department Store

Name: _____   Date:_____

Section: _____

Description of the Problem

Develop a C++ program that will determine if a department-store customer has exceeded the credit limit on a charge account. For each customer, the following information is available:

a) account number (an integer);

b) balance at the beginning of the month;

c) total of all items charged by the customer this month;

d) total of all credits applied to the customer's account this month;

e) allowed credit limit.

The program should input this information, calculate the new balance (= *beginning balance + charges – credits*) and determine if the new balance exceeds the customer's credit limit. For those customers whose credit limit is exceeded, the program should display the customer's account number, credit limit, new balance and the message "Credit limit exceeded."

In this lab, you will practice the top-down, stepwise refinement methodology discussed in the text. You should formulate the algorithm by using pseudocode and top-down, stepwise refinement before you begin coding.

Sample Output

```
Enter account number (-1 to end): 100
Enter beginning balance: 5394.78
Enter total charges: 1000.00
Enter total credits: 500.00
Enter credit limit: 5500.00
Account:        100
Credit limit: 5500.00
Balance:       5894.78
Credit Limit Exceeded.

Enter account number (-1 to end): 200
Enter beginning balance: 1000.00
Enter total charges: 123.45
Enter total credits: 321.00
Enter credit limit: 1500.00

Enter account number (-1 to end): 300
Enter beginning balance: 500.00
Enter total charges: 274.73
Enter total credits: 100.00
Enter credit limit: 800.00

Enter account number (-1 to end): -1
```

Lab Exercises   Name:

Lab Exercise 1 — Department Store

Template

```
1    // Chapter 2 of C++ How to Program
2    // account.cpp
3    #include <iostream>
4
5    using std::cout;
6    using std::cin;
7    using std::endl;
8    using std::fixed;
9
10   #include <iomanip>
11
12   using std::setprecision;
13
14   int main()
15   {
16      int accountNumber; // customers account number
17      double balance; // customers balance
18      double charges; // charges on the account
19      double credits; // credits to the account
20      double limit; // credit limit on the account
21
22      cout << "Enter account number (-1 to end): " << fixed;
23
24      /* write code to read the customer's account number here */
25
26      /* begin loop here */ {
27         /* prompt and read the customer's balance here */
28         /* prompt and read the customer's charges here */
29         /* prompt and read the customer's credits here */
30         /* prompt and read the customer's credit limit here */
31         /* calculate the new customer's balance here */
32
33         /* determine if customer's credit limit is exceeded */
34         /* if customer's limit is exceeded print message */
35
36         cout << "\nEnter account number (-1 to end): ";
37         /* write code to read the customer's account number here */
38      }    // end while loop
39
40      cout << endl;  // ensure all output is displayed
41
42      return 0;
43
44   } // end main
```

Fig. L 2.1   account.cpp.

Problem Solving Tips

1. Notice that the number of customers is not specified in advance. The problem statement implies that you should use a sentinel value to control the loop.

Lab Exercises   Name: _____

Lab Exercise 1 — Department Store

2. The input data consist of one integer and four monetary amounts. The monetary amounts are numbers with decimal points, so you will use type **double** to represent them.

3. You will use a **while** loop to process several sets of customer data.

4. Before the loop, you will prompt for the first set of data. Inside the loop, you will prompt for each new set of data. It is a good practice to remind the user of the sentinel value in each prompting message.

5. What sentinel value should you use? It needs to be a value that will not be confused with a legitimate data value. A good choice for this program would be to use **-1** for the customer's account number, because account numbers are nonnegative integers.

6. While you could prompt each time for all five facts needed for a customer, a better strategy would be to prompt just for the account number. If it is negative, terminate the loop. If it is nonnegative, prompt for the remaining four pieces of data for that customer.

7. How do you determine if the new balance exceeds the credit limit? You already have input the credit limit, but you will need to calculate the new balance which is equal to the starting balance, plus the charges, minus the credits.

8. Be sure to follow the spacing and indentation conventions mentioned in the text. Before and after each control structure, place a line of vertical space to make the control structure stand out. Indent all the body statements of **main**, and indent all the body statements of each control structure.

9. Print your outputs neatly in the indicated format. Use **setprecision(2)** to force two positions of precision to the right of the decimal point when printing monetary amounts. You will need to **#include <iomanip>** to use function **setprecision(2)**.

10. Also remember to use the **fixed** manipulator. This manipulator specifies that the number output should be output in fixed notation, as opposed to scientific notation (i.e., **std::scientific**). Fixed notation always keeps a "fixed" decimal point, regardless of the number of digits displayed. For example, 1.50000000000 is expressed in fixed notation. Scientific notation displays numbers in a format such as 1.5E+10.

11. If you have any questions as you proceed, ask your lab instructor for help.

Follow-Up Questions and Activities

1. Execute the program, and enter a decimal value when you are prompted for an account number. Observe what happens. You are no longer asked to input a **beginning balance**. Your output screen may resemble the output accompanying this question. Instead, the program prompts you to enter only **total charges**, **total credits** and **credit limit**. Why does this situation occur?

```
Enter account number (-1 to end): 123.456
Enter beginning balance: Enter total charges:
```

Lab Exercises

Name:

Lab Exercise 1 — Department Store

2. Why is it necessary to ask the user to input the first account number before you begin the **while** loop? What problems could occur if the user were asked for an account number only inside the **while** loop?

3. Modify the program to use counter-controlled repetition to process 10 accounts at a time. Use a **for** loop to do so. Explain when to use sentinel-controlled repetition and when to use counter-controlled repetition.

4. Change the **while** loop into a **do/while** loop. Execute the program, and enter **-1** as the first customer's account number. What happens? How is this result different from that generated using a **while** loop?

Lab Exercises   Name:

Lab Exercise 2 — Payroll

Name: _____   Date:_____

Section: _____

This problem is intended to be solved in a closed-lab session with a teaching assistant or instructor present. The problem is divided into six parts:

1. Lab Objectives
2. Description of the Problem
3. Sample Output
4. Program Template (Fig. L 2.2)
5. Problem-Solving Tips
6. Follow-Up Questions and Activities

The program template represents a complete working C++ program, with one or more key lines of code replaced with comments. Read the problem description and examine the sample output; then study the template code. Using the problem-solving tips as a guide, replace the **/* */** comments with C++ code. Compile and execute the program. Compare your output with the sample output provided. Then answer the follow-up questions. The source code for the template is available at **www.deitel.com** and **www.prenhall.com./deitel**.

Lab Objectives

This lab was designed to reinforce programming concepts from Chapter 2 of *C++ How To Program: Fourth Edition*. In this lab, you will practice:

*   writing pseudocode.
*   using sentinel-controlled repetition.
*   using **if/else** selection structures.

The follow-up questions and activities also will give you practice:

*   experimenting with **<iomanip>**.
*   using nested **if/else** statements.
*   using **switch** statements.

Description of the Problem

Develop a program that determines the gross pay for several employees. The company pays "straight-time" for the first 40 hours worked by each employee per week and pays "time and a half" for all hours worked in excess of 40 hours. You are given a list of the employees of the company, the number of hours each employee worked last week and the hourly rate of each employee. Your program should input this information for each employee and should determine and display the employee's gross pay. [*Note*: Do not attempt to input the employee's name. You will learn how to do this in Chapter 4 of *C++ How To Program: Fourth Edition*.]

In this problem, you will practice the top-down, stepwise refinement methodology discussed in the text. You should formulate the algorithm by using pseudocode and top-down, stepwise refinement before you begin coding.

Lab Exercises   Name:

Lab Exercise 2 — Payroll

Lab Exercises   Name: _____

Lab Exercise 2 — Payroll

Sample Output

```
Enter hours worked (-1 to end): 39
Enter hourly rate of the worker ($00.00): 10.00
Salary is $390.00

Enter hours worked (-1 to end): 40
Enter hourly rate of the worker ($00.00): 10.00
Salary is $400.00

Enter hours worked (-1 to end): 41
Enter hourly rate of the worker ($00.00): 10.00
Salary is $415.00

Enter hours worked (-1 to end): -1
```

Template

```cpp
1    // Chapter 2 of C++ How to Program
2    // wagecalculator.cpp
3    #include <iostream>
4
5    using std::cout;
6    using std::cin;
7    using std::endl;
8    using std::fixed;
9
10   #include <iomanip>
11
12   using std::setprecision;
13
14   int main()
15   {
16      /* declare program variables here */
17
18      cout << "Enter hours worked (-1 to end): " << fixed;
19
20      cin >> hours;
21
22      /* write code to begin loop here */  {
23         /* write code here to prompt and input hourly rate */
24
25         /* write code here to determine if hours worked are less
26            than or equal to 40 and if so, calculate base pay.
27            If not, calculate base + overtime pay */
28         cout << "Salary is $" << setprecision( 2 ) << salary
29            << "\n\nEnter hours worked (-1 to end): ";
30         cin >> hours;
31      }
32
33      return 0;
34
35   } // end main
```

Fig. L 2.2   wagecalculator.cpp.

Lab Exercises   Name:

Lab Exercise 2 — Payroll

Problem-Solving Tips

1. Notice that the number of employees is not specified in advance. The problem statement implies that you should use a sentinel value to control the loop.

2. The input data consist of two **double**s per employee, one for the number of hours worked and one for the hourly rate.

3. You will use a **while** loop to process several sets of employee data.

4. Before the loop, you will prompt for the number of hours worked. Inside the loop, you will prompt for each new set of data. It is a good programming practice to remind the user of the sentinel value in each prompt.

5. What sentinel value should you use? It needs to be a value that will not be confused with one of the legitimate data input values. A good choice for this program would be to use **-1** for the employee's number of hours worked, because the number of hours worked is a nonnegative value.

6. While you could prompt each time for both pieces of information needed for a customer, a better strategy would be to prompt just for the number of hours worked. If it is **-1**, terminate the loop. If it is not **-1** prompt for the remaining piece of data for that employee, namely, the hourly rate.

7. How do you calculate the pay for each employee? Multiply the number of hours worked by the hourly rate. Actually, it is not this simple because some employees need to be paid overtime (i.e., time and a half) for their overtime hours. So you will need to divide the employees into two groups—those who worked 40 hours or fewer, and those who worked more than 40 hours. You can do this task effectively with an **if/else** statement. If the person worked 40 hours or less, multiply the number of hours worked times the hourly salary; otherwise (**else**), calculate the pay by multiplying 40 times the hourly salary rate and adding to this value to the number of overtime hours times the overtime rate. The number of overtime hours is the number of hours in excess of the first 40 hours worked (i.e., *hours –40*), and the overtime salary is 1.5 times the hourly rate.

8. Be sure to follow the spacing and indentation conventions mentioned in the text. Before and after each control structure, place, a line of vertical space to make the control structure stand out. Indent all the body statements of **main** and indent all of the body statements of each control structure.

9. Print your outputs neatly in the indicated format. Remember to use **setprecision(2)** to force two positions of precision to the right of the decimal point when printing monetary amounts. You will need to **#include <iomanip>** to use function **setprecision(2)**.

10. Also remember to use manipulator **fixed**. This manipulator specifies that the number output should be output in fixed notation, as opposed to scientific notation (**std::scientific**). Fixed notation always keeps a "fixed" decimal point, regardless of the number of digits displayed. For example, 1.50000000000 is expressed in fixed notation. Scientific notation displays numbers in a format such as 1.5E+10.

11. If you have any questions as you proceed, ask your lab instructor for help.

Follow-Up Questions and Activities

1. Remove the **setprecision** command on line 28. The line should now read as follows:

```
cout << "Salary is $" << salary
```

Lab Exercises   Name:

Lab Exercise 2 — Payroll

Run the program again. Compare the output with the prior output. What are the differences? What is the default value for **setprecision**?

2. Modify the code so that if an employee works exactly 55 hours, that employee receives a $100 bonus, but no longer receives overtime for the number of hours worked over 40. Make an additional modification that if the employee works 75 hours or more, that employee receives a $1000 bonus in addition to overtime. Determining how to nest the **if/else** structures properly might seem complicated. It is recommended that your code resemble the following pseudocode:

If worked 40 hours or less
   Calculate salary
Else
   Calculate base salary for 40 hours

   If worked 55 hours
      Add a $100 bonus to base salary
   Else
      Add overtime salary to base salary

   If worked 75 hours or more
      Add a $1000 bonus to base salary

Test your code: How much does someone who worked exactly 55 hours earn? How much does someone who worked 56 hours earn? How much does someone who worked 75 hours earn?

Lab Exercises   Name:

Lab Exercise 2 — Payroll

3. Now modify the program so that workers get a $100 bonus for working exactly 55 hours, a $1000 bonus for working exactly 75 hours and lose $75 for working exactly 20 hours. If workers work any other number of hours, even if it is less than 40, give them overtime pay. Implement this modification using a **switch** statement. Compare the **switch** structure with the **if/else** structure. [*Note*: A **switch** statement works only with integral types, so it is necessary to change the declaration of **hours** to be of type **int**.]

Lab Exercises   Name:

Lab Exercise 3 — Pythagorean Triples

Name: _____   **Date:** _____

Section: _____

This problem is intended to be solved in a closed-lab session with a teaching assistant or instructor present. The problem is divided into six parts:

1. Lab Objectives
2. Description of the Problem
3. Sample Output
4. Program Template (Fig. L 2.3)
5. Problem-Solving Tips
6. Follow-Up Questions and Activities

The program template represents a complete working C++ program, with one or more key lines of code replaced with comments. Read the problem description and examine the sample output; then study the template code. Using the problem-solving tips as a guide, replace the **/* */** comments with C++ code. Compile and execute the program. Compare your output with the sample output provided. Then answer the follow-up questions. The source code for the template is available at **www.deitel.com** and **www.prenhall.com./deitel**.

Lab Objectives

This lab was designed to reinforce programming concepts from Chapter 2 of *C++ How To Program: Fourth Edition*. In this lab, you will practice :

*   using counter-controlled repetition.
*   using "brute force" to solve a problem.
*   nesting **for** loops.

The follow-up questions and activities will also give you practice:

*   using **break** statements.
*   using **continue** statements.
*   using **long** integers.

Description of the Problem

The set of three integer values for the lengths of the sides of a right triangle is called a *Pythagorean triple*. These three sides must satisfy the relationship that the sum of the squares of two of the sides is equal to the square of the hypotenuse. Find all integer Pythagorean triples for **side1**, **side2** and the **hypotenuse**, all no larger than 500. Use a triple-nested **for** loop that tries all possibilities. This program is an example of "brute force" computing. You will learn in more advanced computer science courses that there are many interesting problems for which there is no known algorithmic approach other than using sheer brute force.

Lab Exercises   Name:

Lab Exercise 3 — Pythagorean Triples

Sample Output

```
3       4       5
4       3       5
5       12      13
6       8       10
7       24      25
8       6       10
8       15      17
9       12      15
...
475     132     493
476     93      485
...
483     44      485
A total of 772 triples were found.
```

Template

```cpp
1   // Chapter 2 of C++ How to Program
2   // triples.cpp
3   #include <iostream>
4
5   using std::cout;
6   using std::endl;
7
8   int main()
9   {
10     int count = 0;
11     long hyptSquared; // hypotenuse squared
12     long sidesSquared; // sides squared
13
14     for ( /* write header for side1 */ ) {
15
16        for ( /* write header for side2 */ ) {
17
18           for ( /* write header for hyptSquared */ ) {
19              /* calculate hyptSquared */
20              /* calculate the sum of the sides squared */
21
22              if ( hyptSquared == sidesSquared ) {
23                 cout << side1 << "\t" << side2 << "\t"
24                      << hypt << "\n";
25                 ++count;
26
27              } // end if
28
29           } // end for
30
31        } // end for
32
33     } // end for
34
```

Fig. L2.3   **triples.cpp**. (Part 1 of 2.)

Lab Exercises   Name:

Lab Exercise 3 — Pythagorean Triples

```
35      cout << "A total of " << count << " triples were found."
36          << endl;
37
38      return 0;
39
40   } // end main
```

Fig. L 2.3   `triples.cpp`. (Part 2 of 2.)

Problem-Solving Tips

1. This program does not require any input from the user.

2. This program can take several minutes to run, depending on your computer's processor speed. If you have a CPU monitor available on your system, it is worth taking a look at it when this program is executed.

3. Do not be concerned that you are trying values that do not seem to make sense, such as a 1–500–1 triangle. Remember that brute-force techniques try all possible values.

4. The formula for the Pythagorean Theorem is $hypotenuse^2 = (side1)^2 + (side\ 2)^2$.

5. Be sure to follow the spacing and indentation conventions mentioned in the text. Before and after each control structure, place a line of vertical space to make the control structure stand out. Indent all the body statements of **main**, and indent all of the body statements of each control structure.

6. If you have any questions as you proceed, ask your lab instructor for help.

Follow-Up Questions and Activities

1. How many times did this program execute the inner most **for** loop? Add another counter to the program that counts the number of times this loop iterates. Declare a new variable of type **long** on line 13, named **loopCounter**, and initialize it to **0**. Add a statement on line 21 that increments **loopCounter** by **1**. Before exiting the program, print the value of **loopCounter**. Do the numbers match?

Lab Exercises   Name:

Lab Exercise 3 — Pythagorean Triples

2. Add a **break** statement to the program inside the innermost **for** loop. This **break** statement should be called after the 20th Pythagorean triple is found. Explain what happens to the program after the 20th triple is found. Are all three **for** loops exited, or just the innermost one? What happens when the **break** statement is placed inside the middle loop? The outermost loop?

3. Add a **continue** statement to the program that prevents a Pythagorean triple from being found when **side1** is equal to **8**. Using your solution to Follow-up Question 1, calculate how many times this new program executed the inner **for** loop. Explain why the **continue** statement affected the output.

4. Explain why a **long** variable is used for **hyptSquared** and **sideSquared**. Modify the program so that they are both of type **short** instead of type **long**. Rerun the program. What happens?

Lab Exercises   Name:

Debugging

Name: _____   **Date:**_____

Section: _____

The program in this section does not run properly. Fix all the syntax errors so that the program will compile successfully. Once the program compiles, compare the output with the sample output, and eliminate any logic errors that may exist. The sample output demonstrates what the program's output should be once the program's code has been corrected.

Sample Output

```
i is now equal to 1
        j is now equal to 0
                i + j = 1        i - j = 1
                i * j = 0        i ^ j = 1
        j is now equal to 1
                i + j = 2        i - j = 0
                i * j = 1        i ^ j = 1
                i / j = 1        i % j = 0
        j is now equal to 2
                i + j = 3        i - j = -1
                i * j = 2        i ^ j = 1
                i / j = 0.5      i % j = 1
        j is now equal to 3
                i + j = 4        i - j = -2
                i * j = 3        i ^ j = 1
                i / j = 0.33     i % j = 1
i is now equal to 2
        j is now equal to 0
                i + j = 2        i - j = 2
                i * j = 0        i ^ j = 1
        j is now equal to 1
                i + j = 3        i - j = 1
                i * j = 2        i ^ j = 2
                i / j = 2        i % j = 0
        j is now equal to 2
                i + j = 4        i - j = 0
                i * j = 4        i ^ j = 4
                i / j = 1        i % j = 0
        j is now equal to 3
                i + j = 5        i - j = -1
                i * j = 6        i ^ j = 8
                i / j = 0.67     i % j = 2

The final values of i and j are: 3 and 4
```

Lab Exercises   Name:

Debugging

Broken Code

```
1   // Chapter 2 of C++ How To Program
2   // Debugging problem
3
4   #include <iostream>
5
6   using std::cout;
7   using std::endl;
8
9   #include <iomanip>
10
11  using std::setprecision;
12
13  int main()
14  {
15      int i = 1;
16      double a;
17      double b;
18
19      cout << setprecision( 2 );
20
21      for ( int i; i <= 2; i++ )
22          cout << "i is now equal to " << i << endl;
23
24          for ( int j; j <= 3; j++ ) {
25              cout << "\tj is now equal to " << j << endl;
26
27              cout << "\t\ti + j = " << i + j << "\ti - j = "
28                   << i - j << endl;
29              cout << "\t\ti * j = " << i * j << "\ti ^ j = "
30                   << pow( i, j ) << endl;
31
32              if ( j = 0 )
33                  continue;
34
35              else {
36                  a = i;
37                  b = j;
38                  cout << "\t\ti / j = " << a / b <<
39                           "\ti % j = " << a % b << endl;
40              } // end else
41
42          } // end for
43
44      cout << "\nThe final values of i and j are: " << i
45           << " and " << j << endl;
46
47      return 0;
48
49  } // end main
```

Fig. L 2.4   debugging02.cpp.

Postlab Activities

Coding Exercises

Name: _____   **Date:**_____

Section: _____

These coding exercises reinforce the lessons learned in the lab and provide additional programming experience outside the classroom and laboratory environment. They serve as a review after you have successfully completed the Prelab Activities and Lab Exercises successfully.

For each of the following problems, write a program or a program segment that performs the specified action.

1. Write a **for** loop that prints all the odd integers from **1** to **100**, inclusive.

2. Write a **do/while** loop that counts downward from **10** to **0**.

Postlab Activities

Name:

Coding Exercises

3. Write a program that inputs an integer between **1** and **5** and uses a `switch` structure to print the number's corresponding letter in the alphabet (i.e., A, B, C, D or E).

Postlab Activities

Name: _____

Coding Exercises

4. Write a program that inputs an integer and uses an **if/else** statement to determine if the integer is odd or even. If it is odd, print **x is odd**, and if it is even, print **x is even**.

Postlab Activities   Name:

Coding Exercises

5. Rewrite your solution to Coding Exercise 4 so that it uses the conditional operator (**? :**).

6. Write a **while** loop that sums all the integers between **1** and **10**, inclusive, except for **3** and **6**. Print the sum.

7. Write a loop that reads in a maximum of 10 numbers and sums them. If the user enters the sentinel value of **-1**, terminate the loop prematurely. Print the sum.

8. Write a sentinel-controlled loop (use a sentinel value of **-1**) that contains statements which input and output user integer data. Do not print the number if it is either **7** or **63**.

Postlab Activities   Name:

Coding Exercises

9. Write a program that computes and prints the average of the integers between **1** and **10** inclusive. Print the number as a fixed decimal with three digits of precision.

10. Write a counter-controlled **for** loop that iterates from **1** to **10** and prints the value of its counter. Terminate the loop prematurely when the counter has a value of **6**.

11. Modify your solution to Coding Exercise 10 to use a **continue** statement such that every value except **6** is printed.

Postlab Activities

Name:

Coding Exercises

Postlab Activities   Name:

Programming Challenges

Name: _____   Date:_____

Section: _____

The Programming Challenges are more involved than the Coding Exercises and may require a significant amount of time to complete. Write a C++ program for each of the problems in this section. The answers to these problems are available at **www.deitel.com**, **www.prenhall.com/deitel** and on the *C++ Multimedia Cyber Classroom: Fourth Edition*. Pseudocode, hints and/or sample outputs are provided to aid you in your programming.

12. A large chemical company pays its salespeople on a commission basis. The salespeople receive $200 per week, plus nine percent of their gross sales for that week. For example, a salesperson who sells $5000 worth of chemicals in a week receives $200 plus nine percent of $5000, or a total of $650. Develop a program that will input each salesperson's gross sales for last week and calculate and display that salesperson's earnings. Process one salesperson's figures at a time. The output should resemble that shown below. Pseudocode is provided as a guide.

```
Enter sales in dollars (-1 to end): 5000.00
Salary is: $650.00

Enter sales in dollars (-1 to end): 6000.00
Salary is: $740.00

Enter sales in dollars (-1 to end): 7000.00
Salary is: $830.00

Enter sales in dollars (-1 to end): -1
```

Input the first salesperson's sales in dollars

While the sentinel value (−1) has not been entered for the sales
    Calculate the salesperson's wages for the week
    Print the salesperson's wages for the week
    Input the next salesperson's sales in dollars

13. [*Note*: This problem has three parts.] The factorial of a nonnegative integer n is written $n!$ (pronounced "n factorial") and is defined as follows:

$n! = n \cdot (n - 1) \cdot (n - 2) \cdot \ldots \cdot 1$ (for values of n greater than or equal to 1)

and

$n! = 1$ (for $n = 0$).

For example, $5! = 5 \cdot 4 \cdot 3 \cdot 2 \cdot 1$, which is 120.

a) Write a program that reads a nonnegative integer and computes and prints its factorial. Consider the following suggestions to get you started:

Postlab Activities   Name:

Programming Challenges

Hints:

- Create a variable **factorial**, and initialize it to **1**. Multiply it by a counter each time through the repetition structure.

- Use a repetition structure that initializes its counter to the number input and decrements it until it reaches **1**.

b) Write a program that estimates the value of the mathematical constant e by using the formula:

$$e = 1 + \frac{1}{1!} + \frac{1}{2!} + \frac{1}{3!} + \dots$$

Hints:

- Create a variable **e** of type **double**, and initialize it to **0**.

- Create a **while** loop that will calculate the mathematical constant e by iterating 20 times, with a counter starting at **1**.

- Keep a running product of the factorials in variable **factorial** by multiplying it by the loop counter.

- Each time through the loop, after updating **factorial**, add **1.0 / factorial** to **e**. Use **1.0** in your division to ensure a floating-point result.

c) Write a program that computes the value of e^x by using the formula:

$$e^x = 1 + \frac{x}{1!} + \frac{x^2}{2!} + \frac{x^3}{3!} + \dots$$

Hints:

- Use the solution to Part b as a starting point.

- Create another variable **xToX** to store the value of **x** raised to a power.

- Nest another loop inside of your **while** loop. Have this loop iterate **n** times, where **n** is the value of the counter in the outer loop.

- For each iteration of this inner loop, calculate **xToX** by multiplying **x** by itself.

- Add **xToX / factorial** to **eToX**.

- Make sure that **factorial** is of type **double**. Use casting if necessary.

14. A palindrome is a number or a text phrase that reads the same backwards as forwards. For example, each of the following five-digit integers is a palindrome: 12321, 55555, 45554 and 11611. Write a program that reads in a five-digit integer and determines whether it is a palindrome.

Hints:

- Use the division and modulus operators to separate the number into its individual digits.

- Store each digit in its own variable.

- Compare the first and fifth digits and the second and fourth digits; if they are equal, the number is a palindrome.

15. A company pays its employees as managers (who receive a fixed weekly salary), hourly workers (who receive a fixed hourly wage for up to the first 40 hours they work and time and a half, i.e., 1.5 times their hourly wage, for overtime hours worked), commission workers (who receive $250 plus 5.7% of their gross weekly sales), and pieceworkers (who receive a fixed amount of money per item for each of the items they produce—each

Postlab Activities

Name:

Programming Challenges

pieceworker in this company works on only one type of item). Write a program to compute the weekly pay for each employee. You do not know the number of employees in advance. Each type of employee has its own pay code: Managers have paycode **1**, hourly workers have paycode **2**, commission workers have paycode **3** and pieceworkers have paycode **4**. Use a **switch** structure to compute each employee's pay, based on that employee's paycode. Within the **switch**, prompt the user (i.e., the payroll clerk) to enter the appropriate facts your program needs to calculate each employee's pay based on that employee's paycode. Sample output is provided next. Model your code to produce these results.

```
Enter paycode (-1 to end): 3
Commission worker selected.
Enter gross weekly sales: 4000
Commission Worker's pay is $ 478.00

Enter paycode (-1 to end): 2
Hourly worker selected.
Enter the hourly salary: 4.50
Enter the total hours worked: 20
Worker's pay is $ 90.00

Enter paycode (-1 to end): 4
Piece worker selected.
Enter number of pieces: 50
Enter wage per piece: 3
Piece Worker's pay is $ 150.00

Enter paycode (-1 to end): -1


Total number of managers paid          : 0
Total number of hourly workers paid     : 1
Total number of commission workers paid: 1
Total number of piece workers paid      : 1
```

Postlab Activities

Name:

Programming Challenges

3

Functions

Objectives

- To understand how to construct programs modularly from pieces called functions.
- To create new functions.
- To understand the mechanisms used to pass information between functions.
- To introduce simulation techniques using random number generation.
- To understand how the visibility of identifiers is limited to specific regions of programs.
- To understand how to write and use functions that call themselves.

Assignment Checklist

Name: _____   **Date:** _____

Section: _____

Exercises	Assigned: Circle assignments	Date Due
Prelab Activities		
Matching	YES NO	
Fill in the Blank	13, 14, 15, 16, 17, 18	
Short Answer	19, 20, 21, 22, 23	
Programming Output	24, 25, 26, 27, 28, 29	
Correct the Code	30, 31, 32, 33, 34, 35, 36	
Lab Exercises		
Lab Exercise 1 — Prime Numbers	YES NO	
Follow-Up Questions and Activities Lab	1, 2, 3, 4	
Lab Exercise 2 — Reversing Digits	YES NO	
Follow-Up Questions and Activities Lab	1, 2, 3	
Lab Exercise 3 — Greatest Common Divisor	YES NO	
Follow-Up Questions and Activities Lab	1, 2, 3	
Debugging	YES NO	
Labs Provided by Instructor		
1.		
2.		
3.		
Postlab Activities		
Coding Exercises	1, 2, 3, 4, 5, 6, 7, 8	
Programming Challenges	9, 10, 11	

Assignment Checklist

Name:

Prelab Activities

Matching

Name: _____   **Date:** _____

Section: _____

After reading Chapter 3 of *C++ How to Program: Fourth Edition*, answer the given questions. These questions are intended to test and reinforce your understanding of key concepts and may be done either before the lab or during the lab.

For each term in the column on the left, write the corresponding letter for the description that best matches it from the column on the right.

Term	Description
____ 1. Divide-and-conquer	a) Using existing functions as building blocks to create new programs.
____ 2. Function call	b) Technique for reducing the number returned by **rand** into a specific range.
____ 3. Local variable	c) Contains function prototypes and definitions of various data types.
____ 4. Call-by-reference	d) Seeds the random-number generator.
____ 5. **static**	e) Invokes a function.
____ 6. Call-by-value	f) Known only in the function in which it is defined.
____ 7. Scaling	g) Passes a copy of an argument's value to a function.
____ 8. Scope	h) Technique for constructing a program from smaller, more manageable pieces.
____ 9. **rand**	i) Generates and returns a pseudo-random number.
____ 10. Header file	j) The portion of a program in which an identifier may be referenced.
____ 11. Software reusability	k) Provides a called function with the ability to access the caller's data directly.
____ 12. **srand**	l) Signifies that a variable retains its value after exiting the function in which it was defined.

Prelab Activities   Name:

Matching

Prelab Activities

Name: _____

Fill in the Blank

Name: _____   Date: _____

Section: _____

Fill in the blank for each of the following statements:

13. A function is invoked by a(n) _____.

14. Most functions have a list of _____ that provide the means of communication between functions.

15. Each standard library has a corresponding _____ that contains the function prototypes for all functions in that library and definitions of various data types and constants needed by those functions.

16. To specify that a function does not return a value, keyword _____ is used.

17. The compiler ignores variable names placed in the function _____.

18. To use function **sqrt**, the _____ header file must be included.

Prelab Activities

Name:

Fill in the Blank

Prelab Activities   Name: _____

Short Answer

Name: _____   **Date:**_____

Section: _____

In the space provided, answer each of the given questions. Your answers should be as concise as possible; aim for two or three sentences.

19. Compare and contrast call-by-reference and call-by-value.

20. Give an example of a function prototype. Identify the return type, the function name and the argument list. What is the purpose of the return type? What is the purpose of the argument list?

Prelab Activities

Name:

Short Answer

21. Provide an example of each of the four scopes for an identifier: function scope, file scope, block scope and function-prototype scope. Briefly discuss each scope.

22. Describe the differences between **rand** and **srand** and the role that each plays in the generation of random numbers.

23. What are enumerations?

Prelab Activities   Name:

Programming Output

Name: _____   Date:_____

Section: _____

For each of the given program segments, read the code and write the output in the space provided below each pro-gram. [*Note*: Do not execute these programs on a computer.]

24. What is output by the given program segment? Assume that **<cmath>** has been included.

```
1   double x = -5.49;
2
3   cout << ceil( x ) << endl << fabs( x ) << endl << floor( x );
```

Your answer:

25. What is output by the following program segment when function **f1** is invoked?

```
1   void f1()
2   {
3      int x = 5;
4
5      f2( x );
6      cout << x << endl;
7   }
8
9   void f2( int x )
10  {
11     x += 5;
12     cout << x << endl;
13  }
```

Your answer:

Prelab Activities

Name: _____

Programming Output

26. What is the output of

```
cout << mystery( 6, 2, 5 ) << endl;
```

assuming the following definition of **mystery**?

```
1   int mystery( int x, int y, int z )
2   {
3       int value = x;
4
5       if ( y > value )
6           value = y;
7
8       if ( z > value )
9           value = z;
10
11      return value;
12  }
```

Your answer:

27. What is output by the following program segment when function **f3** is called twice?

```
1   void f3()
2   {
3       static int x = 0;
4
5       x++;
6       cout << x << endl;
7   }
```

Your answer:

Prelab Activities   Name:

Programming Output

28. What is output by the following program?

```
1    #include <iostream>
2
3    using std::cout;
4    using std::endl;
5
6    void f1();
7
8    int main()
9    {
10      int x = 0;
11
12      cout << "Initially, x = " << x << endl;
13      f1();
14      cout << "At the end, x = " << x << endl;
15
16      return 0;
17
18   } // end main
19
20   // definition for f1
21   void f1()
22   {
23      int x = 3;
24
25      cout << "During call to f1, x = " << x << endl;
26
27   } // end function f1
```

Your answer:

Prelab Activities   Name:

Programming Output

29. What is the output of

```
cout << mystery2( 5, 4 ) << endl;
```

assuming the following definition of **mystery2**? [*Note*: This problem is intended for those students who have studied recursion in Sections 3.12–3.14 of *C++ How to Program: Fourth Edition*.]

```
1   int mystery2( int x, int y )
2   {
3      if ( y == 0 )
4         return x;
5
6      else if ( y < 0 )
7         return mystery2( x - 1, y + 1 );
8
9      else
10        return mystery2( x + 1, y - 1 );
11
12  } // end mystery2
```

Your answer:

Prelab Activities   Name:

Correct the Code

Name: _____   Date:_____

Section: _____

For each of the given program segments, determine if there is an error in the code. If there is an error, specify whether it is a logic error or a syntax error, circle the error in the program, and write the corrected code in the space provided after each problem. If the code does not contain an error, write "no error." [*Note*: It is possible that a program segment may contain multiple errors.]

30. The following program segment defines function **maximum**, which returns the largest of three integers:

```
1   int maximum( int x, int y, int z );
2   {
3       int max = x;
4
5       if ( y > max )
6           max = y;
7
8       if ( z > max )
9           max = x;
10
11      return max;
12  }
```

Your answer:

31. The following program segment should output five random numbers in the range from **1** to **6**, inclusive:

```
1   for ( int i = 1; i <= 5; i++ ) {
2       cout << setw( 10 ) << 1 + srand() % 6;
```

Your answer:

Prelab Activities   Name:

Correct the Code

32. The following program segment creates an enumeration **Status** and declares a variable **myStatus** to be of type **Status**:

```
1    enum Status = { CONTINUE; WON; LOST };
2    Status myStatus = 1;
```

Your answer:

33. The following program should display three lines of text:

```
1    #include <iostream>
2
3    using std::cout;
4    using std::endl;
5
6    int main()
7    {
8       cout << "Before call to f1.\n";
9
10      f1();
11
12      cout << "After call to f1.\n";
13
14      return 0;
15
16   } // end main
17
18   // f1 definition
19   void f1()
20   {
21      cout << "During call to f1.\n";
22
23   } // end function f1
```

Your answer:

Prelab Activities

Name:

Correct the Code

34. The following segment should define two functions:

```
1    void f2()
2    {
3       cout << "During call to f2.\n";
4
5       void f3()
6       {
7          cout << "During call to f3.\n";
8       }
9
10   } // end function f2
```

Your answer:

35. The given program segment should recursively calculate factorials. [*Note*: This problem is intended for those students who have studied recursion in Sections 3.12–3.14 of *C++ How to Program: Fourth Edition*.]

```
1    void factorial( unsigned long number )
2    {
3       if ( number <= 1 )
4          return 1;
5
6       else
7          return number * factorial( number + 1 );
8
9    } // end function factorial
```

Your answer:

Prelab Activities   Name:

Correct the Code

36. The following program should display a character input by the user:

```
1    #include <iostream>
2
3    using std::cout;
4    using std::endl;
5
6    void f4( int c );
7
8    int main()
9    {
10       char myChar;
11
12       cout << "Enter a character: ";
13       cin >> myChar;
14
15       f4( myChar )
16
17       return 0;
18
19   } // end main
20
21   // f4 definition
22   void f4( char c )
23   {
24       cout << "You just entered the character: " << myChar << endl;
25       return myChar;
26
27   } // end function f4
```

Your answer:

Lab Exercises

Lab Exercise 1 — Prime Numbers

Name: _____   **Date:**_____

Section: _____

This problem is intended to be solved in a closed-lab session with a teaching assistant or instructor present. The problem is divided into six parts:

1. Lab Objectives
2. Description of the Problem
3. Sample Output
4. Program Template (Fig. L 3.1)
5. Problem-Solving Tips
6. Follow-Up Questions and Activities

The program template represents a complete working C++ program, with one or more key lines of code replaced with comments. Read the problem description and examine the sample output; then study the template code. Using the problem-solving tips as a guide, replace the **/* */** comments with C++ code. Compile and execute the program. Compare your output with the sample output provided. Then answer the follow-up questions. The source code for the template is available at **www.deitel.com** and **www.prenhall.com./deitel**.

Lab Objectives

This lab was designed to reinforce programming concepts from Chapter 3 of *C++ How To Program: Fourth Edition*. In this lab, you will practice:

- writing function prototypes to specify the name of the function, the type of data returned by the function, the number of parameters the function expects to receive, the types of the parameters and the order in which these parameters are expected.

- making function calls and passing arguments to a function.

- returning values from a function.

The follow-up questions and activities also will give you practice:

- using call-by-reference so that the called function is able to modify its arguments

- determining variable scope. A variable, unless it was declared to be a global variable, can be used only in the portion of the program in which it was declared.

Description of the Problem

An integer is said to be *prime* if it is divisible only by two distinct factors 1 and itself. For example, 2, 3, 5 and 7 are prime, but 4, 6, 8 and 9 are not. [*Note*: The number 1 is not a prime number.]

Write a function that determines if a number is prime. Use this function in a program that determines and prints all the prime numbers between 1 and 10,000.

Lab Exercises   Name:

Lab Exercise 1 — Prime Numbers

Sample Output

```
The prime numbers from 1 to 10000 are:
     2     3     5     7    11    13    17    19    23    29
    31    37    41    43    47    53    59    61    67    71
    73    79    83    89    97   101   103   107   109   113
   127   131   137   139   149   151   157   163   167   173
   179   181   191   193   197   199   211   223   227   229
   233   239   241   251   257   263   269   271   277   281
   283   293   307   311   313   317   331   337   347   349
   353   359   367   373   379   383   389   397   401   409
   419   421   431   433   439   443   449   457   461   463
...
  9739  9743  9749  9767  9769  9781  9787  9791  9803  9811
  9817  9829  9833  9839  9851  9857  9859  9871  9883  9887
  9901  9907  9923  9929  9931  9941  9949  9967  9973
```

Template

```cpp
1   // Chapter 3 of C++ How to Program
2   // prime.cpp
3
4   #include <iostream>
5
6   using std::cout;
7   using std::endl;
8
9   #include <iomanip>
10
11  using std::setw;
12
13  /* write prototype for function prime */
14
15  int main()
16  {
17     int count = 0;
18
19     cout << "The prime numbers from 1 to 10000 are:\n";
20
21     for ( int loop = 2; loop <= 10000; ++loop )
22
23        if ( /* make call to function prime */ ) {
24           ++count;
25           cout << setw( 6 ) << loop;
26
27           if ( count % 10 == 0 )
28              cout << '\n';
29
30        } // end if
31
32     cout << '\n' << "There were " << count
33           << " prime numbers\n";
```

Fig. L 3.1   prime.cpp. (Part 1 of 2.)

Lab Exercises   Name:

<hr>

Lab Exercise 1 — Prime Numbers

```
34
35      return 0;
36
37   } // end main
38
39   // function prime definition
40   bool prime( int n )
41   {
42      for ( int i = 2; /* write loop condition */; i++ )
43
44         if ( /* write code to test if n is divisible by i */ )
45            return false;
46
47      return true;    // number is prime
48
49   } // end function prime
```

Fig. L 3.1   prime.cpp. (Part 2 of 2.)

Problem-Solving Tips

1. The program does not require any data to be input by the user.

2. Function **prime** contains an algorithm for determining if a number is prime. Functions should perform only one well-defined task. Function **prime** should return **true** if the number is prime and **false** otherwise. If a number is evenly divisible by another number other than itself or 1, it is not prime. Use the modulus operator, **%**, to test for a remainder.

3. Be sure to follow the spacing and indentation conventions mentioned in the text. Before and after each control structure place a line of vertical space to make the control structure stand out. Indent all the body statements of **main**, and indent all of the body statements of each control structure.

4. If you have any questions as you proceed, ask your lab instructor for assistance.

Follow-Up Questions and Activities

1. Initially, you might think that $n/2$ is the upper limit for which you must test to see if a number is prime, but you need go as high as the square root of n only. Why? Rewrite the program, and run it both ways. Do not forget to include any additional header files needed by your program.

Lab Exercises   Name: _____

Lab Exercise 1 — Prime Numbers

2. Modify function **prime** to return an integer value. If the number it tests is prime, return **1**; otherwise return **0**. Do not make any modifications to your **main** function. Why does the program still work?

3. Add an additional function **increment**, that increments its argument each time that it is called. Now, rather than using **++count** on the line in your solution that corresponds to line 24 in the program template, call **increment**. [*Note*: This problem is intended for students who have studied call-by-reference in Section 3.17 of *C++ How to Program: Fourth Edition*.]

4. In **prime**, replace variable **n** with variable **loop** in the **for** loop's condition. What error do you get? Now, make **loop** a global variable. Does this modification eliminate the error?

Lab Exercises   Name:

Lab Exercise 2 — Reversing Digits

Name: _____   **Date:**_____

Section: _____

This problem is intended to be solved in a closed-lab session with a teaching assistant or instructor present. The problem is divided into six parts:

1. Lab Objectives

2. Description of the Problem

3. Sample Output

4. Program Template (Fig. L 3.2)

5. Problem-Solving Tips

6. Follow-Up Questions and Activities

The program template represents a complete working C++ program, with one or more key lines of code replaced with comments. Read the problem description and examine the sample output; then study the template code. Using the problem-solving tips as a guide, replace the /* */ comments with C++ code. Compile and execute the program. Compare your output with the sample output provided. Then answer the follow-up questions. The source code for the template is available at **www.deitel.com** and **www.prenhall.com./deitel**.

Lab Objectives

This lab was designed to reinforce programming concepts from Chapter 3 of *C++ How To Program: Fourth Edition*. In this lab, you will practice:

- writing function prototypes to specify the name of the function, the type of data returned by the function, the number of parameters the function expects to receive, the types of the parameters and the order in which the parameters are expected.

- using multiple functions to perform specific tasks.

The follow-up questions and activities also will give you practice:

- nesting function calls.

- tracing through a program.

- comparing call-by-reference to call-by-value.

Description of the Problem

Write a function that takes an integer value and returns the number with its digits reversed. For simplicity, use integer numbers that do not contain zeroes. For example, given the number **7631**, the function should return **1367**.

Lab Exercises

Name:

Lab Exercise 2 — Reversing Digits

Sample Output

```
Enter a number between 1 and 9999: 7631
The number with its digits reversed is: 1367
```

Template

```cpp
1   // Chapter 3 of C++ How to Program
2   // reversedigits.cpp
3   #include <iostream>
4
5   using std::cout;
6   using std::cin;
7   using std::endl;
8
9   #include <iomanip>
10
11  using std::setw;
12
13  /* write prototype for reverseDigits */
14  /* write prototype for width */
15
16  int main()
17  {
18      int number;
19
20      cout << "Enter a number between 1 and 9999: ";
21      cin >> number;
22      cout << "The number with its digits reversed is: "
23          << setw( /* write call for width */ )
24          << /* write call for reverseDigits */
25          << endl;
26
27      return 0;
28
29  } // end main
30
31  // function reverseDigits definition
32  /* write function header for reverseDigits */
33  {
34      int reverse = 0;
35      int divisor = 1000;
36      int multiplier = 1;
37
38      while ( n > 10 ) {
39
40          if ( n >= divisor ) {
41              reverse += n / divisor * multiplier;
42              n %= divisor;
43              /* write a line of code that reduces divisor by a factor
44              of 10 */
45          /* write a line of code that increases multiplier
46              by a factor of 10 */
```

Fig. L 3.2   **reversedigits.cpp**. (Part 1 of 2.)

Lab Exercises   Name:

Lab Exercise 2 — Reversing Digits

```
47
48            } // end if
49            else
50               divisor /= 10;
51
52        } // end while
53
54        reverse += n * multiplier;
55        return reverse;
56
57    } // end function reverseDigits
58
59    // function width definition
60    /* write function header for width */
61    {
62        if ( n / 1000 )
63           return 4;
64        else if ( n / 100 )
65           return 3;
66        else if ( n / 10 )
67           return 2;
68        else
69           return 1;
70
71    } // end function width
```

Fig. L 3.2   reversedigits.cpp. (Part 2 of 2.)

Problem-Solving Tips

1. This problem requires that one integer be input by the user.

2. You should write a function called **reverseDigits** that takes the four-digit number as an argument. The algorithm for **reverseDigits** is as follows:

   a) Declare a variable called **divisor**, and assign **1000** to it.

   b) Using a **while** loop, isolate each individual digit and store it in its reverse position. This task is accomplished by dividing the number by **divisor** to get one digit and multiplying the number by its new position (e.g., one's position, ten's position, etc.). For example, the first digit is multiplied by one, the second digit is multiplied by ten, etc. In the body of the loop, during each iteration, the number must be reduced by a factor of 10, the **divisor** must be reduced by a factor of 10 each iteration and the multiplier must be increased by a factor of 10.

3. Be sure to follow the spacing and indentation conventions mentioned in the text. Before and after each control structure place a line of vertical space to make the control structure stand out. Indent all the body statements of **main**, and indent all the body statements of each control structure.

4. If you have any questions as you proceed, ask your lab instructor for assistance.

Lab Exercises   Name:

Lab Exercise 2 — Reversing Digits

Follow-Up Questions and Activities

1. Add code to **main** so that it reverses **number** twice (i.e., reverse it once, then reverse the result of the first function call). Do not store the value of **number** after it has been reversed once. Is the number that has been reversed twice equal to the original number?

2. What happens if **divisor** is initialized to **100** instead of **1000**? Try to solve this problem on paper first; then compare your answer with the one given by the computer. Are they the same?

Lab Exercises   Name: _____

Lab Exercise 2 — Reversing Digits

3. Rewrite **reverse** to take its arguments call-by-reference. It should no longer return a value; it should just modify the number it is passed. [*Note*: This problem is intended for students who have studied call-by-reference in Section 3.17 in *C++ How to Program: Fourth Edition*.]

Lab Exercises   Name:

Lab Exercise 2 — Reversing Digits

Lab Exercises   Name: _____

Lab Exercise 3 — Greatest Common Divisor

Name: _____   Date:_____

Section: _____

This problem is intended to be solved in a closed-lab session with a teaching assistant or instructor present. The problem is divided into six parts:

1. Lab Objectives

2. Description of the Problem

3. Sample Output

4. Program Template (Fig. L 3.3)

5. Problem-Solving Tips

6. Follow-Up Questions and Activities

The program template represents a complete working C++ program, with one or more key lines of code replaced with comments. Read the problem description and examine the sample output; then study the template code. Using the problem-solving tips as a guide, replace the /* */ comments with C++ code. Compile and execute the program. Compare your output with the sample output provided. Then answer the follow-up questions. The source code for the template is available at **www.deitel.com** and **www.prenhall.com./deitel**.

Lab Objectives

This lab was designed to reinforce programming concepts from Chapter 3 of C++ *How To Program: Fourth Edition*. In this lab, you will practice:

- writing function prototypes to specify the name of the function, the type of data returned by the function, the number of parameters the function expects to receive, the types of the parameters and the order in which the parameters are expected.

- passing multiple arguments to a function.

The follow-up questions and activities also will give you practice:

- using global variables. Global variables can be referenced from anywhere inside a program; a variable that is going to be accessed from multiple functions can be declared as global.

- using the conditional operator (**? :**).

- passing arguments via call-by-reference.

Description of the Problem

The greatest common divisor (GCD) of two integers is the largest integer that evenly divides into each of the two integers. Write a function **gcd** that returns the greatest common divisor of two integers.

Lab Exercises   Name:

Lab Exercise 3 — Greatest Common Divisor

Sample Output

```
Enter two integers: 6 8
The greatest common divisor of 6 and 8 is 2

Enter two integers: 789 4
The greatest common divisor of 789 and 4 is 1

Enter two integers: 9999 27
The greatest common divisor of 9999 and 27 is 9

Enter two integers: 73652 8
The greatest common divisor of 73652 and 8 is 4

Enter two integers: 99 11
The greatest common divisor of 99 and 11 is 11
```

Template

```cpp
1   // Chapter 3 of C++ How to Program
2   // gcd.cpp
3   #include <iostream>
4
5   using std::cout;
6   using std::cin;
7   using std::endl;
8
9   /* write prototype for gcd */
10
11  int main()
12  {
13     int a;
14     int b;
15
16     // allow the five sets of numbers to be input
17     for ( int j = 1; j <= 5; ++j ) {
18        cout << "Enter two integers: ";
19        cin >> a >> b;
20        cout << "The greatest common divisor of " << a
21             << " and " << b << " is "
22             <<  /* write call for gcd */ << "\n\n";
23
24     } // end for
25
26     return 0;
27
28  } // end main
29
30  // function gcd definition
31  /* write header for gcd */
```

Fig. L 3.3   gcd.cpp. (Part 1 of 2.)

Lab Exercises   Name:

Lab Exercise 3 — Greatest Common Divisor

```
32   {
33       int greatest = 1;
34
35       for ( int i = 2; i <= ( ( x < y ) ? x : y ); ++i )
36
37          if ( /* write condition to determine if both x and y are
38                 divisible by i */ )
39             greatest = i;
40
41       /* write a statement to return greatest */
42
43   } // end function gcd
```

Fig. L 3.3   gcd.cpp. (Part 2 of 2.)

Problem-Solving Tips

1. The program requires that two integers be input. Write a loop that allows several pairs of integers to be input during execution. This structure will allow you to test the program more thoroughly.

2. The program should contain one function **gcd** that implements the greatest-common-divisor algorithm. Every value up to and including the smallest of the two numbers must be divided into both the numbers. Use the modulus operator to check for a remainder. If the remainder is zero for both numbers, a common divisor has been found. Return the greatest common divisor from the function.

3. Be sure to follow the spacing and indentation conventions mentioned in the text. Before and after each control structure place a line of vertical space to make the control structure stand out. Indent all of the body statements of **main**, and indent all the body statements of each control structure.

4. If you have any questions as you proceed, ask your lab instructor for assistance.

Follow-Up Questions and Activities

1. Use global variables to rewrite the program so that **gcd** takes no arguments. Why is it considered bad programming practice to use global variables?

Lab Exercises

Name:

Lab Exercise 3 — Greatest Common Divisor

2. Rewrite the **for** loop in your solution that corresponds to line 35 in the program template so that it does not use the conditional operator (**? :**). [*Hint*: You will need to use the logical AND operator (**&&**).]

3. Create another function called **input**, that takes two integer values passed via call-by-reference and replaces their values with two input by the user. Use this function to input the values for **a** and **b**.

Lab Exercises   Name: _____

Debugging

Name: _____   Date: _____

Section: _____

The program (Fig. L 3.4) in this section does not run properly. Fix all the syntax errors so that the program will compile successfully. Once the program compiles, compare the output with the sample output, and eliminate any logic errors that may exist. The sample output demonstrates what the program's output should be once the program's code has been corrected.

Sample Output

[*Note*: This program uses random-number generation. The output will vary each time the program is executed. Run the program multiple times to confirm that it is working properly.]

```
January 1, 1900
February 8, 1985
```

```
January 1, 1900
May 25, 1913
```

```
January 1, 1900
August 6, 1912
```

Broken Code

```cpp
1    // Chapter 3 of C++ How to Program
2    // Debugging problem
3
4    #include <iostream>
5
6    using std::cout;
7    using std::endl;
8
9    #include <ctime>
10
11   #include <cstdlib>
12
13   enum Months { JAN = 1, FEB, MAR, APR, MAY, JUN,
14                 JUL, AUG, SEP, OCT, NOV, DEC };
15
16   void generateDate( int &, int &, int );
17   void printDate( Months, int, int );
18   int validDate( int, int );
19
```

Fig. L 3.4   debugging03.cpp. (Part 1 of 4.)

Lab Exercises

Debugging

```
20   int main()
21   {
22      int month = 1;
23      int day = 1;
24      int year = 1900;
25
26      srand( time( 0 ) );
27
28      printDate( month, day, year );
29      year = getYear( year );
30      getMonth();
31      day = getDay();
32
33      if ( validDate( month, day, year ) == true )
34         printDate( month, day, year );
35
36      return 0;
37
38   } // end main
39
40   // return month
41   int getMonth()
42   {
43      Month myMonth = rand() % 12 + 1;
44
45      return myMonth;
46
47   } // end getMonth
48
49   // return year
50   int getYear( int aYear )
51   {
52      return rand() % 101 + 1900;
53
54   } // end getYear
55
56   // return day
57   void getDay() { }
58   {
59      return rand() % 31 + 1;
60
61   } // end getDay
62
63   // output date
64   void printDate( Months month, int day, year );
65   {
66      switch ( month ) {
67
68         case JAN:
69            cout << "January " << day << ", " << year << endl;
70
71         case FEB:
72            cout << "February " << day << ", " << year << endl;
73            break;
74
```

Fig. L 3.4   debugging03.cpp. (Part 2 of 4.)

Lab Exercises   Name:

Debugging

```
75          case MAR:
76             cout << "March " << day << ", " << year << endl;
77             break;
78
79          case APR:
80             cout << "April " << day << ", " << year << endl;
81             break;
82          case MAY:
83             cout << "May " << day << ", " << year << endl;
84             break;
85
86          case JUN:
87             cout << "June " << day << ", " << year << endl;
88             break;
89
90          case JUL:
91             cout << "July " << day << ", " << year << endl;
92             break;
93
94          case AUG:
95             cout << "August " << day << ", " << year << endl;
96             break;
97
98          case SEP:
99             cout << "September " << day << ", " << year << endl;
100            break;
101         case OCT:
102            cout << "October " << day << ", " << year << endl;
103            break;
104
105         case NOV:
106            cout << "November " << day << ", " << year << endl;
107            break;
108
109         case DEC:
110            cout << "December " << day << ", " << year << endl;
111            break;
112
113         default:
114            cout << "invalid month\n";
115
116      } // end switch
117
118 } // end printDate
119
120 // check for validDate
121 bool validDate( int month, int day, int year )
122 {
123    int month;
124    int day;
125    int year;
126
127    if ( year < 1900 || year > 2001 )
128       return false;
129
130    else if ( month < 1 || month > 12 )
131       return false;
```

Fig. L 3.4   **debugging03.cpp**. (Part 3 of 4.)

Lab Exercises

Debugging

```
132      else if ( day < 1 || day > 31 )
133         return false;
134
135      else if ( day == 31 && month == APR || month == JUN
136              || month == SEP || month == NOV )
137         return false;
138
139      else if ( month == 2 && day > 28 )
140         return false;
141
142  } // end validDate
```

Fig. L 3.4   **debugging03.cpp**. (Part 4 of 4.)

Postlab Activities

Coding Exercises

Name: _____   Date:_____

Section: _____

These coding exercises reinforce the lessons learned in the lab and provide additional programming experience outside the classroom and laboratory environment. They serve as a review after you have completed the Prelab Activities and Lab Exercises successfully.

For each of the following problems, write a program or a program segment that performs the specified action.

1. Write a function that takes an integer parameter and returns the value of that integer modulus **7** (e.g., **n % 7**).

2. Write a short program that simulates 10 flips of a coin. Produce random results.

Postlab Activities

Coding Exercises

3. Change your coin-flipping program into a game: Every time heads comes up, the player wins $2; every time tails comes up, the player loses $1. Write a function **calculateTotal** that adds up the player's winnings after 10 flips of the coin.

4. Write a function **divides** that takes two integer parameters and returns **true** if the first integer divides evenly into the second one (i.e., the remainder is **0**).

Postlab Activities   Name: _____

Coding Exercises

5. Write a function **byTen** that uses a **static** variable **count**. Each call to the function should increment the **count** by **10**. Initialize **count** to be **0** at the start of the program.

6. Write a function **halve** that takes an integer parameter and returns the value of that integer divided by **2**.

Postlab Activities

Name:

Coding Exercises

7. Modify **halve** to take its parameter via call-by-reference.
    [*Note*: This problem is intended for those students who have studied call-by-reference in Section 3.17 in *C++ How to Program: Third Edition*.]

8. Write a function **minimumValue** that prints and returns the minimum of its five integer parameters.

Postlab Activities   Name:

Programming Challenges

Name: _____   Date:_____

Section: _____

The Programming Challenges are more involved than the Coding Exercises and may require a significant amount of time to complete. Write a C++ program for each of the problems in this section. The answers to these problems are available at **www.deitel.com**, **www.prenhall.com/deitel** and on the *C++ Multimedia Cyber Classroom: Fourth Edition*. Pseudocode, hints and/or sample outputs are provided to aid you in your programming.

9. A parking garage charges a $2.00 minimum fee to park for up to three hours. The garage charges an additional $0.50 per hour for each hour *or part thereof* in excess of three hours. The maximum charge for any given 24-hour period is $10.00. Assume that no car parks for longer than 24 hours at a time. Write a program that calculates and prints the parking charges for each of three customers who parked their cars in this garage yesterday. You should enter the number of hours parked for each customer. Your program should print the results in a neat tabular format and should calculate and print the total of yesterday's receipts. The program should use the function **calculateCharges** to determine the charge for each customer. Your output should appear in the following format:

```
Enter the hours parked for three cars: 1.5 4.0 24.0

Car        Hours       Charge
1           1.5         2.00
2           4.0         2.50
3          24.0        10.00
TOTAL      29.5        14.50
```

Hints:

-   Use a **for** loop to prompt the user for the number of hours parked for each of the three customers.
-   Declare variables to store the total number of hours and the total charges for each customer.
-   The variables for all charges and numbers of hours should be of type **double**.
-   Function **calculateCharges** should use a nested **if/else** structure to determine the customer charge.

10. Write a function **integerPower(base, exponent)** that returns the value of

    $base^{exponent}$

For example, **integerPower(3, 4) = 3 * 3 * 3 * 3**. Assume that **exponent** is a positive, nonzero integer and that **base** is an integer. The function **integerPower** should use **for** or **while** loop to control the calculation. Do not use any math library functions.

Hints:

-   Use a **for** loop to loop X times where X is the exponent that **integerPower** is passed.
-   During each iteration of the loop, multiply variable **product** by the value of **base**.
-   Return the value of **product** after X iterations of the **for** loop.

Postlab Activities   Name:

Programming Challenges

11. Computers are playing an increasing role in education. Write a program that will help an elementary school student learn multiplication. Use **rand** to produce two positive one-digit integers. The program should then output a question using the numbers, such as:

```
How much is 6 times 7?
```

The student then types the answer. The program checks the student's answer. If it is correct, print **"Very good!"**, and ask another multiplication question. If the answer is wrong, print **"No. Please try again."**, and let the student try the same question repeatedly until the student gets it right.

Hints:

• Use sentinel-controlled repetition to limit the number of questions that the program asks the user. At the same time, check that the user has entered the correct answer.

• Seed the **rand** function with **srand** to randomize the program

Arrays

Objectives

- To declare arrays, initialize arrays and refer to individual array elements.
- To be able to pass arrays to functions.
- To understand basic sorting techniques.
- To understand basic searching techniques.
- To be able to declare, initialize and manipulate multiple-subscript arrays.

Assignment Checklist

Name: _____   **Date:** _____

Section: _____

Exercises	Assigned: Circle assignments	Date Due
Prelab Activities		
Matching	YES NO	
Fill in the Blank	12, 13, 14, 15, 16, 17, 18, 19	
Short Answer	20, 21, 22, 23, 24	
Programming Output	25, 26, 27, 28, 29, 30	
Correct the Code	31, 32, 33, 34, 35, 36, 37, 38	
Lab Exercises		
Lab Exercise 1—**Rolling Dice**	YES NO	
Follow-Up Questions and Activities	1, 2, 3, 4	
Lab Exercise 2—**Bubble Sort**	YES NO	
Follow-Up Questions and Activities	1, 2, 3	
Lab Exercise 3—**Salespeople**	YES NO	
Follow-Up Questions and Activities	1, 2, 3	
Debugging	YES NO	
Labs Provided by Instructor		
1.		
2.		
3.		
Postlab Activities		
Coding Exercises	1, 2, 3, 4, 5, 6, 7, 8,	
Programming Challenges	9, 10, 11, 12	

Assignment Checklist

Name:

Prelab Activities

Matching

Name: _____   **Date:** _____

Section: _____

After reading Chapter 4 of *C++ How to Program: Fourth Edition*, answer the given questions. These questions are intended to test and reinforce your understanding of key concepts and may be done either before the lab or during the lab.

For each term in the column on the left, write the corresponding letter for the description that best matches it from the column on the right.

Term	Description
___ 1. Subscript	a) Qualifier that prevents modification of a variable's value.
___ 2. Zeroth element	b) Refers to a particular location or element in an array.
___ 3. Scalar quantities	c) Data such as individual array elements.
___ 4. Bubble sort	d) String termination character.
___ 5. Sorting	e) Sequence of characters enclosed in double quotes.
___ 6. Search key	f) Value for which a search is made.
___ 7. Double-subscripted arrays	g) First element in an array.
___ 8. Null character	h) Discrepancy between "i^{th} element of the array" and "array element i."
___ 9. `const`	i) Sorting technique in which several passes of the array are made. On each pass, successive pairs of elements are compared.
___ 10. Off-by-one errors	j) Arrays that require two subscripts to identify an array element.
___ 11. String	k) Placing data in some particular order (such as descending or ascending).

Prelab Activities   Name:

Matching

Prelab Activities   Name:

Fill in the Blank

Name: _____   **Date:**_____

Section: _____

Fill in the blank for each of the following statements:

12. To pass an array to a function, the _____ of the array is passed.

13. To pass one row of a double-subscripted array to a function that receives a single-subscripted array, pass the name of the array followed by the _____.

14. In a worst case scenario, searching an array with 1024 elements will take only _____ comparisons using a binary search.

15. C++ stores lists of values in _____.

16. Assigning a value to a(n) _____ variable in an executable statement is a syntax error.

17. Arrays are passed to functions call-by _____.

18. All strings end with the _____ character.

19. A(n) _____ may be an integer or an integer expression and identifies a particular array element.

Prelab Activities

Name:

Fill in the Blank

Prelab Activities   Name:

Short Answer

Name: _____   **Date:**_____

Section: _____

In the space provided, answer each of the given questions. Your answers should be as concise as possible; aim for two or three sentences.

20. What is an "off-by-one error?" Provide an example.

21. Describe how a binary search works. Why is it more efficient than a linear search?

22. What is the **const** qualifier? What happens when the programmer tries to modify the contents of an array that has been qualified with keyword **const**?

23. How is a bubble sort implemented? Is this implementation efficient for sorting large arrays?

24. Describe how multi-dimensional arrays might represent a table in which information is arranged in rows and columns.

Prelab Activities

Name: _____

Short Answer

Prelab Activities   Name:

Programming Output

Name: _____   **Date:**_____

Section: _____

For each of the given program segments, read the code and write the output in the space provided below each program. [*Note*: Do not execute these programs on a computer.]

25. What is output by the following program segment?

```
1   int i;
2   int values[ 10 ] = { 4, 1, 1, 3, 4, 9, 9, 2, 1, 7 };
3
4   cout << "Element" << setw( 13 ) << "Value" << endl;
5
6   for ( i = 0; i < 10; i++ )
7       cout << setw( 7 ) << i << setw( 13 ) << values[ i ] << endl;
```

Your answer:

26. What is output by the following code segment?

```
1   char string1[] = "How are you?";
2
3   cout << "string1 is: " << string1 << endl;
4
5   for ( int i = 0; string1[ i ] != '\0'; i++ )
6       cout << string1[ i ] << "_";
```

Your answer:

Prelab Activities

Name:

Programming Output

27. What is output by the following program segment?

```
1   int main()
2   {
3      cout << "First call to function:\n";
4      fn();
5
6      cout << "\n\nSecond call to fn:\n";
7      fn();
8      cout << endl;
9
10     return 0;
11
12  } // end main
13
14  // function fn definition
15  void fn()
16  {
17     static int array1[ 3 ];
18     int i;
19
20     cout << "\nValues on entering fn:\n";
21
22     for ( i = 0; i < 3; i++ )
23        cout << "array1[" << i << "] = " << array1[ i ] << "  ";
24
25     cout << "\nValues on exiting fn:\n";
26
27     for ( i = 0; i < 3; i++ )
28        cout << "array1[" << i << "] = "
29            << ( array1[ i ] += 2 ) << "   ";
30
31  } // end function fn
```

Your answer:

Prelab Activities

Name:

Programming Output

28. What is output by the following program segment? What algorithm does this segment implement?

```
1   int main()
2   {
3      const int arraySize = 10;
4      int a[ arraySize ] = { 2, 62, 4, 33, 10, 12, 89, 68,
5                             45, 7 };
6      int i;
7      int hold;
8
9      cout << "Data items in original order\n";
10
11     for ( i = 0; i < arraySize; i++ )
12        cout << setw( 4 ) << a[ i ];
13
14     for ( int pass = 0; pass < arraySize - 1; pass++ )
15
16        for ( i = 0; i < arraySize - 1; i++ )
17
18           if ( a[ i ] < a[ i + 1 ] ) {
19              hold = a[ i ];
20              a[ i ] = a[ i + 1 ];
21              a[ i + 1 ] = hold;
22
23           } // end if
24
25     cout << "\nData items in new order\n";
26
27     for ( i = 0; i < arraySize; i++ )
28        cout << setw( 4 ) << a[ i ];
29
30     cout << endl;
31
32     return 0;
33
34   } // end main
```

Your answer:

Prelab Activities

Name:

Programming Output

29. What is output by the following program segment?

```
1   const int arraySize = 10;
2   int a[ arraySize ] = { 4, 3, 7, 1, 13, 6, 0, 2, 9, 5 };
3
4   for ( int i = 0; i < arraySize; i++ ) {
5
6      for ( int j = 0; j < a [ i ]; j++ )
7         cout << "*";
8
9      cout << endl;
10  }
```

Your answer:

30. Which searching algorithm is implemented in the following code? What value is returned by the function call **search(a, 7, 0, 4)**, where **a** is defined as

    int a[5] = { 1, 2, 3, 7, 9 };?

```
1   int search( const int b[], int searchKey, int low, int high )
2   {
3      int middle;
4
5      while ( low <= high ) {
6         middle = ( low + high ) / 2;
7
8         if ( searchKey == b[ middle ] )
9            return middle;
10
11         else if ( searchKey < b[ middle ] )
12            high = middle - 1;
13
14         else
15            low = middle + 1;
16
17      } // end while
18
19      return -1;
20
21  } // end function search
```

Your answer:

Prelab Activities   Name: _____

Correct the Code

Name: _____   **Date:** _____

Section: _____

For each of the given program segments, determine if there is an error in the code. If there is an error, specify whether it is a logic error or a syntax error, circle the error in the program, and write the corrected code in the space provided after each problem. If the code does not contain an error, write "no error." [*Note*: It is possible that a program segment may contain multiple errors.]

31. The following code should assign **8** to the 105th subscript of **array**:

```
1   array[ 105 ] = [ 8 ];
```

Your answer:

32. The **for** loop should initialize all array values to **-1**.

```
1   int array[ 10 ];
2
3   for ( int i = 0; i < 9; i++ )
4      array[ i ] = -1;
```

Your answer:

33. Array **array** should contain all the integers from **0** and **10**, inclusive.

```
1   int aarray[ 10 ] = { 0, 1, 2, 3, 4, 5, 6, 7, 8, 9, 10 };
```

Your answer:

Prelab Activities   Name:

Correct the Code

34. The following code segment should declare two arrays containing five and six elements, respectively:

```
1   const int arraySize = 5;
2   int a[ arraySize ];
3
4   arraySize = 6;
5
6   int b[ arraySize ];
```

Your answer:

35. The **for** loop that follows should print array **array**'s values:

```
1   int array[ 10 ] = { 0 };
2
3   for ( int i = 0; i <= 10; i++ )
4       cout << array[ i ];
```

Your answer:

36. This **for** loop should print double-subscripted array **array**'s values:

```
1   int array[ 10 ][ 5 ] = { 10, 5 };
2
3   for ( int i = 0; i < 5; i++ )
4
5       for ( int k = 0; k < 10; k++ )
6           cout << array[ i ][ k ];
```

Your answer:

Prelab Activities

Name: _____

Correct the Code

37. This program segment should read a character string from the user. Assume that the input can be any word in the English language.

```
1   char string1[ 2 ];
2
3   cout << "Please enter any word: ";
4   cin >> string1;
```

Your answer:

38. In the code segment, **10** should be assigned to the array element that corresponds to the third row and fourth column.

```
1   int table[ 100, 100 ] = { { 0 }, { 0 } };
2
3   table[ 3, 4 ] = 10;
```

Your answer:

Prelab Activities   Name:

Correct the Code

Lab Exercises

Lab Exercise 1 — Rolling Dice

Name: _____   **Date:** _____

Section: _____

This problem is intended to be solved in a closed-lab session with a teaching assistant or instructor present. The problem is divided into six parts:

1. Lab Objectives

2. Description of the Problem

3. Sample Output

4. Program Template (Fig. L 4.2)

5. Problem-Solving Tips

6. Follow-Up Questions and Activities

The program template represents a complete working C++ program, with one or more key lines of code replaced with comments. Read the problem description and examine the sample output; then study the template code. Using the problem-solving tips as a guide, replace the **/* */** comments with C++ code. Compile and execute the program. Compare your output with the sample output provided. Then answer the follow-up questions. The source code for the template is available at **www.deitel.com** and **www.prenhall.com./deitel**.

Lab Objectives

This lab was designed to reinforce programming concepts from Chapter 4 of *C++ How To Program: Fourth Edition*. In this lab, you will practice:

- using **rand** to generate random numbers and using **srand** to seed the random-number generator.

- declaring, initializing and referencing arrays.

The follow-up questions and activities also will give you practice:

- remembering that arrays begin with subscript 0 and recognizing off-by-one errors.

- preventing array out-of-bounds errors.

- using two-dimensional arrays.

Description of the Problem

Write a program that simulates the rolling of two dice. The program should call **rand** to roll the first die, and should call **rand** again to roll the second die. The sum of the two values should then be calculated. [*Note:* Because each die has an integer value from 1 to 6, then the sum of the two values will vary from 2 to 12 with 7 being the most frequent sum and 2 and 12 being the least frequent sums. Figure L 4.1 shows the 36 possible combinations of the two dice.] Your program should roll the two dice 36,000 times. Use a single-subscripted array to tally the numbers of times each sum appears. Print the results in a tabular format. Also, determine if the totals are reasonable, (i.e., there are six ways to roll a 7), so approximately one sixth of all the rolls should be 7.

Lab Exercises

Name:

Lab Exercise 1 — Rolling Dice

	1	2	3	4	5	6
1	2	3	4	5	6	7
2	3	4	5	6	7	8
3	4	5	6	7	8	9
4	5	6	7	8	9	10
5	6	7	8	9	10	11
6	7	8	9	10	11	12

Fig. L 4.1   36 possible outcomes of rolling two dice.

Sample Output

Sum	Total	Expected	Actual
2	1000	2.778%	2.778%
3	1958	5.556%	5.439%
4	3048	8.333%	8.467%
5	3979	11.111%	11.053%
6	5007	13.889%	13.908%
7	6087	16.667%	16.908%
8	4996	13.889%	13.878%
9	3971	11.111%	11.031%
10	2996	8.333%	8.322%
11	2008	5.556%	5.578%
12	950	2.778%	2.639%

Lab Exercises   Name:

Lab Exercise 1 — Rolling Dice

Template

```
 1   // Chapter 4 of C++ How to Program
 2   // rolldie.cpp
 3   #include <iostream>
 4
 5   using std::cout;
 6   using std::endl;
 7   using std::fixed;
 8
 9   #include <iomanip>
10
11   using std::setprecision;
12   using std::setw;
13
14   #include <cstdlib>
15   #include <ctime>
16
17   int main()
18   {
19      const long ROLLS = 36000;
20      const int SIZE = 13;
21
22      // array expected contains counts for the expected
23      // number of times each sum occurs in 36 rolls of the dice
24
25      /* Write the declaration of array expected here. Assign an
26         initializer list containing the expected values here. Use
27         SIZE for the number of elements */
28
29      /* Write declaration for array sum here. Initialize all
30         elements to zero. Use SIZE for the number of elements */
31
32      int die1;
33      int die2;
34
35      srand( time( 0 ) );
36
37      /* Write a for loop that iterates ROLLS times. Randomly
38         generate values for x (i.e., die1) and y (i.e., die2)
39         and increment the appropriate counter in array sum that
40         corresponds to the sum of x and y */
41
42      cout << setw( 10 ) << "Sum" << setw( 10 ) << "Total"
43           << setw( 10 ) << "Expected" << setw( 10 ) << "Actual\n" << fixed
44           << setprecision( 3 );
45
46      for ( int j = 2; j < SIZE; ++j )
47         cout << setw( 10 ) << j << setw( 10 ) << sum[ j ]
48              << setw( 9 ) << 100.0 * expected[ j ] / 36 << "%"
49              << setw( 9 ) << 100.0 * sum[ j ] / ROLLS << "%\n";
50
51      return 0;
52
53   } // end main
```

Fig. L 4.2   **rolldie.cpp**.

Lab Exercises

Name:

Lab Exercise 1 — Rolling Dice

Problem-Solving Tips

1. Remember that array subscripts always begin with zero. This is also true for each dimension of a multiple-subscripted array (which this lab does not use).

2. The actual percentage is the likelihood, based on the results of your program, that a dice roll produced a certain result. In other words, if you roll the dice 36,000 times the actual percentage will be the *(number of times a result occurred / 36000) * 100.*

3. The expected percentage is the statistical probability that a dice roll will produce a certain result. This can be calculated from the diagram "36 possible outcomes of rolling two dice," shown in the problem description. For instance there is only one combination that will produce the sum of 2 and there are 36 total combinations. Therefore, the expected percentage of rolling a 2 is 1/36 or 2.778%.

Follow-Up Questions and Activities

1. Why is the variable **SIZE** initialized to **13** when there are only 11 possible die-roll outcomes?

2. What happens if the **<** operator, on the line in your solution that corresponds to the **<** operator on line 46 of the program template, is changed to **<=**? Why?

3. What happens if the array is not initialized to zeros? Try running the program without initializing the array. Show your results.

4. Modify the program to use a two-dimensional array as shown in the diagram "36 possible outcomes of rolling two dice," provided in the problem description section. Now, rather than counting the number of times each sum appears, increment the correct cell in the array. Print this array with the number of times each dice combination occurred. A sample output may look like the following:

	1	2	3	4	5	6
1	1011	971	1027	1025	971	1015
2	1013	968	990	968	1081	993
3	993	1014	983	973	1019	977
4	980	1004	974	1022	946	1046
5	1003	1021	1019	979	1004	1056
6	1026	1015	931	989	1014	979

Lab Exercises   Name:

Lab Exercise 2 — Bubble Sort

Name: _____   Date:_____

Section: _____

This problem is intended to be solved in a closed-lab session with a teaching assistant or instructor present. The problem is divided into six parts:

1. Lab Objectives
2. Description of the Problem
3. Sample Output
4. Program Template (Fig. L 4.3–Fig. L 4.4)
5. Problem-Solving Tips
6. Follow-Up Questions and Activities

The program template represents a complete working C++ program, with one or more key lines of code replaced with comments. Read the problem description and examine the sample output; then study the template code. Using the problem-solving tips as a guide, replace the **/* */** comments with C++ code. Compile and execute the program. Compare your output with the sample output provided. Then answer the follow-up questions. The source code for the template is available at **www.deitel.com** and **www.prenhall.com./deitel**.

Lab Objectives

This lab was designed to reinforce programming concepts from Chapter 4 of *C++ How To Program: Fourth Edition*. In this lab, you will practice:

- sorting data using the bubble sort algorithm, which makes several passes through an array and on each pass, compares successive pairs of elements. If a pair is in the proper order, a swap is not made. If a pair is in the incorrect order, the values are swapped.

- optimizing a program to be more efficient. The bubble sort algorithm is an inefficient sorting algorithm. To improve its efficiency, the program can determine if the data is already in order and avoid making duplicate comparisons.

The follow-up questions and activities also will give you practice:

- passing arrays as arguments. When passing arrays as arguments, it is important to remember that arrays are passed call-by-reference.

- recognizing array-out-of-bounds errors and off-by-one errors.

Description of the Problem

The bubble sort presented in Fig. 4.16 of *C++ How to Program: Fourth Edition* is inefficient for large arrays. For parts a, b and c do the following:

1. Save each modification in a different source-code file.
2. Record the "Number of comparisons" after each modification.
3. Make the requested modification(s).

Lab Exercises

Name:

Lab Exercise 2 — Bubble Sort

a) Modify the bubble sort implementation to produce the following output:

```
Data items in original order
   2   6   4   8  10  12  89  68  45  37

After pass 0:   2   4   6   8  10  12  68  45  37  89
After pass 1:   2   4   6   8  10  12  45  37  68  89
After pass 2:   2   4   6   8  10  12  37  45  68  89
After pass 3:   2   4   6   8  10  12  37  45  68  89
After pass 4:   2   4   6   8  10  12  37  45  68  89
After pass 5:   2   4   6   8  10  12  37  45  68  89
After pass 6:   2   4   6   8  10  12  37  45  68  89
After pass 7:   2   4   6   8  10  12  37  45  68  89
After pass 8:   2   4   6   8  10  12  37  45  68  89

Data items in ascending order
   2   4   6   8  10  12  37  45  68  89
Number of comparisons = 81
```

b) After the first pass, the largest number is guaranteed to be in the highest-numbered element of the array; after the second pass, the two highest numbers are "in place," and so on. Instead of making nine comparisons on every pass, modify the bubble sort to make eight comparisons on the second pass, seven on the third pass, and so on. The output should look as follows: [*Note:* Each subsequent line prints one less array element. This shows that the number of comparisons decreased by 1 on each pass.]

```
Data items in original order
   2   6   4   8  10  12  89  68  45  37

After pass 0:   2   4   6   8  10  12  68  45  37  89
After pass 1:   2   4   6   8  10  12  45  37  68
After pass 2:   2   4   6   8  10  12  37  45
After pass 3:   2   4   6   8  10  12  37
After pass 4:   2   4   6   8  10  12
After pass 5:   2   4   6   8  10
After pass 6:   2   4   6   8
After pass 7:   2   4   6
After pass 8:   2   4

Data items in ascending order
   2   4   6   8  10  12  37  45  68  89
Number of comparisons = 45
```

c) The data in the array may already be in the proper order or near-proper order, so why make nine passes if fewer will suffice? Modify the bubble sort to check at the end of each pass if any swaps have been made. If none has been made, then the data must be in the proper order, so the program should terminate. If swaps have been made, then at least one more pass is needed. Do the following:

   1) Use the data set [2, 6, 4, 8, 10, 12, 89, 68, 45, 37] from parts a and b. Did the program appear to run any differently?

   2) Now use the data set shown in the following output box. Did the program appear to run any differently?

Lab Exercises   Name:

Lab Exercise 2 — Bubble Sort

```
Data items in original order
   6   4   2   8  10  12  37  45  68  89

After pass 0:   4   2   6   8  10  12  37  45  68  89
After pass 1:   2   4   6   8  10  12  37  45  68
After pass 2:   2   4   6   8  10  12  37  45

Data items in ascending order
   2   4   6   8  10  12  37  45  68  89
Number of comparisons = 24
```

Template (Part a)

```cpp
 1   // Chapter 4 of C++ How to Program
 2   // bubblesorta.cpp
 3   #include <iostream>
 4
 5   using std::cout;
 6   using std::endl;
 7
 8   #include <iomanip>
 9
10   using std::setw;
11
12   int main()
13   {
14      const int SIZE = 10;
15      int a[ SIZE ] = { 2, 6, 4, 8, 10, 12, 89, 68, 45, 37 };
16      int hold;
17      int numberOfComparisons = 0;
18      int compare;
19
20      cout << "Data items in original order\n";
21
22      for ( int i = 0; i < SIZE; ++i )
23         cout << setw( 4 ) << a[ i ];
24
25      cout << "\n\n";
26
27      /* Write bubble sort implementation here */
28
29      cout << "\nData items in ascending order\n";
30
31      for ( int j = 0; j < SIZE; ++j )
32         cout << setw( 4 ) << a[ j ];
33
34      cout << "\nNumber of comparisons = " << numberOfComparisons
35           << endl;
36
37      return 0;
38
39   } // end main
```

Fig. L 4.3   bubblesorta.cpp.

Lab Exercises

Name:

Lab Exercise 2 — Bubble Sort

Template (Parts b and c)

```cpp
1   // Chapter 4 of C++ How to Program
2   // bubblesortbc.cpp
3   #include <iostream>
4
5   using std::cout;
6   using std::endl;
7
8   #include <iomanip>
9
10  using std::setw;
11
12  int main()
13  {
14     const int SIZE = 10;
15     int a[ SIZE ] = { 6, 4, 2, 8, 10, 12, 37, 45, 68, 89 };
16     int hold;
17     int numberOfComparisons = 0;
18     int compare;
19     bool swapCheck = true;
20
21     cout << "Data items in original order\n";
22
23     for ( int i = 0; i < SIZE; ++i )
24        cout << setw( 4 ) << a[ i ];
25
26     cout << "\n\n";
27
28     /* Write bubble sort implementation here */
29
30     cout << "\nData items in ascending order\n";
31
32     for ( int q = 0; q < SIZE; ++q )
33        cout << setw( 4 ) << a[ q ];
34
35     cout << "\nNumber of comparisons = " << numberOfComp
36           << endl;
37
38     return 0;
39
40  } // end main
```

Fig. L 4.4   `bubblesortbc.cpp`.

Problem-Solving Tips

1. (Part a) Follow the template carefully. You can print the new output simply by adding **cout** statements within the bubble sort implementation (in between the **for** loops). You should not have more than four **for** loops in your solution.

2. (Part b) The number of comparisons made per pass must equal the value of the current pass (i.e., if the current pass is five then a maximum of five comparisons should be made).

Lab Exercises   Name:

Lab Exercise 2 — Bubble Sort

3. (Part c) Note that only three swaps are needed to order the data. This particular data set shows that this algorithm is efficient for arrays that are either almost sorted or completely sorted. The modification requires an extra variable (e.g., **swapCheck**). Use this new variable as a flag. When entering the loop, disable the flag. When a swap is made, enable the flag. The condition of the outer loop should test for this value being enabled. If the value is enabled, the loop iterates. Otherwise the loop terminates.

Follow-Up Questions and Activities

1. Why was there a difference in program execution of Part c between the two different data sets? Try another data set and observe the differences.

2. Add a function, **xthSmallest**, that determines what the Xth smallest number in the array is after it has been sorted. This function should take two arguments: The array and the Xth smallest number. For example, if the data set stored in array **myArray** was

    ```
    { -1, 8, 12, 42, 54, 62, 73, 75, 110, 299 }
    ```

    the value returned by **xthSmallest(myArray, 4)** would be **42**. [*Note:* The Xth element is different from the element with subscript X, because the first element has subscript value **0**.]

Lab Exercises

Lab Exercise 2 — Bubble Sort

3. Remove bubble sort from **main** and place it in a function named **bubbleSort** that takes an array argument and a constant integer representing the array's size. What should this function return? Is the array passed call-by-reference or call-by-value?

Lab Exercises   Name:

Lab Exercise 3 — Salespeople

Name: _____   Date:_____

Section: _____

This problem is intended to be solved in a closed-lab session with a teaching assistant or instructor present. The problem is divided into six parts:

1. Lab Objectives
2. Description of the Problem
3. Sample Output
4. Program Template (Fig. L 4.5)
5. Problem-Solving Tips
6. Follow-Up Questions and Activities

The program template represents a complete working C++ program, with one or more key lines of code replaced with comments. Read the problem description and examine the sample output; then study the template code. Using the problem-solving tips as a guide, replace the /* */ comments with C++ code. Compile and execute the program. Compare your output with the sample output provided. Then answer the follow-up questions. The source code for the template is available at **www.deitel.com** and **www.prenhall.com./deitel**.

Lab Objectives

This lab was designed to reinforce programming concepts from Chapter 4 of *C++ How To Program: Fourth Edition*. In this lab, you will practice:

*   using double-subscripted arrays to store tables of information.
*   nesting **for** loops to access multiple-subscripted arrays.

The follow-up question and activities also will give you practice:

*   using **const int**s to declare identifiers that are used in an array declaration.
*   initializing multi-dimensional arrays.
*   using character arrays to store strings.

Description of the Problem

Use a double-subscripted array to solve the following problem. A company has four salespeople (1 to 4) who sell five different products (1 to 5). Each salesperson passes in slips for each different type of product sold. Each slip contains the following:

a) The salesperson number
b) The product number
c) The total dollar value of that product sold that day

Assume that multiple slips are available. Write a program that reads all this information and summarize the total sales by salesperson by product. All totals should be stored in the double-subscripted array **sales**. After processing all the sales information, print the results in tabular format with each of the columns representing a particular product and each of the rows representing a particular salesperson. Cross total each row to get the total sales of each product;

Lab Exercises

Name:

Lab Exercise 3 — Salespeople

cross total each column to get the total sales by salesperson. Your tabular printout should include these cross totals to the right of the totaled rows and to the bottom of the totaled columns.

Sample Output

```
Enter the salesperson (1 - 4), product number (1 - 5)
and total sales.Enter -1 for the salesperson to end input.
1 1 9.99
3 3 5.99
2 2 4.99
-1

The total sales for each sales person are displayed
at the end of each row, and the total sales for each
product are displayed at the bottom of each column.
           1         2         3         4         5      Total
1        9.99      0.00      0.00      0.00      0.00      9.99
2        0.00      4.99      0.00      0.00      0.00      4.99
3        0.00      0.00      5.99      0.00      0.00      5.99
4        0.00      0.00      0.00      0.00      0.00      0.00

Total  9.99      4.99      5.99      0.00      0.00
```

Template

```cpp
1   // Chapter 4 of C++ How to Program
2   // Exercise 3 (sales.cpp)
3
4   #include <iostream>
5
6   using std::cout;
7   using std::cin;
8   using std::endl;
9   using std::fixed;
10
11  #include <iomanip>
12
13  using std::setprecision;
14  using std::setw;
15
16  int main()
17  {
18     const int PEOPLE = 5;
19     const int PRODUCTS = 6;
20
21     /* Write the declaration for array sales here */
22
23     double value;
24     double totalSales;
25     double productSales[ PRODUCTS ] = { 0.0 };
26     int salesperson;
27     int product;
```

Fig. L 4.5   sales.cpp. (Part 1 of 3.)

Lab Exercises   Name:

Lab Exercise 3 — Salespeople

```
28
29     cout << "Enter the salesperson (1 - 4), "
30         << "product number (1 - 5)\nand total sales."
31         << "Enter -1 for the salesperson to end input.\n";
32
33     cin >> salesPerson;
34
35     // process sales
36     while ( salesPerson != -1 ) {
37        cin >> product >> value;
38        /* Write a statement that adds values to the
39           sales array */
40        cin >> salesPerson;
41
42     } // end while
43
44     // table header: describes output and prints
45     // column header(product numbers 1-5)
46     cout << "\nThe total sales for each sales person "
47         << "are displayed\nat the end of each row,"
48         << "and the total sales for each\nproduct "
49         << "are displayed at the bottom of each column.\n"
50         << setw( 10 ) << 1 << setw( 10 ) << 2
51         << setw( 10 ) << 3 << setw( 10 ) << 4
52         << setw( 10 ) << 5 << setw( 12 ) << "Total\n" << fixed
53         << setprecision( 2 );
54
55     // nested loop structure: prints salesperson number
56     // followed by the amounts sold for each product
57     for ( int i = 1; /* Write condition here */ ; ++i ) {
58        totalSales = 0.0;
59
60        // print salesperson number
61        cout << i;
62
63        // inner loop: prints amounts sold for each product
64        for ( int j = 1; /* Write condition here */; ++j ) {
65
66           /* Write a statement that adds the current sales
67              element to totalSales */
68
69           // print sales for each salesperson for each product
70           cout << setw( 10 )
71              << sales[ i ][ j ];
72
73           /* Write a statement that adds the current sales
74              element to productSales */
75
76        } // end for
77
78        // print the last column item (total sales of each
79        // product). The totalSales value is 9.99 under
80        // "Total" in the output box. After this value is
81        // printed, the next table line can be created
82        cout << setw( 10 ) << totalSales << '\n';
83
84     } // end for
```

Fig. L 4.5   **sales.cpp**. (Part 2 of 3.)

Lab Exercises

Name:

Lab Exercise 3 — Salespeople

```
85
86
87      // header for last row
88      cout << "\nTotal" << setw( 6 ) << productSales[ 1 ];
89
90      // prints last row which displays total sales
91      // for each product
92      for ( int j = 2; j < PRODUCTS; ++j )
93         cout << setw( 10 ) << productSales[ j ];
94
95      cout << endl;
96
97      return 0;
98
99   } // end main
```

Fig. L 4.5   sales.cpp. (Part 3 of 3.)

Problem-Solving Tips

1. This problem asks the reader to input a series of numbers representing the salesperson number, product number and the dollar amount. The product number and salesperson number represent the row subscript and column subscript in the **sales** array where the dollar amount is added. Each array begins with subscript zero; therefore, it is recommended that you oversize the array by one element in each dimension. This allows you to map the product number and salesperson number directly to a subscript without having to subtract one.

2. Table columns contain the total sales for each product. Table rows contain the sales figures for each salesperson. To create the output, the table header must first be printed. (See template.) When program control reaches the outer **for** loop, the salesperson number is printed. The inner **for** loop prints the amount of each product that the salesperson sold. When the inner loop finishes, control returns to the outer loop and the **\n** character is printed.

3. To display totals in the right-most column, simply sum each element in the row and display the total. This is best done when the array is output. To display the totals at the bottom, declare a one-dimensional array of five elements. While outputting **sales**, simply add the current column's value to the appropriate element of the single-subscripted array. After outputting **sales** and the totals for each row, iterate through the single-subscripted array and output its values.

Follow-Up Questions and Activities

1. Explain why keyword **const** must be present when declaring the variables **PRODUCTS** and **PEOPLE**. Why do these two constants have the values **6** and **5** rather than **5** and **4**?

Lab Exercises   Name: _____

Lab Exercise 3 — Salespeople

2. Change the declaration of **productSales**, in your solution that corresponds to line 25 in the program template, so that salesperson 1 has sold $75.00 of product 3 initially and so that salesperson 4 has sold $63.00 of product 1 initially. All other array values should be initialized to **0.0**. [*Hint*: Use curly braces to initialize the array.]

3. Create an additional array that stores the names of all of the salespeople. Allow the user to input the names of the five employees. Limit the names to 20 characters. When generating the output table, use the names of the salespeople rather than numbers.

Lab Exercises   Name:

Lab Exercise 3 — Salespeople

Lab Exercises   Name:

Debugging

Name: _____   **Date:**_____

Section: _____

The program (Fig. L 4.6) in this section does not run properly. Fix all the syntax errors so that the program will compile successfully. Once the program compiles, compare the output with the sample output, and eliminate any logic errors that may exist. The sample output demonstrates what the program's output should be once the program's code has been corrected.

Sample Output

```
Here is the grade database

        Name    1    2    3    4    5    6    7    8    9   10
         Bob   56   67   83   81   70   84   94   64   68   86
        John   76   89   81   42   66   93  104   91   71   85
         Joe   65   69   91   89   82   93   72   76   79   99

Bob's highest grade is: 94
Bob's lowest grade is: 56
John's highest grade is: 104
John's lowest grade is: 42
Joe's highest grade is: 99
Joe's lowest grade is: 65
```

Broken Code

```cpp
1   // Chapter 4 of C++ How to Program
2   // Debugging Problem
3
4   #include <iostream>
5
6   using std::cout;
7   using std::endl;
8
9   #include <iomanip>
10
11  using std::setw;
12
13  #include <ctime>
14
15  const int NUM_GRADES = 10;
16  const int NUM_SUDENTS = 3;
17
18  int findHighest( int );
19  int findLowest( int * );
20  void printDatabase( const int [][], const char [][ 20 ] );
21
```

Fig. L 4.6   **debugging04.cpp**. (Part 1 of 3.)

Lab Exercises

Name:

Debugging

```
22  int main()
23  {
24     int student1[ NUM_GRADES ] = { 0 };
25     int student2[ NUM_GRADES ] = { 76, 89, 81, 42, 66, 93, 104,
26                                     91, 71, 85, 105 };
27     int student3[ NUM_GRADES ] = { 65, 69, 91, 89, 82, 93, 72,
28                                     76, 79, 99 };
29     char names[ NUM_SUDENTS ][ 20 ] = { "Bob", "John", "Joe" };
30
31     int database[ NUM_SUDENTS ][ NUM_GRADES ];
32     int i = 0;
33
34     srand( time( 0 ) );
35
36     // initialize student1
37     for ( i = 0; i < NUM_GRADES; i++ )
38        student1[ NUM_GRADES ] = rand() % 50 + 50;
39
40     // initialize database
41     for ( i = 1; i < NUM_GRADES; i++ ) {
42        database[ 0 ][ i ] = student1[ i ];
43        database[ 1 ][ i ] = student2[ i ];
44        database[ 2 ][ i ] = student3[ i ];
45
46     } // end for
47
48     printDatabase( database, studentNames );
49
50     for ( i = 0; i < NUM_SUDENTS; i++ ) {
51        cout << studentNames[ i ] << "'s highest grade is: "
52             << findHighest( student1 ) << endl
53             << studentNames[ i ] << "'s lowest grade is: "
54             << findLowest( database[ i ] ) << endl;
55
56     } // end for
57
58
59     return 0;
60
61  } // end main
62
63  // determine largest grade
64  int findHighest( int )
65  {
66     int highest = a[ 0 ];
67
68     for ( int i = 1; i <= NUM_GRADES; i++ )
69        if ( a[ i ] > highest )
70           highest = a[ i ];
71
72     return highest;
73
74  } // end function findHighest
75
```

Fig. L 4.6   **debugging04.cpp**. (Part 2 of 3.)

Lab Exercises   Name:

Debugging

```
76   // determine lowest grade
77   int findLowest( int a[] )
78   {
79      int lowest = a[ 0 ];
80
81      for ( int i = 1; i < NUM_GRADES; i++ )
82         if ( a[ i ] < lowest )
83            lowest = a[ i ];
84
85      return lowest;
86
87   } // end lowestGrade
88
89   // output data
90   void printDatabase( int a[][ NUM_GRADES ], char names[][ 20 ] )
91   {
92      cout << "Here is the grade database\n\n"
93           << setw( 10 ) << "Name";
94
95      for ( int n = 1; n <= NUM_GRADES; n++ )
96         cout << setw( 4 ) << n;
97
98      cout << endl;
99
100     for ( int i = 0; i < NUM_SUDENTS; i++ ) {
101        cout << setw( 10 ) << names[ i ];
102
103        for ( int j = 0; j < NUM_GRADES; j++ )
104           cout << setw( 4 ) << a[ i, j ];
105
106        cout << endl;
107
108     } // end for
109
110     cout << endl;
111
112  } // end printDatabase
```

Fig. L 4.6   **debugging04.cpp**. (Part 3 of 3.)

Lab Exercises   Name:

Debugging

Postlab Activities

Coding Exercises

Name: _____   **Date:**_____

Section: _____

These coding exercises reinforce the lessons learned in the lab and provide additional programming experience outside the classroom and laboratory environment. They serve as a review after you have completed the Prelab Activities and Lab Exercises successfully.

For each of the following problems, write a program or a program segment that performs the specified action:

1. Write a line of code that declares a 101-element array.

2. Modify your solution to Coding Exercise 1 by writing additional code to initialize all elements of the array to **-1**.

3. Write a line of code that accesses element seven of the array in Coding Exercise 2 and sets its value to **7**.

4. Use the **rand** function to select randomly an array element of the array created in Coding Exercise 1. Assign that element a value of **2**.

Postlab Activities   Name:

Coding Exercises

5. Write a function **printArray** that prints the contents of the array created in Coding Exercise 1. Place a space between every number that is printed. In addition, print a new line after every 20 elements.

6. Declare an array and initialize it to the value of the string "**Hi there**." Print this array's contents.

7. Write a **for** loop that prints only **Hi** from the array created in Coding Exercise 6.

8. Write a program that generates a multiplication table. Use a double-subscripted array to represent your table. All multiplications from 1 to 5 should be included (i.e., 5 * 5 = 25 is largest value in this table). Initialize the array's elements to **0** and have your program populate the array with the proper values.

Postlab Activities   Name:

Programming Challenges

Name: _____   Date: _____

Section: _____

The Programming Challenges are more involved than the Coding Exercises and may require a significant amount of time to complete. Write a C++ program for each of the problems in this section. The answers to these problems are available at **www.deitel.com**, **www.prenhall.com/deitel** and on the *C++ Multimedia Cyber Classroom: Fourth Edition*. Pseudocode, hints and/or sample outputs are provided to aid you in your programming.

9. Use a single-subscripted array to solve the following problem. A company pays its salespeople on a commission basis. The salespeople receive $200 per week plus 9 percent of their gross sales for that week. For example, a salesperson who grosses $5000 in sales in a week receives $200 plus 9 percent of $5000, or a total of $650. Write a program (using an array of counters) that determines how many of the salespeople earned salaries in each of the following ranges (assume that each salesperson's salary is truncated to an integer amount):

    a) $200–$299

    b) $300–$399

    c) $400–$499

    d) $500–$599

    e) $600–$699

    f) $700–$799

    g) $800–$899

    h) $900–$999

    i) $1000 and over

Hints:

  • Calculate salary as a **double**. Then use **static_cast< int >** to truncate the salaries and convert them to integers. Divide by **100** to obtain an array index.

  • Make use of the **?:** operator to index the array. (What happens if the index is **>= 10**?)

10. Use a 20-element single-subscripted integer array to solve the following problem: Read in 20 numbers, each of which is between 10 and 100, inclusive. As each number is input, print it only if it is not a duplicate of a number previously input.

Hints:

  • Compare every value input to all existing array elements. If it is a duplicate, set a flag variable to **1**. This flag should be used to determine whether it is necessary to print the value.

  • Use a counter variable to keep track of the number of elements entered into the array and the array position where the next value should be stored.

11. *(The Sieve of Eratosthenes)* A prime integer is any integer that is evenly divisible only by itself and 1. The Sieve of Eratosthenes is a method of finding prime numbers. It operates as follows:

    a) Create an array with all elements initialized to **1** (true). Array elements with prime subscripts will remain

Postlab Activities   Name:

Programming Challenges

1. All other array elements eventually will be set to zero.

b) Starting with array subscript 2 (subscript 1 is not prime), every time an array element is found whose value is **1**, iterate through the remainder of the array and set to zero every element whose subscript is a multiple of the subscript for the element with value **1**. For array subscript 2, all elements beyond 2 in the array that are multiples of 2 will be set to zero (subscripts 4, 6, 8, 10, etc.); for array subscript 3, all elements beyond 3 in the array that are multiples of 3 will be set to zero (subscripts 6, 9, 12, 15, etc.); and so on.

When this process is complete, the array elements that contain **1** indicate that the subscript is a prime number. These subscripts can then be printed. Write a program that uses an array of 1000 elements to determine and print the prime numbers between 1 and 999. Ignore the element with 0.

Hints:

- Use a loop to find all elements that are set to **1**. (This must be done in order.) Set all multiples of that element to **0**.

- Print the primes by looping through the array searching for elements equal to **1**. Print their subscript. Increment a counter by one each time a prime number is printed.

12. Write a recursive function **recursiveMinimum** that takes an integer array and the array size as arguments and returns the element with the smallest value in the array. The function should stop processing and return control to its caller if it receives a one-element array. [*Note:* This problem is intended for those students who have studied recursion in Section 3.12–3.14 of *C++ How to Program: Fourth Edition*.]

Hints:

- Write a program to test your function. Populate an array with randomly generated integers.

- Function **recursiveMinimum** should take as its arguments the array, a low value and a high value. The low and high values represent the boundaries of the array, respectively.

- Recursive functions involving arrays approach their base case by reducing the size of the array using boundaries, not by literally passing a smaller array. Your function should approach the base case in the following manner: **low++** until **low == high**.

Pointers and Strings

Objectives

- To use pointers. Pointers enable programmers to simulate passing arguments call-by-reference.
- To understand the close relationships among pointers, arrays and strings. The variable name of an array or a string is a pointer to the address at which that array or string is stored.
- To declare and use arrays of strings. Strings are used to store and manipulate character data. In C++, strings are stored as arrays of characters. The string manipulation library, **<cstring>**, is used to compare, copy, tokenize and determine the length of strings.

Assignment Checklist

Name: _____   **Date:** _____

Section: _____

Exercises	Assigned: Circle assignments	Date Due
Prelab Activities		
Matching	YES NO	
Fill in the Blank	11, 12, 13, 14, 15, 16, 17, 18	
Short Answer	19, 20, 21, 22	
Programming Output	23, 24, 25, 26, 27, 28, 29	
Correct the Code	30, 31, 32, 33, 34, 35, 36	
Lab Exercises		
Lab Exercise 1 — The Tortoise and the Hare	YES NO	
Follow-Up Questions and Activities	1, 2, 3, 4	
Lab Exercise 2 — Encryption/Decryption	YES NO	
Follow-Up Questions and Activities	1, 2, 3	
Lab Exercise 3 — Shuffling and Dealing	YES NO	
Follow-Up Questions and Activities	1, 2, 3	
Debugging	YES NO	
Labs Provided by Instructor		
1.		
2.		
3.		
Postlab Activities		
Coding Exercises	1, 2, 3, 4, 5, 6, 7, 8, 9, 10	
Programming Challenges	11, 12, 13, 14	

Assignment Checklist

Name:

Prelab Activities

Matching

Name: _____   **Date:**_____

Section: _____

After reading Chapter 5 of *C++ How to Program: Fourth Edition*, answer the given questions. These questions are intended to test and reinforce your understanding of key concepts and may be done either before the lab or during the lab.

For each term in the column on the left, write the corresponding letter for the description that best matches it from the column on the right.

.

Term	Description
____ 1. `&`	a) `ptr[ 3 ]`
____ 2. *rvalue*	b) A character in single quotes that corresponds to an integer value.
____ 3. Pointer-offset notation	c) Can be used to determine the size of an array in bytes.
____ 4. Dereferencing operator	d) A series of characters enclosed in double quotation marks.
____ 5. lvalue	e) `ptr + 3`
____ 6. Pointer-subscript notation	f) Series of characters delimited by characters such as spaces or punctuation marks.
____ 7. `sizeof`	g) Can be used on the left side of an assignment operator (e.g., variables).
____ 8. Character constant	h) `*`
____ 9. String literal	i) Unary operator that returns the address of its operand.
____ 10. Token	j) Can be used on the right side of an assignment operator (e.g., constants) only.

Prelab Activities

Name:

Matching

Prelab Activities   Name:

Fill in the Blank

Name: _____   **Date:**_____

Section: _____

Fill in the blank for each of the following statements:

11. Pointers are variables that contain other variables' _____.

12. All elements of an array are stored _____ in memory.

13. In many cases, pointers can be accessed exactly like arrays (known as pointer _____ notation).

14. The only integer value that can be assigned to a pointer without casting is _____.

15. It is not necessary to include names of pointers in function prototypes; it is necessary only to include the pointer _____.

16. The * operator is referred to as the _____, or _____, operator.

17. Subtracting or comparing two pointers that do not refer to elements of the same _____ is usually a logic error.

18. Function _____ copies its second argument—a string—into its first argument—a character array.

Prelab Activities   Name:

Fill in the Blank

Prelab Activities   Name: _____

Short Answer

Name: _____   **Date:** _____

Section: _____

In the space provided, answer each of the given questions. Your answers should be as concise as possible; aim for two or three sentences.

19. What are the three kinds of things that can be assigned to a pointer?

20. What happens when a programmer tries to dereference a pointer that has not been properly initialized or has not been assigned to point to a specific location in memory? What sort of error(s) will this dereferencing cause?

21. What is pointer arithmetic? Why is it applicable to arrays only?

Prelab Activities   Name:

Short Answer

22. Array names are like constant pointers to the beginning of the array. Can programmers modify array names in the same way as they modify pointers (i.e., in arithmetic expressions)? What about operators **++**, **--**. **+=**, **-=**, and **=?** Can these be used with an array name?

Prelab Activities

Name: _____

Programming Output

Name: _____   Date:_____

Section: _____

For each of the given program segments, read the code and write the output in the space provided below each program. [*Note*: Do not execute these programs on a computer.]

23. What is output by the following program segment?

```
1   int number = 99;
2   int *ptr = &number;    // address of number is 0012FF7C
3
4   cout << number << " " << *ptr << " " << ptr;
```

Your answer:

24. What is output by the following code?

```
1   char c[] = "Hello you";
2   char *sPtr = c;
3
4   for ( ; *sPtr != 'u'; sPtr++ )
5      cout << *sPtr;
```

Your answer:

Prelab Activities   Name:

Programming Output

25. What is output by the following program segment?

```
1   int a[] = { 1, 2, 3, 4, 5 };
2   int *ptr = a;
3
4   cout << a[ 3 ] << " " << *( ptr + 3 ) << " " << ptr[ 3 ];
```

Your answer:

26. What is output by the following program segment?

```
1   int main()
2   {
3      char s1[] = "Boston, Massachusetts";
4      char *sPtr2 = "New York, NY";
5
6      cout << s1 << setw( 4 ) << sPtr2;
7
8      for ( int i = 0; ( s1[ i ] = sPtr2[ i ] ) != '\0'; i++ )
9         ;
10
11     cout << endl << s1 << setw( 4 ) << sPtr2 << endl;
12
13     return 0;
14
15  } // end main
```

Your answer:

Prelab Activities

Name: _____

Programming Output

27. What is output by the following program segment?

```
1   char x[] = "It is a nice day";
2   char y[ 25 ];
3   char z[ 15 ];
4
5   cout << "The string in array x is: " << x
6        << "\nThe string in array y is: " << strcpy( y, x )
7        << '\n';
8
9   strncpy( z, x, 9 );
10  z[ 9 ] = '\0';
11  cout << "The string in array z is: " << z << endl;
```

Your answer:

28. What is output by the following program segment?

```
1   char *s1Ptr = "C++ is fun";
2   char *s2Ptr = "C++ is fun everyday";
3
4   if ( strncmp( s1Ptr, s2Ptr, 10 ) == 0 )
5       cout << "Equal ";
6
7   else
8       cout << "Not Equal";
```

Your answer:

29. What is output by the following program segment?

```
1   char *sPtr = "Boston, MA";
2
3   cout << strlen( sPtr );
```

Your answer:

Prelab Activities

Name:

Programming Output

Prelab Activities

Name:

Correct the Code

Name: _____   Date:_____

Section: _____

For each of the given program segments, determine if there is an error in the code. If there is an error, specify whether it is a logic error or a syntax error, circle the error in the program, and write the corrected code in the space provided after each problem. If the code does not contain an error, write "no error." [*Note*: It is possible that a program segment may contain multiple errors.]

30. The following declarations should declare three pointers:

```
1   int *ptr1;
2   int &ptr2;
3   int ptr2;
```

Your answer:

31. The following code should print **a** and the contents of **a** via the pointer:

```
1   int a = 7;
2   int *aptr = &a;
3
4   cout << *a << aptr
```

Your answer:

Prelab Activities

Name: _____

Correct the Code

32. The following code should print the elements of the array, using pointer arithmetic:

```
1   int a[ 5 ] = { 1, 2, 3, 4, 5 };
2   int *aptr = &a[ 0 ];
3
4   for ( int i = 0; i <= 5; i++ )
5       cout << *( aptr + i );
```

Your answer:

33. The following code should print **Hello** when **strPrint** is called:

```
char *ptr = "Hello";
strPrint( ptr );
```

```
1   void print( char *sPtr )
2   {
3       for ( ; *sPtr != '\0'; sPtr++ )
4           cout << *sPtr;
5   }
```

Your answer:

34. The following program segment should copy part of **s1Ptr** into **s2**:

```
1   char *s1Ptr = "United States of America";
2   char s2[ 15 ];
3
4   for ( int i = 0; *( s1Ptr + i ) != 'o'; i++ )
5       s2[ i ] = *( s1Ptr + i );
6
7   cout << s1Ptr << endl << s2;
```

Your answer:

Prelab Activities   Name:

Correct the Code

35. The following code should compare two strings:

```
1   char *s1Ptr = "Hello";
2   char *s2Ptr = "Hello";
3
4   if ( strcmp( s1Ptr, s2Ptr ) == true )
5      cout << "Equal ";
6
7   else
8      cout << "Not Equal";
```

Your answer:

36. The following code should print the result of calling **strcat** to the screen:

```
1   char s1[] = "How are you";
2   char s2[] = "Good night";
3
4   cout << strcat( s1, s2 );
```

Your answer:

Prelab Activities

Name:

Correct the Code

Lab Exercises

Lab Exercise 1 — Tortoise and the Hare

Name: _____   Date:_____

Section: _____

This problem is intended to be solved in a closed-lab session with a teaching assistant or instructor present. The problem is divided into six parts:

1. Lab Objectives

2. Description of the Problem

3. Sample Output

4. Program Template (Fig. L 5.1)

5. Problem-Solving Tips

6. Follow-Up Questions and Activities

The program template represents a complete working C++ program, with one or more key lines of code replaced with comments. Read the problem description and examine the sample output; then study the template code. Using the problem-solving tips as a guide, replace the **/* */** comments with C++ code. Compile and execute the program. Compare your output with the sample output provided. Then answer the follow-up questions. The source code for the template is available at **www.deitel.com** and **www.prenhall.com./deitel**.

Lab Objectives

This lab was designed to reinforce programming concepts from Chapter 5 of *C++ How To Program: Fourth Edition*. In this lab, you will practice:

- Call-by-reference using reference notation.

- Call-by-reference using pointer notation.

The follow-up questions and activities also give you practice:

- Comparing call-by-value functions with call-by-reference functions. In call-by-value functions a copy of the argument is passed, whereas in call-by-reference functions the address of the argument is passed.

- Dereferencing pointers to access the data stored at a specific memory address.

- Using the address operator (**&**) to obtain the memory address of a variable.

Description of the Problem

In this problem you will recreate the classic race between the tortoise and the hare. You will use random number generation to develop a simulation of this memorable event.

Our contenders begin the race at "square 1" of 70 squares. Each square represents a possible position along the race course. The finish line is at square 70.

Lab Exercises

Name:

Lab Exercise 1 — Tortoise and the Hare

There is a clock that ticks once per second. With each tick of the clock, your program should adjust the position of the animals according to the following rules:

Animal	Move type	Percentage of the time	Actual move
Tortoise	Fast plod	50%	3 squares to the right
	Slip	20%	6 squares to the left
	Slow plod	30%	1 square to the right
Hare	Sleep	20%	No move at all
	Big hop	20%	9 squares to the right
	Big slip	10%	12 squares to the left
	Small hop	30%	1 square to the right
	Small slip	20%	2 squares to the left

Begin the race by printing

```
BANG !!!!!
AND THEY'RE OFF !!!!!
```

Start each animal at position 1 (i.e., the "starting gate"). If an animal slips left before square 1, move the animal back to square 1. For each tick of the clock (i.e., each repetition of a loop), print a 70-position line showing the letter **T** in the tortoise's position and the letter **H** in the hare's position. Occasionally, the contenders will land on the same square. In this case, the tortoise bites the hare, and your program should print **OUCH!!!** beginning at that position. All print positions other than the **T**, the **H** or the **OUCH!!!** should be blank.

After printing each line, determine whether either animal has reached or passed square 70. If so, print the name of the winner, and terminate the simulation. If the tortoise wins, print **TORTOISE WINS!!! YAY!!!** If the hare wins, print **Hare wins. Yuch.**. If neither animal wins, perform the loop again to simulate the next tick of the clock.

In this program, you will be passing arguments via call by reference, using reference notation. After successfully completing the exercise, rewrite your solution to use pointer notation.

Lab Exercises   Name:

Lab Exercise 1 — Tortoise and the Hare

Sample Output:

```
ON YOUR MARK, GET SET
BANG                  !!!!
AND THEY'RE OFF    !!!!
H   T
 H      T
 H           T
   HT
OUCH!!!
     T       H
H        T
T               H
    T         H
       T      H
T                        H
   T    H
     T             H
       T        H
        T             H
    T                     H
        T                    H
        T                           H
          T                H
           T               H
           T                H
      T          H
         T                H
         T                  H
       T                H
        T                H
       T                H
     T       H
         T         H
           T         H
     T                H
      T
        T                      H
         T                     H
          T                      H
         T                       H
           T
        T                            H
          T                      H
           T                       H
            T                         H
          T                  H
            T                           H
             T
Hare wins. Yuch.
TIME ELAPSED = 41 seconds
```

Lab Exercises   Name:

Lab Exercise 1 — Tortoise and the Hare

Template

```cpp
1    // Chapter 5 of C++ How to Program
2    // tortoiseandhare.cpp
3    #include <iostream>
4
5    using std::cout;
6    using std::endl;
7
8    #include <cstdlib>
9
10   #include <ctime>
11
12   #include <iomanip>
13
14   using std::setw;
15
16   const int RACE_END = 70;
17
18   /* Write prototype for moveTortoise here */
19   /* Write prototype for moveHare here */
20   /* Write prototype for printCurrentPositions here */
21
22   int main()
23   {
24       int tortoise = 1;
25       int hare = 1;
26       int timer = 0;
27
28       srand( time( 0 ) );
29
30       cout << "ON YOUR MARK, GET SET\nBANG               !!!!"
31            << "\nAND THEY'RE OFF     !!!!\n";
32
33       // controls race
34       while ( tortoise != RACE_END && hare != RACE_END ) {
35           /* Write call for moveTortoise here */
36           /* Write call for moveHare here */
37           /* Write call for printCurrentPositions here */
38           ++timer;
39
40       } // end while
41
42       // determine winner
43       if ( tortoise >= hare )
44           cout << "\nTORTOISE WINS!!! YAY!!!\n";
45
46       else
47           cout << "Hare wins. Yuch.\n";
48
49       cout << "TIME ELAPSED = " << timer << " seconds" << endl;
50
51       return 0;
52
53   } // end main
54
```

Fig. L 5.1   tortoiseandhare.cpp. (Part 1 of 2.)

Lab Exercises   Name:

Lab Exercise 1 — Tortoise and the Hare

```
55   // move tortoise
56   /* Write function definition header for moveTortoise here */
57   {
58      int x = 1 + rand() % 10;
59
60      // determine which move to make
61      if ( x >= 1 && x <= 5 )          // fast plod
62         turtlePtr += 3;
63
64      else if ( x == 6 || x == 7 )    // slip
65         turtlePtr -= 6;
66
67      else                             // slow plod
68         ++( turtlePtr );
69
70      // ensure that tortoise remains within subscript range
71      if ( turtlePtr < 1 )
72         turtlePtr = 1;
73
74      else if ( turtlePtr > RACE_END )
75         turtlePtr = RACE_END;
76
77   } // end function moveTortoise
78
79   // move hare
80   /* Write function definition for moveHare here */
81   {
82      int y = 1 + rand() % 10;
83
84      /* Write statements that move hare */
85
86      /* Write statements that test if hare is before
87         the starting point or has finished the race */
88
89   } // end function moveHare
90
91   // output positions of animals
92   /* Write function definition for printCurrentPositions here */
93   {
94      if ( bunnyPtr == snapperPtr )
95         cout << setw( bunnyPtr ) << "OUCH!!!";
96
97      else if ( bunnyPtr < snapperPtr )
98         cout << setw( bunnyPtr ) << "H"
99              << setw( snapperPtr - bunnyPtr ) << "T";
100
101     else
102        cout << setw( snapperPtr ) << "T"
103             << setw( bunnyPtr - snapperPtr ) << "H";
104
105     cout << "\n";
106
107  } // end function printCurrentPositions
```

Fig. L 5.1   `tortoiseandhare.cpp`. (Part 2 of 2.)

Lab Exercises   Name:

Lab Exercise 1 — Tortoise and the Hare

Problem-Solving Tips

1. Variable **tortoise** and variable **hare** store the animal's current positions (i.e., an **int** in the range 1 to 70), respectively. Because these variables are owned by **main** and we wish to modify them in the called function (i.e., **moveTortoise** and **moveHare**), they must be passed by reference. Remember that nonarray types are passed by-value.

2. (*References*) Remember that references are declared using the ampersand (**&**) in a function definition header and that they are used in the same way as non-pointer parameters, but enable the called function to modify the caller's data.

3. (*Pointers*) Remember that pointers must be declared using the dereferencing operator (*****). Valid pointer assignments include addresses, **0** and **NULL**, and that pointers must be dereferenced (using the dereferencing operator) to manipulate the data of the address to which they point.

4. Generate the percentages in the table in the "Problem Description" by producing a random integer, i, in the range $1 \leq i \leq 10$. For the tortoise, perform a "fast plod" when $1 \leq i \leq 5$, a "slip" when $6 \leq i \leq 7$, and a "slow plod" when $8 \leq i \leq 10$. Use a similar technique to move the hare.

Follow-Up Questions and Activities

1. Could this race have been simulated by passing the arguments call-by-value to the functions? Why is it more convenient for programmers to pass arguments call-by-reference to functions?

2. What would happen if you forgot to dereference one of the pointers in the program? Is this a syntax error? Describe the effects of such a mistake.

3. How would you determine the memory addresses at which variables **tortoise** and **hare** are stored? Modify the program to print the addresses.

Lab Exercises

Name:

Lab Exercise 1 — Tortoise and the Hare

4. Why is the following statement an error?

```
int *RACE_END_ptr = RACE_END;
```

Lab Exercises   Name:

Lab Exercise 1 — Tortoise and the Hare

Lab Exercises   Name:

Lab Exercise 2 — Encryption/Decryption

Name: _____   **Date:** _____

Section: _____

This problem is intended to be solved in a closed-lab session with a teaching assistant or instructor present. The problem is divided into six parts:

1. Lab Objectives
2. Description of the Problem
3. Sample Output
4. Program Template (Fig. L 5.2)
5. Problem-Solving Tips
6. Follow-Up Questions and Activities

The program template represents a complete working C++ program, with one or more key lines of code replaced with comments. Read the problem description and examine the sample output; then study the template code. Using the problem-solving tips as a guide, replace the **/* */** comments with C++ code. Compile and execute the program. Compare your output with the sample output provided. Then answer the follow-up questions. The source code for the template is available at **www.deitel.com** and **www.prenhall.com./deitel**.

Lab Objectives

This lab was designed to reinforce programming concepts from Chapter 5 of *C++ How To Program: Fourth Edition*. In this lab, you will practice:

- Using pointer-subscript notation to access data stored in an array.

- Using pointer-offset notation to access data stored in an array.

- Using strings to store and manipulate textual input, and to output text-based messages.

The follow-up questions and activities also will give you practice:

- Learning the values of character constants.

- Contrasting pointer-offset and pointer-subscript notations.

- Using the string manipulation functions to compare and copy strings.

Description of the Problem

Write a simple encryption/decryption program. Function **encrypt** takes a character pointer as a parameter and uses pointer-subscript notation to change the value in the address pointed to by adding **1** to it. Function **decrypt** takes a character pointer as a parameter and uses pointer notation to change the value in the address pointed to by subtracting **1** from it. Function **main** calls functions **encrypt** and **decrypt** and prints the encrypted string.

Lab Exercises   Name:

Lab Exercise 2 — Encryption/Decryption

Sample Output

```
Original string is: this is a secret!
Encrypted string is: uijt!jt!b!tfdsfu"
Decrypted string is: this is a secret!
```

Template

```cpp
 1   // Chapter 5 of C++ How to Program
 2   // Exercise2.cpp
 3
 4   #include <iostream>
 5
 6   using std::cout;
 7   using std::endl;
 8
 9   /* Write the prototype for function encrypt */
10   /* Write the prototype for function decrypt */
11
12   int main()
13   {
14      // create a string to encrypt
15      char string[] = "this is a secret!";
16
17      cout << "Original string is: " << string << endl;
18
19      encrypt( string );
20      cout << "Encrypted string is: " << string << endl;
21
22      decrypt( string );
23      cout << "Decrypted string is: " << string << endl;
24
25      return 0;
26
27   } // end main
28
29   // encrypt data
30   void encrypt( char e[] )
31   {
32      /* Write implementation for function encrypt */
33
34   } // end function encrypt
35
36   // decrypt data
37   void decrypt( char *ePtr )
38   {
39      /* Write implementation for function decrypt */
40
41   } // end function decrypt
```

Fig. L 5.2   encryption.cpp.

Lab Exercises   Name:

Lab Exercise 2 — Encryption/Decryption

Problem-Solving Tips

1. Remember that pointer-subscript notation uses the pointer name and brackets, `[]`. Pointer-offset notation uses the pointer name and the dereferencing operator.

2. Remember that characters are represented by an integer value in the ASCII character set.

3. For more information on character constants and the ASCII character set, see Appendix B in *C++ How to Program: Fourth Edition*.

Follow-Up Questions and Activities

1. This program performs arithmetic with character constants to encrypt and decrypt text. This character manipulation is fundamental to C++. Fill in the accompanying table. Use Appendix B in *C++ How to Program: Fourth Edition* as a guide.

Character	Integer Value
`'0'`	___
`'A'`	___
___	98
___	7

2. In examining the program template provided, you will notice that function **encrypt** takes an argument **char e[]** and function **decrypt** takes an argument **char *ePtr**. Is there a difference between **e** and **ePtr**? Explain why or why not.

3. Assume that the program you just completed will be used to protect passwords. Most password systems limit the number of characters a password can have. Modify your program to take as input strings up to 25 characters in length, but if the user enters a password containing more than 10 characters, the password should be truncated. Some password systems also prompt users to enter their password a second time to verify that it was entered correctly. Add this feature to the program as well. The program dialog should be similar to the following:

```
Enter your password: abcdefg
Re-enter your password: hello
Invalid password
Enter your password again: abcdefg
Re-enter your password: abcdefg
Your encrypted password is: bcdefgh
```

Lab Exercises   Name:

Lab Exercise 2 — Encryption/Decryption

Lab Exercises   Name:

Lab Exercise 3 — Shuffling and Dealing

Name: _____   **Date:**_____

Section: _____

This problem is intended to be solved in a closed-lab session with a teaching assistant or instructor present. The problem is divided into six parts:

1. Lab Objectives
2. Description of the Problem
3. Sample Output
4. Program Template (Fig. L 5.3)
5. Problem-Solving Tips
6. Follow-Up Questions and Activities

The program template represents a complete working C++ program, with one or more key lines of code replaced with comments. Read the problem description and examine the sample output; then study the template code. Using the problem-solving tips as a guide, replace the **/* */** comments with C++ code. Compile and execute the program. Compare your output with the sample output provided. Then answer the follow-up questions. The source code for the template is available at **www.deitel.com** and **www.prenhall.com./deitel**.

Lab Objectives

This lab was designed to reinforce programming concepts from Chapter 5 of *C++ How To Program: Fourth Edition*. In this lab, you will practice:

- Using arrays of pointers to create an array of strings.

- String comparison using function **strcmp** from the string manipulation library.

The follow-up questions and activities also will give you practice:

- Recognizing indefinite postponement and designing mechanisms to avoid it.

- Using **enum** to create an enumerated type **Suits**.

Description of the Problem

Modify the card-shuffling and -dealing program of Fig. 5.24 in *C++ How to Program: Fourth Edition* to display the color (red or black) of each card dealt. Indicate that a card is a face card (i.e., jack, queen and king) by displaying an asterisk when that card is output.

Lab Exercises   Name:

Lab Exercise 3 — Shuffling and Dealing

Sample Output

```
   Six of Clubs      [ Black ]     Deuce of Hearts    [ Red ]
  King of Hearts     [ Red ]*     Queen of Clubs      [ Black ]*
  King of Spades     [ Black ]*    Nine of Hearts     [ Red ]
   Ten of Hearts     [ Red ]       Six of Diamonds    [ Red ]
  Jack of Hearts     [ Red ]*     Five of Spades      [ Black ]
 Seven of Clubs      [ Black ]    Deuce of Clubs      [ Black ]
  Jack of Diamonds   [ Red ]*     Four of Spades      [ Black ]
   Ace of Clubs      [ Black ]     Ten of Clubs       [ Black ]
  King of Diamonds   [ Red ]*     Nine of Diamonds    [ Red ]
  Jack of Spades     [ Black ]*   Three of Clubs      [ Black ]
   Ten of Spades     [ Black ]     Ace of Spades      [ Black ]
  Five of Clubs      [ Black ]    Seven of Spades     [ Black ]
 Eight of Spades     [ Black ]    Queen of Diamonds   [ Red ]*
 Deuce of Spades     [ Black ]    Eight of Clubs      [ Black ]
 Seven of Hearts     [ Red ]       Six of Spades      [ Black ]
 Deuce of Diamonds   [ Red ]     Eight of Hearts     [ Red ]
  Four of Clubs      [ Black ]     Six of Hearts      [ Red ]
  Four of Hearts     [ Red ]      Nine of Clubs       [ Black ]
 Three of Diamonds   [ Red ]      Four of Diamonds    [ Red ]
 Three of Hearts     [ Red ]     Queen of Hearts      [ Red ]*
 Three of Spades     [ Black ]     Ace of Diamonds    [ Red ]
 Eight of Diamonds   [ Red ]       Ace of Hearts      [ Red ]
  Jack of Clubs      [ Black ]*   Queen of Spades     [ Black ]*
 Seven of Diamonds   [ Red ]       Ten of Diamonds    [ Red ]
  Five of Hearts     [ Red ]      King of Clubs       [ Black ]*
  Nine of Spades     [ Black ]    Five of Diamonds    [ Red ]
```

Template

```cpp
1    // Chapter 5 of C++ How to Program
2    // shuffle.cpp
3
4    #include <iostream>
5
6    using std::cout;
7    using std::endl;
8    using std::fixed;
9    using std::left;
10
11   #include <iomanip>
12
13   using std::setw;
14
15   #include <cstring>
16
17   #include <ctime>
18
19   #include <cstdlib>
20
```

Fig. L 5.3   `shuffle.cpp`. (Part 1 of 3.)

Lab Exercises   Name:

Lab Exercise 3 — Shuffling and Dealing

```
21   // prototypes
22   void deal( const int [][ 13 ], const char *[],
23            const char *[],
24               /* Write additional argument here */ );
25
26   void shuffle( int [][ 13 ] );
27
28   int main()
29   {
30      // initialize suit array
31      const char *suit[ 4 ] =
32         { "Hearts", "Clubs", "Diamonds", "Spades" };
33
34      // initialize face array
35      const char *face[ 13 ] =
36         { "Ace", "Deuce", "Three", "Four",
37           "Five", "Six", "Seven", "Eight",
38           "Nine", "Ten", "Jack", "Queen", "King" };
39      /* Write declaration for color here */
40
41      // initialize deck array
42      int deck[ 4 ][ 13 ] = { 0 };
43
44      shuffle( deck );
45      deal( deck, face, suit,
46            /* Write additional argument here */ );
47
48      return 0;
49
50   } // end main
51
52   // deal cards in deck
53   void deal( const int wDeck[][ 13 ], const char *wFace[],
54            const char *wSuit[], const char *wColor[] )
55   {
56      // for each of the 52 cards
57      for ( int card = 1; card <= 52; card++ )
58
59         // loop through rows of wDeck
60         for ( int row = 0; row <= 3; row++ )
61
62            // loop through columns of wDeck for current row
63            for ( int column = 0; column <= 12; column++ )
64
65               // if slot contains current card, display card
66               if ( wDeck[ row ][ column ] == card ){
67
68                  /* Write statement to declare a boolean
69                     variable isFace */
70
71                  /* Write statement to determine if the current
72                     card is a face card. If it is, assign true
73                     to variable isFace. If it is not, assign
74                     false to variable isFace */
75
```

Fig. L 5.3   shuffle.cpp. (Part 2 of 3.)

Lab Exercises   Name:

Lab Exercise 3 — Shuffling and Dealing

```
76                  cout << right << setw( 5 )
77                       << wFace[ column ] << " of "
78                       << setw( 8 ) << left
79                       << wSuit[ row ] << "  ";
80
81                  /* Write statement to display Red or Black */
82                  /* Write statement to display an asterisk
83                     if it is necessary */
84
85                  cout << ( card % 2 == 0 ? '\n' : '\t' );
86
87            } // end if
88
89      } // end function deal
90
91      // shuffle cards in deck
92      void shuffle( int wDeck[][ 13 ] )
93      {
94         int row;
95         int column;
96
97         srand( time( 0 ) ); // seed random number generator
98
99         // for each of the 52 cards, choose slot of deck randomly
100        for ( int card = 1; card <= 52; card++ ) {
101           do {
102              row = rand() % 4;
103              column = rand() % 13;
104           } while( wDeck[ row ][ column ] != 0 );
105
106           // place card number in chosen slot of deck
107           wDeck[ row ][ column ] = card;
108
109        } // end for
110
111     } // end function shuffle
```

Fig. L 5.3   `shuffle.cpp`. (Part 3 of 3.)

Problem-Solving Tips

1. Declare an array of pointers to characters named **color**. This array should contain the strings **"Red"** and **"Black"**.

2. In the template, we changed the order of the strings assigned to **suit**. This modified order will aid you in displaying the color.

3. You will need to use **strcmp** from the string manipulation library to determine if a card is a face card.

Lab Exercises   Name: _____

Lab Exercise 3 — Shuffling and Dealing

Follow-Up Questions and Activities

1. What is indefinite postponement? Could this implementation exhibit indefinite postponement? Why or why not?

2. In your solution, you probably used function **strcmp** to compare strings. Write a function named **compare** for comparing strings. Do not use any **<cstring>** library functions. Use pointer-subscript notation.

3. The second problem-solving tip notes that our **suit** array needs to be arranged in a specific order. Create an enumeration **Suits** to replace the **suit** array. Modify function **deal** to use a **switch** statement and the **Suits** enumeration to print the correct suit.

Lab Exercises   Name:

Lab Exercise 3 — Shuffling and Dealing

Lab Exercises   Name:

Debugging

Name: _____   **Date:** _____

Section: _____

The program (Fig. L 5.4) in this section does not run properly. Fix all the syntax errors so that the program will compile successfully. Once the program compiles, compare the output with the sample output, and eliminate any logic errors that may exist. The sample output demonstrates what the program's output should be once the program's code has been corrected.

Sample Output

```
The value stored in variable name is:
The value stored in variable age is: 0

The value stored in variable name is:
The value stored in variable age is: 0

Enter a name: John
Enter an age: 44

Enter a name: John
Enter an age: 43

The value stored in variable name is: John
The value stored in variable age is: 44

The value stored in variable name is: John
The value stored in variable age is: 43

John has grown one year older

Both people have the same name and age
```

Lab Exercises

Name:

Debugging

Broken Code

```
1   // Chapter 5 of C++ How to Program
2   // Debugging Problem
3
4   #include <iostream>
5
6   using std::cout;
7   using std::cin;
8   using std::endl;
9
10  #include <cstring>
11
12  void initialize( char [], int * );
13  void input( const char [], int & );
14  void print( const char *, const int );
15  void growOlder( const char [], int * );
16  bool comparePeople( const char *, const int *,
17                      const char *, const int * );
18
19  int main()
20  {
21     char name1[ 25 ];
22     char name2[ 25 ];
23     int age1;
24     int age2;
25
26     initialize( name1, &age1 );
27     initialize( name2, &age2 );
28
29     print( name1, *age1 );
30     print( name2, *age2 );
31
32     input( name1, age1 );
33     input( name2, age2 );
34
35     print( &name1, &age1Ptr );
36     print( &name2, &age1Ptr );
37
38     growOlder( name2, age2 );
39
40     if ( comparePeople( name1, &age1, name2, &age2 ) )
41        cout << "Both people have the same name and age"
42             << endl;
43
44     return 0;
45
46  } // end main
47
48  // function input definition
49  void input( const char name[], int &age )
50  {
51     cout << "Enter a name: ";
52     cin >> name;
53
54     cout << "Enter an age: ";
55     cin >> age;
```

Fig. L 5.4   debugging05.cpp. (Part 1 of 2.)

Lab Exercises

Name:

Debugging

```cpp
56       cout << endl;
57
58  } // end function input
59
60  // function initialize definition
61  void initialize( char name[], int *age )
62  {
63     name = "";
64     age = 0;
65
66  } // end function initialize
67
68  // function print definition
69  void print( const char name[], const int age )
70  {
71     cout << "The value stored in variable name is: "
72          << name << endl
73          << "The value stored in variable age is: "
74          << age << endl << endl;
75
76  } // end function print
77
78  // function growOlder definition
79  void growOlder( const char name[], int *age )
80  {
81     cout << name << " has grown one year older\n\n";
82     *age++;
83
84  } // end function growOlder
85
86  // function comparePeople definition
87  bool comparePeople( const char *name1, const int *age1,
88                      const char *name2, const int *age2 )
89  {
90     return ( age1 == age2 && strcmp( name1, name2 ) );
91
92  } // end function comparePeople
```

Fig. L 5.4   debugging05.cpp. (Part 2 of 2.)

Lab Exercises

Name:

Debugging

Postlab Activities

Coding Exercises

Name: _____   Date:_____

Section: _____

These coding exercises reinforce the lessons learned in the lab and provide additional programming experience outside the classroom and laboratory environment. They serve as a review after you have completed the Prelab Activities and Lab Exercises successfully.

For each of the following problems, write a program or a program segment that performs the specified action.

1. Write three lines of code that declare three pointers to integers. Initialize one to **NULL**, another to **0** and the third to point to the address of **x**.

2. Using the pointer you declared in Coding Exercise 1, that points to the address of **x**, modify **x** by assigning to it the value of **4**.

3. Write a function prototype for the function **fn** that takes two pointers to integers as arguments and returns nothing.

4. Call function **fn** that you declared in Coding Exercise 3, and pass to it two of the pointers from Coding Exercise 1 as arguments.

5. Apply the **sizeof** operator to all pointers from Coding Exercises 1.

Postlab Activities

Name:

Coding Exercises

6. Initialize a character string to a phrase of your choice. Traverse the contents of the string, using pointer-offset notation, and print each character, separated from adjacent characters by a '+' character.

7. Traverse the contents of the string from Coding Exercise 6, this time using pointer subscript notation. In this exercise, each character output should be separated from adjacent characters by a '-' character.

8. Compare the first and third characters in the string from Coding Exercises 6–7. If they are equal, print "**equal**." Use pointer-offset notation.

9. Write a program that inputs two strings—**s1** and **s2**—from the user. Use **strcpy** to copy the contents of **s2** into **s1**. Assume that user input is limited to 50 characters.

10. Use **strncat** to append the first five characters of **"today is a nice day"** to **"how old are you "**.

Postlab Activities   Name:

Programming Challenges

Name: _____   Date:_____

Section: _____

The Programming Challenges are more involved than the Coding Exercises and may require a significant amount of time to complete. Write a C++ program for each of the problems in this section. The answers to these problems are available at **www.deitel.com**, **www.prenhall.com/deitel** and on the *C++ Multimedia Cyber Classroom: Fourth Edition*. Pseudocode, hints and/or sample outputs are provided to aid you in your programming.

11. Modify the program in Fig. 5.24 of *C++ How to Program: Fourth Edition* so that the card-dealing function deals a five-card poker hand. Then write functions to accomplish each of the following tasks:

   a) Determine if the hand contains a pair.

   b) Determine if the hand contains two pairs.

   c) Determine if the hand contains three of a kind (e.g., three jacks).

   d) Determine if the hand contains four of a kind (e.g., four aces).

   e) Determine if the hand contains a flush (i.e., all five cards of the same suit).

   f) Determine if the hand contains a straight (i.e., five cards of consecutive face values).

Hints:

   • Each function should be passed the dealt hand, the deck of cards and **face**.

   • To determine if two (or more) cards are of the same suit, create an array of 13 elements—one for each card—and initialize its elements to **0**. Iterate through the hand, incrementing the appropriate card within your array. Finally, loop through the resulting array, checking for elements greater than or equal to **2** (or **3** or **4**).

   • Similarly, check for a flush by creating a four-element array, where each element represents a different suit.

   • Check for a straight by using the bubble sort.

12. [*Note*: This problem is intended for those students who have studied recursion in Section 3.17 of *C++ How to Program: Fourth Edition*.] The following grid of hashes (**#**) and dots (**.**) is a double-subscripted array representation of a maze:

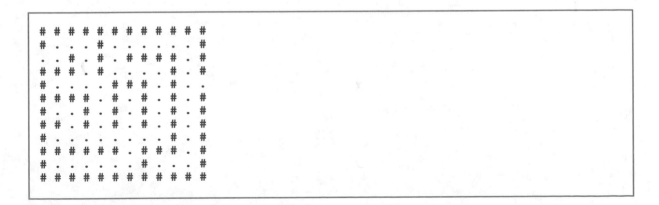

Postlab Activities   Name:

Programming Challenges

In the preceding double-subscripted array, the hashes represent the walls of the maze, and the dots represent squares in the possible paths through the maze. Moves can be made only to a location in the array that contains a dot.

There is a simple algorithm for walking through a maze which guarantees that you will find the exit (assuming that there is an exit). If there is no exit, you will arrive at the starting location again. Place your right hand on the wall to your right, and begin walking forward. Never remove your hand from the wall. If the maze turns to the right, you follow the wall to the right. As long as you do not remove your hand from the wall, you will arrive at the exit of the maze eventually. There may be a shorter path than the one you have taken, but you are guaranteed to get out of the maze if you follow the algorithm.

Write recursive function **mazeTraverse** to walk through the maze. The function should receive as arguments a 12-by-12 character array representing the maze, and the starting location of the maze. As **maze-Traverse** attempts to locate the exit of the maze, it should place the character **X** in each square in the path. The function should display the maze after each move so the user can watch as the maze is solved.

Hints:

- The **mazeTraverse** function should be passed the array representing the maze, two starting coordinates (**x** and **y**) and the "right" wall.

- Write functions to determine if the coordinates are on the edge of the maze (only the starting and ending points are in this position) and if a move is legal. Also include a function to print the maze.

13. Write a program that inputs a line of text, tokenizes the line with function **strtok** and outputs the tokens in reverse order.

Hints:

- Allow the maximum amount of text input to be 100 characters long.

- Use **strtok** to tokenize the text, inserting all tokens into an array (because the maximum input is only 100 characters, there should be no more than 60 tokens).

- Print the contents of this array, from the last element to the first.

14. Many computerized check-writing systems do not print the amount of the check in words. Perhaps the main reason for this omission is the fact that most high-level computer languages used in commercial applications do not contain adequate string manipulation features. Another reason is that the logic for writing word equivalents of check amounts is somewhat involved.

    Write a program that inputs a numeric check amount and writes the word equivalent of the amount. For example, the amount 112.43 should be written as

    ONE HUNDRED TWELVE and 43/100

Hints:

- Handle only amounts from 0 to 100.

- Create arrays of characters to pointers containing the words for all the digits and the tens places (forty, fifty, sixty, etc.) do not forget about the teens!

- Use the **%** operator to isolate certain digits.

- Implementation for amounts larger than 100 is similar.

6

Classes and
Data Abstraction

Objectives

- To understand the software and engineering concepts of encapsulation and data hiding.
- To understand the notions of data abstraction and abstract data types (ADTs).
- To create C++ ADTs, namely, classes. Class definitions include member access specifiers, member function prototypes, constructors, destructors and data members.
- To understand how to create, use and destroy class objects.
- To understand how to design constructors to initialize objects.
- To control access to object data members and member functions by using the **private** member-access specifier.
- To appreciate the value of object orientation.

Assignment Checklist

Name: _____   **Date:** _____

Section: _____

Exercises	Assigned: *Circle assignments*	Date Due
Prelab Activities		
Matching	YES NO	
Fill in the Blank	11, 12, 13, 14, 15, 16, 17, 18, 19, 20, 21, 22, 23	
Short Answer	24, 25, 26, 27	
Programming Output	28, 29, 30, 31	
Correct the Code	32, 33, 34, 35, 36, 37, 38	
Lab Exercises		
Lab Exercise 1 — Complex Numbers	YES NO	
Follow-Up Questions and Activities	1, 2, 3	
Lab Exercise 2 — Dates	YES NO	
Follow-Up Questions and Activities	1, 2, 3, 4	
Debugging	YES NO	
Labs Provided by Instructor		
1.		
2.		
3.		
Postlab Activities		
Coding Exercises	1, 2, 3, 4, 5, 6, 7, 8	
Programming Challenges	9, 10, 11, 12	

Assignment Checklist

Name:

Prelab Activities

Matching

Name: _____   **Date:** _____

Section: _____

After reading Chapter 6 of *C++ How to Program: Fourth Edition*, answer the given questions. These questions are intended to test and reinforce your understanding of key concepts and may be done either before the lab or during the lab.

For each term in the column on the left, write the corresponding letter for the description that best matches it from the column on the right.

Term	Description
___ 1. Data members	a) **public** or **private**.
___ 2. Scope resolution operator	b) Hiding implementation within classes themselves.
___ 3. Constructor	c) Data components of a class.
___ 4. Class interface	d) Function components of a class.
___ 5. Destructor	e) Initializes data members to appropriate values.
___ 6. Member functions	f) **::**.
___ 7. Information hiding	g) **public** member functions.
___ 8. Member-access operator	h) Carries out "termination housekeeping."
___ 9. Message	i) Member function call sent from one object to another.
___ 10. Member-access specifier	j) Dot operator (**.**) or the arrow operator (**->**).

Prelab Activities

Name:

Matching

Prelab Activities   Name: _____

Fill in the Blank

Name: _____   Date: _____

Section: _____

Fill in the blank for each of the following statements:

11. _____ enable the programmer to model objects that have attributes and behaviors or operations.

12. Classes in C++ are a natural evolution of the C notion of _____.

13. The class _____ instantiates objects of that class.

14. The body of a class definition is delimited with _____.

15. **private** member functions are visible only to _____ of the same class.

16. Member-access specifiers always end with a(n) _____ and can appear multiple times and in any order in a class definition.

17. The implementation details of a class should be _____ from its clients.

18. When a member function is defined outside the class definition, the function name is preceded by the _____ name and the _____ operator.

19. A fundamental principle of good software engineering is separating _____ from _____.

20. _____ of a class normally are made **private** and _____ of a class normally are made **public**.

21. Data members can be initialized in a(n) _____, or their values may be *set* after an instance of the object is instantiated.

22. Constructors may not _____ a value.

23. Assigning an object to another object of the same type is performed using _____ copy.

Prelab Activities

Name:

Fill in the Blank

Prelab Activities

Name:

Short Answer

Name: _____   **Date:** _____

Section: _____

In the space provided, answer each of the given questions. Your answers should be as concise as possible; aim for two or three sentences.

24. What is information hiding? Why is it important?

25. Describe the major drawbacks of using **struct**s as opposed to **class**es.

Prelab Activities   Name:

Short Answer

26. Explain when to use the dot operator (`.`) and when to use the arrow operator (`->`).

27. What is the difference between class scope and file scope?

Prelab Activities　　　　　　　　　　　　　Name:

Programming Output

Name: _____　　　　　　Date:_____

Section: _____

For each of the given program segments, read the code and write the output in the space provided below each program. [*Note*: Do not execute these programs on a computer.]

28. What is output by the following code segment? Use the definition of the class **Time** shown in Fig. L 6.1.

```
1   Time t1();
2
3   t1.setTime( 18, 22, 9 );
4   cout << "The time is: ";
5   t1.printStandard();
```

```
6   // Time abstract data type (ADT) definition
7   class Time {
8
9   public:
10      Time();                          // constructor
11      void setTime( int, int, int );   // set hour, minute, second
12      void printUniversal();           // print universal time format
13      void printStandard();            // print standard time format
14
15   private:
16      int hour;      // 0 - 23 ( 24-hour clock format )
17      int minute;    // 0 - 59
18      int second;    // 0 - 59
19
20   }; // end class Time
21
22   // Time constructor initializes each data member to zero.
23   // Ensures all Time objects start in a consistent state.
24   Time::Time()
25   {
26      hour = minute = second = 0;
27
28   } // end Time constructor
29
30   // Set a new Time value using universal time. Perform validity
31   // checks on the data values. Set invalid values to zero.
32   void Time::setTime( int h, int m, int s )
33   {
34      hour = ( h >= 0 && h < 24 ) ? h : 0;
35      minute = ( m >= 0 && m < 60 ) ? m : 0;
36      second = ( s >= 0 && s < 60 ) ? s : 0;
37
38   } // end function setTime
```

Fig. L 6.1　　**Time** class. (Part 1 of 2.)

Prelab Activities   Name: _____

Programming Output

```
39
40   // Print Time in universal format
41   void Time::printUniversal()
42   {
43      cout << setfill( '0' ) << setw( 2 ) << hour << ":"
44           << setw( 2 ) << minute << ":"
45           << setw( 2 ) << second;
46
47   } // end function printUniversal
48
49   // Print Time in standard format
50   void Time::printStandard()
51   {
52      cout << ( ( hour == 0 || hour == 12 ) ? 12 : hour % 12 )
53           << ":" << setfill( '0' ) << setw( 2 ) << minute
54           << ":" << setw( 2 ) << second
55           << ( hour < 12 ? " AM" : " PM" );
56
57   } // end function printStandard
```

Fig. L 6.1   **Time** class. (Part 2 of 2.)

Your answer:

29. What is output by the following program?

```
1    #include <iostream>
2
3    using std::cout;
4    using std::endl;
5
6    class M {
7
8    public:
9       M( int );
10      int mystery( int );
11
12   private:
13      int data;
14      double number;
15
16   }; // end class M
17
18   // constructor
19   M::M( int q )
20   {
21      data = q;
22      number = .5;
23
24   } // end class M constructor
```

Prelab Activities   Name:

Programming Output

```
25
26   // function mystery definition
27   int M::mystery( int q )
28   {
29      data += q;
30      return data * number;
31
32   } // end function mystery
33
34   int main()
35   {
36      M stuff( 44 );
37      cout << stuff.mystery( 78 );
38
39      return 0;
40
41   } // end main
```

(Part 2 of 2.)

Your answer:

30. What is output by the following program?

```
1    #include <iostream>
2
3    using std::cout;
4    using std::endl;
5
6    class M {
7
8    public:
9       M( int );
10      int mystery( int );
11
12   private:
13      int data;
14      int number;
15
16   }; // end class M
17
18   // constructor
19   M::M( int q = 0 )
20   {
21      data = q;
22      number = 2;
23
24   } // end class M constructor
25
26   // function mystery definition
27   int M::mystery( int q )
28   {
```

(Part 1 of 2.)

Prelab Activities   Name:

Programming Output

```
29      data += q;
30      return data;
31
32  } // end function mystery definition
33
34  int main()
35  {
36     M mObject( 2 );
37     M *mPtr = &mObject;
38
39     cout << mObject.mystery( 20 ) << endl;
40     cout << mPtr->mystery( 30 );
41
42     return 0;
43
44  } // end main
```

(Part 2 of 2.)

Your answer:

31. What is the output of the following program segment? Assume use of the **Time** class shown in Fig. L 6.1.

```
1   Time t( 3, 4, 5 );
2
3   t.printStandard();
4   cout << endl;
5
6   t.printUniversal();
7   cout << endl;
8
9   t.setTime( 99, 3, 4 );
10
11  t.printUniversal();
12  cout << endl;
```

Your answer:

Prelab Activities   Name:

Correct the Code

Name: _____   Date:_____

Section: _____

For each of the given program segments, determine if there is an error in the code. If there is an error, specify whether it is a logic error or a syntax error, circle the error in the program, and write the corrected code in the space provided after each problem. If the code does not contain an error, write "no error." [*Note*: It is possible that a program segment may contain multiple errors.]

32. The following code should set the **hour**, **minute**, and **second** variables within a **Time struct**. Use the definition for the **Time struct** defined in Fig. L 6.2.

```
1   Time clock;
2   Time *clockPtr = &clock;
3
4   clock.hour = 8;
5   clock.minute = 12
6   *clockPtr.second = 0;
```

```
1   struct Time {
2      int hour;        // 0-23
3      int minute;      // 0-59
4      int second;      // 0-59
5
6   }; // end struct Time
```

Fig. L 6.2   **Time** structure definition.

Your answer:

Prelab Activities   Name:

Correct the Code

33. The following defines class **Time**:

```
1    class Time {
2
3    public:
4       Time( int = 0, int = 0, int = 0 );
5       void setTime( int, int, int );
6       void printUniversal();
7       void printStandard();
8
9    private:
10      int hour;
11      int minute;
12      int second;
13
14   } // end class Time
```

Your answer:

34. The following code defines class **Q**:

```
1    class Q {
2
3    public:
4       int Q( int );
5       void setQ( int );
6       void printQ();
7       int operateQ( int );
8
9    private:
10      int qData;
11
12   }; // end class Q
```

Your answer:

Prelab Activities   Name:

Correct the Code

35. The following is another version of class **Q**'s definition:

```
1   class Q {
2
3   public:
4       Q( int );
5       void setQ( int );
6       void printQ();
7       int operateQ( int );
8
9   private:
10      int qData = 1;
11
12  }; // end class Q
```

Your answer:

36. The following defines **Q**'s **setQ** method. This definition resides outside class **Q**'s definition. Use the corrected class **Q** from Correct the Code 35:

```
1   void setQ( int input )
2   {
3       qData = input;
4   }
```

Your answer:

Prelab Activities   Name:

Correct the Code

37. The following defines **setHour**, a member function of the **Time** class, Fig. L 6.1.

```
1   int &Time::setHour( int hh )
2   {
3      hour = ( hh >= 0 && hh < 24 ) ? hh : 0;
4
5      return hour;
6   }
```

Your answer:

38. The following code should call member function **printUniversal** of the **Time** class defined in Fig. L 6.1.

```
1   Time clock( 11, 22, 43 );
2   Time *clockPtr = &clock;
3
4   clockPtr.printUniversal();
```

Your answer:

Lab Exercises

Lab Exercise 1 — Complex Numbers

Name: _____   **Date:**_____

Section: _____

This problem is intended to be solved in a closed-lab session with a teaching assistant or instructor present. The problem is divided into six parts:

1. Lab Objectives
2. Description of the Problem
3. Sample Output
4. Program Template (Fig. L 6.3–Fig. L 6.5)
5. Problem-Solving Tips
6. Follow-Up Questions and Activities

The program template represents a complete working C++ program, with one or more key lines of code replaced with comments. Read the problem description and examine the sample output; then study the template code. Using the problem-solving tips as a guide, replace the **/* */** comments with C++ code. Compile and execute the program. Compare your output with the sample output provided. Then answer the follow-up questions. The source code for the template is available at **www.deitel.com** and **www.prenhall.com./deitel**.

Lab Objectives

This lab was designed to reinforce programming concepts from Chapter 6 of *C++ How To Program: Fourth Edition*. In this lab, you will practice:

*   creating new data types by writing class definitions.
*   defining member functions of programmer-defined classes.
*   instantiating objects from programmer-defined classes.
*   calling member functions of programmer-defined classes.

The follow-up questions and activities will also give you practice:

*   initializing programmer-defined class data members with class constructors.

Description of the Problem

Create a class called **Complex** for performing arithmetic with complex numbers. Write a driver program to test your class. Complex numbers have the form

        realPart + imaginaryPart * i

where *i* is

$$\sqrt{-1}$$

Use floating-point variables to represent the **private** data of the class. Provide a constructor function that enables an object of this class to be initialized when it is declared. The constructor should contain default values in case no initializers are provided. Provide **public** member functions for each of the following:

a) Addition of two **Complex** numbers: The real parts are added together and the imaginary parts are added together.

Lab Exercises   Name:

Lab Exercise 1 — Complex Numbers

b) Subtraction of two **Complex** numbers: The real part of the right operand is subtracted from the real part of the left operand and the imaginary part of the right operand is subtracted from the imaginary part of the left operand.

c) Printing **Complex** numbers in the form **(a, b)** where **a** is the real part and **b** is the imaginary part.

Sample Output

```
(1, 7) + (9, 2) = (10, 9)
(10, 1) - (11, 5) = (-1, -4)
```

Template

```
1   // Chapter 6 of C++ How to Program
2   // complex.h
3   #ifndef COMPLEX_H
4   #define COMPLEX_H
5
6   /* Write class definition for Complex */
7
8   #endif // Complex_H
```

Fig. L 6.3   Contents of **complex.h**.

```
1   // Chapter 6 of C++ How to Program
2   // complexm.cpp
3   // member function definitions for class Complex
4   #include <iostream>
5
6   using std::cout;
7
8   #include "complex.h"
9
10  // constructor
11  Complex::Complex( double real, double imaginary )
12  {
13      setComplexNumber( real, imaginary );
14
15  } // end class Complex constructor
16
17  // add complex numbers
18  void Complex::addition( const Complex &a )
19  {
20     /* Write statement to add the realPart of a to the class
21        realPart */
22     /* Write statement to add the imaginaryPart of a to the
23        class imaginaryPart */
24
25  } // end function addition
26
```

Fig. L 6.4   Contents of **complexm.cpp**. (Part 1 of 2.)

Lab Exercises   Name:

Lab Exercise 1 — Complex Numbers

```
27    // subtract complex numbers
28    void Complex::subtraction( const Complex &s )
29    {
30       /* Write a statement to subtract the realPart of s from the
31          class realPart */
32       /* Write a statement to subtract the imaginaryPart of s from
33          the class imaginaryPart */
34
35    } // end function subtraction
36
37    // print complex numbers
38    void Complex::printComplex()
39    {
40       cout << '(' << realPart << ", " << imaginaryPart << ')';
41
42    } // end function printComplex
43
44    // set complex number
45    void Complex::setComplexNumber( double real, double imaginary )
46    {
47       realPart = real;
48       imaginaryPart = imaginary;
49
50    } // end function setComplexNumber
```

Fig. L 6.4   Contents of **complexm.cpp**. (Part 2 of 2.)

```
1     // Chapter 6 of C++ How to Program
2     // complex.cpp
3     #include <iostream>
4
5     using std::cout;
6     using std::endl;
7
8     #include "complex.h"
9
10    int main()
11    {
12       Complex b( 1, 7 ), c( 9, 2 );
13
14       b.printComplex();
15       cout << " + ";
16       c.printComplex();
17       cout << " = ";
18       b.addition( c );
19       b.printComplex();
20
21       cout << '\n';
22       b.setComplexNumber( 10, 1 );
23       c.setComplexNumber( 11, 5 );
24       b.printComplex();
25       cout << " - ";
26       c.printComplex();
27       cout << " = ";
```

Fig. L 6.5   Contents of **complex.cpp**. (Part 1 of 2.)

Lab Exercises   Name:

Lab Exercise 1 — Complex Numbers

```
28      b.subtraction( c );
29      b.printComplex();
30      cout << endl;
31
32      return 0;
33
34   }  // end main
```

Fig. L 6.5   Contents of **complex.cpp**. (Part 2 of 2.)

Problem-Solving Tips

1. In this lab, you must write the definition for class **Complex**. Use the details provided in the member definition (**complexM.cpp**) file to assist you.

2. Remember to use member-access specifiers **public** and **private** to specify the access level of data members and functions. Carefully consider which access specifier to use for each class member. In general, data members should be **private** and member functions should be **public**.

Follow-Up Questions and Activities

1. Why do you think **const** was used in the parameter list of **addition** and **subtraction**?

2. Can **addition** and **subtraction**'s parameters be passed call-by-value instead of call-by-reference? How might this affect the design of class **Complex**? Write a new class definition that illustrates how the parameters would be placed call-by-value.

Lab Exercises   Name: _____

Lab Exercise 1 — Complex Numbers

3. Declare a **Complex** number, as follows, without passing any arguments to the constructor. What happens? Does the default constructor handle this declaration?

    Complex a;

Lab Exercises

Name:

Lab Exercise 1 — Complex Numbers

Lab Exercises   Name:

Lab Exercise 2 — Dates

Name: _____   Date:_____

Section: _____

This problem is intended to be solved in a closed-lab session with a teaching assistant or instructor present. The problem is divided into six parts:

1. Lab Objectives

2. Description of the Problem

3. Sample Output

4. Program Template (Fig. L 6.6–Fig. L 6.8)

5. Problem-Solving Tips

6. Follow-Up Questions and Activities

The program template represents a complete working C++ program, with one or more key lines of code replaced with comments. Read the problem description and examine the sample output; then study the template code. Using the problem-solving tips as a guide, replace the **/* */** comments with C++ code. Compile and execute the program. Compare your output with the sample output provided. Then answer the follow-up questions. The source code for the template is available at **www.deitel.com** and **www.prenhall.com./deitel**.

Lab Objectives

This lab was designed to reinforce programming concepts from Chapter 6 of *C++ How To Program: Fourth Edition*. In this lab, you will practice:

*   modular design of classes.

*   using access functions and utility functions so that it is not necessary for non-member functions to be able to access a class' data members.

The follow-up questions and activities also will give you practice:

*   overloading class constructors and using default arguments with constructors.

*   defining a destructor. A destructor is a special member function that is called when an object is destroyed— for example, automatic objects are destroyed when program execution leaves the scope in which those objects reside.

Description of the Problem

Modify the **Date** class of Fig. 6.24 of *C++ How to Program: Fourth Edition* to perform error checking on the initializer values for data members **month, day** and **year**. Also, provide a member function **nextDay** to increment the day by one. The **Date** object should always remain in a consistent state. Write a driver program that tests the **nextDay** function in a loop that prints the date during each iteration of the loop to illustrate that the **nextDay** function works correctly. Be sure to test the following cases:

a) Incrementing into the next month.

b) Incrementing into the next year.

Lab Exercises

Lab Exercise 2 — Dates

Sample Output

```
10-2-2002
10-3-2002
10-4-2002
10-5-2002
10-6-2002
10-7-2002
10-8-2002
10-9-2002
10-10-2002
...
2-27-2003
2-28-2003
3-1-2003
3-2-2003
3-3-2003
3-4-2003
3-5-2003
3-6-2003
3-7-2003
3-8-2003
3-9-2003
3-10-2003
```

Template

```cpp
1   // Chapter 6 of C++ How to Program
2   // date.h
3   #ifndef DATE_H
4   #define DATE_H
5
6   // class Date definition
7   class Date {
8
9   public:
10     Date( int = 1, int = 1, int = 1900 ); // default constructor
11     void print();
12
13     void setDate( int, int, int );
14
15     void setMonth( int );
16     int getMonth();
17
18     void setDay( int );
19     int getDay();
20
21     void setYear( int );
22     int getYear();
23
24     bool isLeapYear();
25     int monthDays();
26     /* Write prototype for nextDay */
```

Fig. L 6.6   Contents of **date.h**. (Part 1 of 2.)

Lab Exercises   Name:

Lab Exercise 2 — Dates

```
27
28  private:
29      int month;
30      int day;
31      int year;
32
33  }; // end class Date
34
35  #endif // DATE_H
```

Fig. L 6.6   Contents of **date.h**. (Part 2 of 2.)

```
1   // Chapter 6 of C++ How to Program
2   // datem.cpp
3   // member function definitions for date.cpp
4   #include <iostream>
5
6   using std::cout;
7
8   #include "date.h"
9
10  // constructor
11  Date::Date( int m, int d, int y )
12  {
13      setDate( m, d, y );
14
15  } // end class Date constructor
16
17  // return day
18  int Date::getDay()
19  {
20      return day;
21
22  } // end function getDay
23
24  // return month
25  int Date::getMonth()
26  {
27      return month;
28
29  } // end function getMonth
30
31  // return year
32  int Date::getYear()
33  {
34      return year;
35
36  } // end function getYear
37
38  // set day
39  void Date::setDay( int d )
40  {
41      if ( month == 2 && isLeapYear() )
42          day = ( d <= 29 && d >= 1 ) ? d : 1;
43
```

Fig. L 6.7   Contents of **datem.cpp**. (Part 1 of 2.)

Lab Exercises

Lab Exercise 2 — Dates

```
44        else
45            day = ( d <= monthDays() && d >= 1 ) ? d : 1;
46
47    } // end function setDay
48
49    // set month
50    void Date::setMonth( int m )
51    {
52        month = m <= 12 && m >= 1 ? m : 1;
53
54    } // end function setMonth
55
56    // set year
57    void Date::setYear( int y )
58    {
59        year = y <= 2010 && y >= 1900 ? y : 1900;
60
61    } // end function setYear
62
63    // set date
64    void Date::setDate( int mo, int dy, int yr )
65    {
66        setMonth( mo );
67        setDay( dy );
68        setYear( yr );
69
70    } // end function setDate
71
72    // output Date
73    void Date::print()
74    {
75        cout << month << '-' << day << '-' << year << '\n';
76
77    } // end function print
78
79    /* Write function nextDay here */
80
81    // test if it is a leap year
82    bool Date::isLeapYear()
83    {
84        if ( year % 400 == 0 || ( year % 4 == 0 && year % 100 != 0 ) )
85            return true;
86
87        else
88            return false;      // not a leap year
89
90    } // end function isLeapYear
91
92    // return days in month
93    int Date::monthDays()
94    {
95        const int days[ 12 ] = { 31, 28, 31, 30, 31, 30, 31, 31, 30,
96                                  31, 30, 31 };
97
98        return month == 2 && leapYear() ? 29 : days[ month - 1 ];
99
100   } // end function monthDays
```

Fig. L 6.7   Contents of **datem.cpp**. (Part 2 of 2.)

Lab Exercises   Name:

Lab Exercise 2 — Dates

```
1   // Chapter 6 of C++ How to Program
2   // date.cpp
3   #include <iostream>
4
5   using std::cout;
6   using std::endl;
7
8   #include "date.h"
9
10  int main()
11  {
12     const int MAXDAYS = 160;
13     Date d( 10, 2, 2002 );
14
15     // test print and nextDay
16     for ( int loop = 1; loop <= MAXDAYS; ++loop ) {
17        d.print();
18        /* Write call to nextDay */
19
20     } // end for
21
22     cout << endl;
23
24     return 0;
25
26  } // end main
```

Fig. L 6.8   Contents of **date.cpp**.

Problem-Solving Tips

1. In this lab you will implement function **nextDay**. This function should increment into the next day and determine if the next month has occurred. When the next month occurs, determine if the next year has occurred.

2. If you examine function **setDay**, you will notice that it determines if a new month has started. If so, it sets the **day** to one. When **day** is set to one, the **month** must be incremented by one as well. If **month** is one, the next year has been entered. Use functions **setDay**, **setMonth** and **setYear** as part of your **nextDay** implementation.

Follow-Up Questions and Activities

1. The **Date** class has only one constructor. Is it possible to have more than one constructor?

2. What happens when a member function that takes no arguments is called without the parentheses (i.e., **dateObject.nextDay**)?

Lab Exercises   Name:

Lab Exercise 2 — Dates

3. Create a destructor for the **Date** class. The destructor should print text indicating that the destructor for the **Date** class was called successfully.

4. In **main**, try to change **d**'s **year** to **2003** using an assignment statement. Do not call function **setYear**. What happens? Are you able to change the value?

Lab Exercises   Name:

Debugging

Name: _____   **Date:** _____

Section: _____

The program (Fig. L 6.9–Fig. L 6.11) in this section does not run properly. Fix all the syntax errors so that the program will compile successfully. Once the program compiles, compare the output with the sample output, and eliminate any logic errors that may exist. The sample output demonstrates what the program's output should be once the program's code has been corrected.

Sample Output

```
This is the: Ace of spades
This is the: 4 of hearts
This card is not valid
This is the: 4 of hearts

This is the: Ace of hearts
This is the: 5 of hearts
This is the: Queen of clubs
This is the: 5 of hearts

The destructor has been invoked
The destructor has been invoked
The destructor has been invoked
```

Lab Exercises

Name:

Debugging

Broken Code

```
1   // Chapter 6 of C++ How to Program
2   // Debugging Problem (card.h)
3
4   #ifndef CARD_H
5   #define CARD_H
6
7   // class card definition
8   class Card {
9
10  public
11      void Card();
12      void Card( int, int );
13      void ~Card();
14
15      void setSuit( int );
16      int getSuit() const;
17
18      void setValue( int );
19      int getValue() const;
20
21      void print() const;
22
23  private
24      int suit = 4;
25      int value = 1;
26      bool validCard() const;
27
28  } // end class Card
29
30  #endif // CARD_H
```

Fig. L 6.9   Contents of `card.h`.

```
1   // Chapter 6 of C++ How to Program
2   // Debugging Problem (card.cpp)
3
4   #include <iostream>
5
6   using std::cout;
7   using std::endl;
8
9   // default constructor
10  void Card::Card()
11  {
12      suit = 4;
13      value = 1;
14
15  } // end class Card constructor
16
```

Fig. L 6.10   Contents of `card.cpp`. (Part 1 of 3.)

Lab Exercises   Name:

Debugging

```cpp
17  // constructor
18  Card::Card( int s, int v )
19  {
20     suit = s; value = v;
21
22  } // end class Card constructor
23
24  // destructor
25  Card::~Card()
26  {
27     cout << "The destructor has been invoked\n";
28
29  } // end class Card destructor
30
31  // set suit
32  void Card::setSuit( int s )
33  {
34     suit = s;
35
36  } // end function setSuit
37
38  // set value
39  void Card::setValue( int v )
40  {
41     value = v;
42
43  } // end function setValue
44
45  // function print definition
46  void print()
47  {
48     // is card valid
49     if ( !validCard() ) {
50        cout << "This card is not valid\n";
51        return;
52
53     } // end if
54
55     cout << "This is the: ";
56
57     // determine face of card
58     switch ( value ) {
59        case 1:
60           cout << "Ace ";
61           break;
62
63        case 11:
64           cout << "Jack ";
65           break;
66
67        case 12:
68           cout << "Queen ";
69           break;
70
71        case 13:
72           cout << "King ";
73           break;
```

Fig. L 6.10   Contents of **card.cpp**. (Part 2 of 3.)

Lab Exercises   Name:

Debugging

```
74
75          default:
76             cout << value << " ";
77
78       } // end switch
79
80       // determine suit
81       switch ( suit ) {
82          case 1:
83             cout << "of clubs\n";
84             break;
85
86          case 2:
87             cout << "of diamonds\n";
88             break;
89
90          case 3:
91             cout << "of hearts\n";
92             break;
93
94          case 4:
95             cout << "of spades\n";
96             break;
97
98          default:
99             cout << "\ninvalid suit\n";
100
101       } // end switch
102
103    } // end function print
104
105    // return suit
106    int Card::getSuit()
107    {
108       return suit;
109
110    } // end function getSuit
111
112    // return value
113    int Card::getValue()
114    {
115       return value;
116
117    } // end function getValue
118
119    // function validCard definition
120    bool validCard()
121    {
122       return value >= 1 && value <= 13 && suit >= 1 && suit <= 4;
123
124    } // end function validCard
```

Fig. L 6.10   Contents of **card.cpp**. (Part 3 of 3.)

```
1    // Chapter 6 of C++ How to Program
2    // Debugging Problem (debugging06.cpp)
```

Fig. L 6.11   Contents of **debugging06.cpp**. (Part 1 of 2.)

Lab Exercises   Name:

Debugging

```
3
4    #include <iostream>
5
6    using std::cout;
7    using std::endl;
8
9    int main()
10   {
11      Card c1;
12      Card c2( 3, 4 );
13      Card c3( 1, 14 );
14
15      Card *p1 = &c2;
16
17      c1.print();
18      c2.print();
19      c3.print();
20      p1->print();
21      cout << endl;
22
23      c1.setSuit( p1->getSuit() );
24      c3.value = 12;
25      p1->value = 5;
26
27      c1.print();
28      c2.print();
29      c3.print();
30      *p1.print();
31      cout << endl;
32
33      return 0;
34
35   } // end main
```

Fig. L 6.11   Contents of **debugging06.cpp**. (Part 2 of 2.)

Lab Exercises

Name: _____

Debugging

Postlab Activities

Coding Exercises

Name: _____　　　　　　　　Date:_____

Section: _____

These coding exercises reinforce the lessons learned in the lab and provide additional programming experience outside the classroom and laboratory environment. They serve as a review after you have completed the Prelab Activities and Lab Exercises successfully.

For each of the following problems, write a program or a program segment that performs the specified action:

1. Write the class definition (do not define any methods) for a polynomial of the form

    $a0 + a1x + a2x + \ldots + anx$

    where n is the degree of the **Polynomial**. Assume that the largest polynomial to be used has degree **10**. The class definition should contain a constructor, data members and member function prototypes.

2. Instantiate an object of type **Polynomial** with degree **3**.

3. Set the coefficients of your **Polynomial** object to **3**, **−10**, **4** and **1**, respectively.

Postlab Activities   Name:

Coding Exercises

4. Write the class definition for class **BookIndex**, which contains information found in a library's card catalog. It should contain the title, author and copyright year (in the form *yyyy*) as well as member functions for retrieving and manipulating data.

5. The title and author of most books never change after the initial publication. However, copyrights often get updated. Redefine the class **BookIndex** with this information in mind. [*Hint*: Use keyword **const** where appropriate.]

Postlab Activities   Name: _____

Coding Exercises

6. Instantiate an object of type **BookIndex**. Now declare a pointer and assign the object's address to it. Change the book's copyright via the pointer and **->** operator.

7. Change the copyright through the pointer again, this time using the ***** operator instead of the **->** operator.

8. Change the copyright a third time using a reference (**&**) to the **BookIndex** object.

Postlab Activities

Name:

Coding Exercises

Postlab Activities

Programming Challenges

Name: _____   Date:_____

Section: _____

The Programming Challenges are more involved than the Coding Exercises and may require a significant amount of time to complete. Write a C++ program for each of the problems in this section. The answers to these problems are available at **www.deitel.com**, **www.prenhall.com/deitel** and on the *C++ Multimedia Cyber Classroom: Fourth Edition.* Pseudocode, hints and/or sample outputs are provided to aid you in your programming.

9. Provide a constructor that is capable of using the current time from the **time** function—declared in the C Standard Library header **<ctime>**—to initialize an object of the **Time** class.

Hints:

- Write a new constructor that sets the members of the **time** function to the current time.

- Determine the current year using the following formula: *current year – 1970.*

- Depending on the time zone you are in, you must shift the time by a certain number of hours. For this problem, 5 hours is the current shift for Eastern Standard Time (EST).

10. Create a class called **Rational** for performing arithmetic with fractions. Write a driver program to test your class. Use integer variables to represent the **private** data of the class—the numerator and the denominator. Provide a constructor that enables an object of this class to be initialized when it is instantiated. The constructor should contain default values in case no initializers are provided and should store the fraction in reduced form (i.e., the fraction

$$\frac{2}{4}$$

would store 1 for the numerator and 2 for the denominator). Provide **public** member functions for each of the following:

a) Addition of two **Rational** numbers. The result should be stored in reduced form.

b) Subtraction of two **Rational** numbers. The result should be stored in reduced form.

c) Multiplication of two **Rational** numbers. The result should be stored in reduced form.

d) Division of two **Rational** numbers. The result should be stored in reduced form.

e) Printing **Rational** numbers in the form **a/b** where **a** is the numerator and **b** is the denominator.

f) Printing **Rational** numbers in floating-point format.

Hints:

- Write a **private** helper function to reduce numbers.

- The parameters of addition, subtraction, multiplication and division should all be **const**.

- Write a function to perform reduction and call this function after every operation to assure that the fraction is in reduced form.

11. Modify the **Time** class of Fig. 6.18–6.19 of *C++ How to Program: Fourth Edition* to include a **tick** member function that increments the time stored in a **Time** object by one second. The **Time** object should always

Postlab Activities

Programming Challenges

remain in a consistent state. Write a driver program that tests the **tick** member function in a loop that prints the time in standard format during each iteration of the loop to illustrate that the **tick** member function works correctly. Be sure to test the following cases:

a) incrementing into the next minute

b) incrementing into the next hour

c) incrementing into the next day (i.e., 11:59:59 PM to 12:00:00 AM)

Hints:

- **tick** should increment **second** by one (use **++**).

- Determine if the next minute has began. Remember, when **setSecond** gets an invalid value (i.e., 60 or higher), it sets second to **0**. This is a built-in check on whether another minute has begun.

- Do not forget to provide similar implementation for hours.

12. Create a class **Rectangle**, which has attributes **length** and **width**, each of which defaults to **1**. It has member functions that calculate the **perimeter** and the **area** of the rectangle. It has *set* and *get* functions for both **length** and **width**. The *set* functions should verify that **length** and **width** are each floating-point numbers larger than 0.0 and less than 20.0.

Hints:

- *Perimeter = 2 ∞ (length + width)*

- *Area = length ∞ width*

7

Classes: Part II

Objectives

- To create and destroy objects dynamically, using the **new** and **delete** operators. The **new** operator creates an object of the proper size, calls the constructor for the object and returns a pointer of the correct type. The **delete** operator destroys an object that was created with **new**, and releases the object's memory.
- To specify **const** (constant) objects and **const** member functions to enforce the principle of least privilege.
- To understand the purpose of **friend** functions and **friend** classes. A **friend** function of a class is defined outside that class' scope, yet has the right to access **private** members of that class.
- To understand how to use **static** data members and member functions to enable multiple objects of the same class to share one copy of a variable.
- To understand the use of the **this** pointer and to use that pointer to make cascaded function calls. The **this** pointer provides access to an object's own memory address.
- To understand data abstraction and information hiding and to design classes which hide their implementation details from the clients of other classes.
- To use copy constructors to initialize a class to the values of another class object.

Assignment Checklist

Name: _____   **Date:** _____

Section: _____

Exercises	Assigned: Circle assignments	Date Due
Prelab Activities		
Matching	YES NO	
Fill in the Blank	9, 10, 11, 12, 13, 14, 15, 16, 17, 18, 19, 20	
Short Answer	21, 22, 23, 24, 25, 26, 27, 28, 29	
Programming Output	30, 31, 32	
Correct the Code	33, 34, 35, 36, 37	
Lab Exercises		
Lab Exercise 1 — Simple Calculator	YES NO	
Follow-Up Questions and Activities	1, 2, 3, 4	
Lab Exercise 2 — Integer Set	YES NO	
Follow-Up Questions and Activities	1, 2, 3	
Lab Exercise 3 — Cats	YES NO	
Follow-Up Questions and Activities	1, 2, 3	
Debugging	YES NO	
Labs Provided by Instructor		
1.		
2.		
3.		
Postlab Activities		
Coding Exercises	1, 2, 3, 4, 5, 6, 7, 8, 9, 10	
Programming Challenges	11, 12	

Assignment Checklist

Name:

Prelab Activities

Matching

Name: _____   **Date:** _____

Section: _____

After reading Chapter 7 of *C++ How to Program: Fourth Edition*, answer the given questions. These questions are intended to test and reinforce your understanding of key concepts and may be done either before the lab or during the lab.

For each term in the column on the left, write the corresponding letter for the description that best matches it from the column on the right.

Term	Description
____ 1. Object-based programming	a) Used when only one copy of a variable should be shared by all instances of a class.
____ 2. **new** and **delete**	b) Describing functionality of a class independent of its implementation.
____ 3. Assertion	c) Determines whether a line of code (usually involving the **new** operator) was able to fulfill a request.
____ 4. **static** class variable	d) Using objects in programming.
____ 5. Data abstraction	e) Data structure wherein the last item inserted is the first one removed.
____ 6. **friend** function	f) Defined outside the class' scope, yet has access to **private** members of the class.
____ 7. FIFO	g) Data structure wherein the first item inserted is the first one removed.
____ 8. LIFO	h) Operators used for performing dynamic memory allocation and deallocation.

Prelab Activities   Name:

Matching

Prelab Activities   Name:

Fill in the Blank

Name: _____   **Date:**_____

Section: _____

Fill in the blank for each of the following statements:

9.   Classes can be composed of _____ of other classes.

10. Keyword _____ specifies that an object is not modifiable.

11. A **const** object must be initialized in the _____.

12. If a member initializer is not provided for a member object, the member object's _____ is called.

13. The _____ pointer references both the non-**static** member functions and non-**static** data members of the object.

14. The _____ operator allocates space for an object, runs the object's constructor and returns a pointer of the correct type.

15. To destroy an object, the _____ operator is used.

16. _____ can be allocated dynamically and later **delete**d by using **[]**.

17. A(n) _____ data member represents "class-wide" information.

18. _____ are known as last-in, first-out (LIFO) data structures; _____ are known as first-in, first-out (FIFO) data structures.

19. _____ are designed to hold collections of objects. They provide services such as insertion, deletion, searching and sorting.

20. A(n) _____ captures two notions: a data representation and the operations that are allowed on those data.

Prelab Activities

Name:

Fill in the Blank

Prelab Activities   Name:

Short Answer

Name: _____   **Date:**_____

Section: _____

In the space provided, answer each of the given questions. Your answers should be as concise as possible; aim for two or three sentences.

21. What is the purpose of declaring certain objects with keyword **const**?

22. What are **friend** functions? Where in a class definition is a **friend** function specified?

Prelab Activities   Name:

Short Answer

23. What are **static** data members? Why might they be used? What is their scope?

24. What is a stack?

25. What is a queue?

26. What is a proxy class? Why might it be used?

27. What features does C++ provide for dynamic memory allocation?

28. What is meant by "cascading function calls"? How is such cascading accomplished in designing a class?

Prelab Activities

Name:

Programming Output

Name: _____

Date: _____

Section: _____

For each of the given program segments, read the code and write the output in the space provided below each program. [*Note*: Do not execute these programs on a computer.]

29. What is output by the following code? Assume the use of the **Increment** class defined in Fig. L 7.1.

```
1   Increment object( 65, 7 );
2
3   cout << "Before incrementing: ";
4   object.print();
5
6   for ( int j = 0; j < 6; j++ ) {
7      object.addIncrement();
8      cout << "After increment " << j + 1 << ": ";
9      object.print();
10
11  } // end for
```

```
1   // class Increment declaration
2   class Increment {
3
4   public:
5      Increment( int c = 0, int i = 1 );
6      void addIncrement() { count += increment; }
7      void print() const;
8
9   private:
10     int count;
11     const int increment;   // const data member
12
13  }; // end class Increment
14
15  // Constructor for class Increment
16  Increment::Increment( int c, int i )
17     : increment( i )   // initializer for const member
18  {
19     count = c;
20
21  } // end class Increment constructor
22
23  // Print the data
24  void Increment::print() const
25  {
26     cout << "count = " << count
27          << ", increment = " << increment << endl;
28
29  } // end function print
```

Fig. L 7.1   **Increment** class.

Prelab Activities   Name:

Programming Output

Your answer:

30. What is output by the following code? Assume the use of the **Employee** and **Date** classes defined in Fig. L 7.2–Fig. L 7.5.

```
1    Employee e( "John", "Doe", 2, 14, 1963, 1, 29, 2001 );
2
3    cout << '\n';
4    e.print();
```

```
5    // date1.h
6    // Declaration of the Date class.
7    // Member functions defined in date1.cpp
8    #ifndef DATE1_H
9    #define DATE1_H
10
11   // class Date definition
12   class Date {
13   public:
14      Date( int = 1, int = 1, int = 1900 ); // default constructor
15      void print() const;   // print date in month/day/year format
16      ~Date();  // provided to confirm destruction order
17
18   private:
19      int month;  // 1-12
20      int day;    // 1-31 based on month
21      int year;   // any year
22
23      // utility function to test proper day for month and year
24      int checkDay( int );
25
26   }; // end class Date
27
28   #endif // DATE1_H
```

Fig. L 7.2   **date.h**.

```
29   // date1.cpp
30   // Member function definitions for Date class.
31   #include <iostream>
32
33   using std::cout;
34   using std::endl;
35
36   #include "date1.h"
37
```

Fig. L 7.3   **date1.h**. (Part 1 of 3.)

Prelab Activities

Name:

Programming Output

```
38   // constructor: Confirm proper value for month;
39   // call utility function checkDay to confirm proper
40   // value for day.
41   Date::Date( int mn, int dy, int yr )
42   {
43      if ( mn > 0 && mn <= 12 )           // validate month
44         month = mn;
45
46      else {
47         month = 1;
48         cout << "Month " << mn << " invalid. Set to month 1.\n";
49
50      } // end else
51
52       year = yr;
53      day = checkDay( dy );              // validate day
54
55      cout << "Date object constructor for date ";
56      print();
57      cout << endl;
58
59   } // end class Date constructor
60
61   // print Date object in form month/day/year
62   void Date::print() const
63   {
64      cout << month << '/' << day << '/' << year;
65
66   } // end function print
67
68   // destructor: provided to confirm destruction order
69   Date::~Date()
70   {
71      cout << "Date object destructor for date ";
72      print();
73      cout << endl;
74
75   } // end class Date destructor
76
77   // Utility function to confirm proper day value based on month and year.
78   int Date::checkDay( int testDay )
79   {
80      static const int daysPerMonth[ 13 ] =
81         { 0, 31, 28, 31, 30, 31, 30, 31, 31, 30, 31, 30, 31 };
82
83      if ( testDay > 0 && testDay <= daysPerMonth[ month ] )
84         return testDay;
85
86      if ( month == 2 &&        // February: check for leap year
87           testDay == 29 &&
88          ( year % 400 == 0 ||
89           ( year % 4 == 0 && year % 100 != 0 ) ) )
90         return testDay;
91
92      cout << "Day " << testDay << " invalid. Set to day 1.\n";
93
```

Fig. L 7.3   **date1.h**. (Part 2 of 3.)

Prelab Activities   Name:

Programming Output

```
94        return 1;   // leave object in consistent state if bad value
95
96   } // end function checkDay
```

Fig. L 7.3   **date1.h**. (Part 3 of 3.)

```
1    // emply1.h
2    // Declaration of the Employee class.
3    // Member functions defined in emply1.cpp
4    #ifndef EMPLY1_H
5    #define EMPLY1_H
6
7    #include "date1.h"
8
9    // class Employee definition
10   class Employee {
11
12   public:
13      Employee( char *, char *, int, int, int, int, int, int );
14      void print() const;
15      ~Employee();   // provided to confirm destruction order
16
17   private:
18      char firstName[ 25 ];
19      char lastName[ 25 ];
20      const Date birthDate;
21      const Date hireDate;
22
23   }; // end class Employee
24
25   #endif // EMPLY1_H
```

Fig. L 7.4   **emply1.h**.

```
26   // emply1.cpp
27   // Member function definitions for Employee class.
28   #include <iostream>
29
30   using std::cout;
31   using std::endl;
32
33   #include <cstring>
34
35   #include "emply1.h"
36
37   #include "date1.h"
38
```

Fig. L 7.5   **emply1.cpp**. (Part 1 of 2.)

Prelab Activities

Name:

Programming Output

```
39    // constructor
40    Employee::Employee( char *fname, char *lname,
41                        int bmonth, int bday, int byear,
42                        int hmonth, int hday, int hyear )
43       : birthDate( bmonth, bday, byear ),
44         hireDate( hmonth, hday, hyear )
45    {
46       // copy fname into firstName and ensure that it fits
47       int length = strlen( fname );
48
49       length = ( length < 25 ? length : 24 );
50       strncpy( firstName, fname, length );
51       firstName[ length ] = '\0';
52
53       // copy lname into lastName and ensure that it fits
54       length = strlen( lname );
55       length = ( length < 25 ? length : 24 );
56       strncpy( lastName, lname, length );
57       lastName[ length ] = '\0';
58
59       cout << "Employee object constructor: "
60            << firstName << ' ' << lastName << endl;
61
62    } // end class Employee constructor
63
64    // print employee information
65    void Employee::print() const
66    {
67       cout << lastName << ", " << firstName << "\nHired: ";
68       hireDate.print();
69       cout << "   Birth date: ";
70       birthDate.print();
71       cout << endl;
72
73    } // end function print
74
75    // destructor: provided to confirm destruction order
76    Employee::~Employee()
77    {
78       cout << "Employee object destructor: "
79            << lastName << ", " << firstName << endl;
80
81    } // end class Employee destructor
```

Fig. L 7.5   **emply1.cpp**. (Part 2 of 2.)

Your answer:

Prelab Activities

Name:

Programming Output

31. What is output by of the following program?

```cpp
1   #include <iostream>
2
3   using std::cout;
4   using std::endl;
5
6   // class Test definition
7   class Test {
8
9   public:
10     Test( int = 0 );
11     void print() const;
12
13  private:
14     int x;
15
16  }; // end class Test
17
18  // default constructor
19  Test::Test( int a )
20  {
21     x = a;
22
23  } // end class Test constructor
24
25  // function print definition
26  void Test::print() const
27  {
28     cout << x
29          << this->x
30          << ( *this ).x << endl;
31
32  } // end function print
33
34  int main()
35  {
36     Test testObject( 4 );
37
38     testObject.print();
39
40     return 0;
41
42  } // end main
```

Your answer:

Prelab Activities

Name:

Programming Output

32. What happens to program execution when an **Employee** object is instantiated with the use of the following constructor? Assume on line 3 that **new** fails to allocate memory.

```
1   Employee::Employee( const char *first, const char *last )
2   {
3       firstName = new char[ strlen( first ) + 1 ];
4       strcpy( firstName, first );
5
6       lastName = new char[ strlen( last ) + 1 ];
7       strcpy( lastName, last );
8
9       ++count;
10      cout << "Employee constructor for " << firstName
11           << ' ' << lastName << " called." << endl;
12  }
```

Your answer:

Prelab Activities

Programming Output

Prelab Activities

Name:

Correct the Code

Name: _____   Date:_____

Section: _____

For each of the given program segments, determine if there is an error in the code. If there is an error, specify whether it is a logic error or a syntax error, circle the error in the program, and write the corrected code in the space provided after each problem. If the code does not contain an error, write "no error." [*Note*: It is possible that a program segment may contain multiple errors.]

33. The following defines class **Increment**. [*Note*: the use of **const** data member **increment**.]:

```
1    #include <iostream>
2
3    using std::cout;
4    using std::endl;
5
6    // class Increment definition
7    class Increment {
8
9    public:
10       Increment( int c = 0, int i = 1 );
11       void addIncrement() { count += increment; }
12       void print() const;
13
14    private:
15       int count;
16       const int increment;
17
18    }; // end class Increment
19
20    // constructor
21    Increment::Increment( int c, int i )
22    {
23       count = c;
24       increment = i;
25
26    } // end class Increment constructor
27
28    // function print definition
29    void Increment::print() const
30    {
31       cout << "count = " << count
32           << ", increment = " << increment << endl;
33
34    } // end function print
```

Your answer:

Prelab Activities

Name:

Correct the Code

34. The code that follows is a definition for class **Time** and its member functions.

```
1    // class Time definition
2    class Time {
3
4    public:
5       Time( int = 0, int = 0, int = 0 );
6
7       void setTime( int, int, int ) const;
8
9       void setHour( int ) const;
10      int getHour() const;
11
12      void setMinute( int ) const;
13      int getMinute() const;
14
15      void setSecond( int ) const;
16      int getSecond() const;
17
18      void printUniversal() const;
19      void printStandard();
20
21   private:
22      int hour;
23      int minute;
24      int second;
25
26   }; // end class Time
```

```
27   // Member function definitions for Time class.
28   #include <iostream>
29
30   using std::cout;
31
32   #include "time.h"
33
34   // constructor function to initialize private data
35   // default values are 0 (see class definition)
36   Time::Time( int hr, int min, int sec )
37   {
38      setTime( hr, min, sec );
39
40   } // end class Time constructor
41
42   // set values of hour, minute and second.
43   void Time::setTime( int h, int m, int s )
44   {
45      setHour( h );
46      setMinute( m );
47      setSecond( s );
48
49   } // end function setTime
50
51   // set hour value
52   void Time::setHour( int h )
```

Prelab Activities   Name:

Correct the Code

```
53   {
54      hour = ( h >= 0 && h < 24 ) ? h : 0;
55
56   } // end function setHour
57
58   // set minute value
59   void Time::setMinute( int m )
60   {
61      minute = ( m >= 0 && m < 60 ) ? m : 0;
62
63   } // end function setMinute
64
65   // set second value
66   void Time::setSecond( int s )
67   {
68      second = ( s >= 0 && s < 60 ) ? s : 0;
69
70   } // end function setSecond
71
72   // get hour value
73   int Time::getHour() const
74   {
75      return hour;
76
77   } // end functiongetHour
78
79   // get minute value
80   int Time::getMinute() const
81   {
82      return minute;
83
84   } // end function setMinute
85
86   // get second value
87   int Time::getSecond() const
88   {
89      return second;
90
91   } // end function getSecond
92
93   // display universal format time: HH:MM
94   void Time::printUniversal() const
95   {
96      cout << ( hour < 10 ? "0" : "" ) << hour << ":"
97           << ( minute < 10 ? "0" : "" ) << minute;
98
99   } // end function printUniversal
100
101  // display standard format time: HH:MM:SS AM (or PM)
102  void Time::printStandard()
103  {
104      cout << ( ( hour == 12 ) ? 12 : hour % 12 ) << ":"
105           << ( minute < 10 ? "0" : "" ) << minute << ":"
106           << ( second < 10 ? "0" : "" ) << second
107           << ( hour < 12 ? " AM" : " PM" );
108
109  } // end function printStandard
```

(Part 2 of 2.)

Prelab Activities

Name:

Correct the Code

Your answer:

35. The code that follows is a definition for class **Time**. Note the member function which begins a new day by resetting the **hour** to zero.

```
1    // class Time definition
2    class Time {
3
4    public:
5       Time( int = 0, int = 0, int = 0 );
6
7       void setTime( int, int, int );
8
9       void setHour( int );
10      int getHour() const;
11
12      void setMinute( int );
13      int getMinute() const;
14
15      void setSecond( int );
16      int getSecond() const;
17
18      // function newDay definition
19      void newDay() const
20      {
21         setHour( 0 );
22
23      } // end function newDay
24
25      void printUniversal() const;
26      void printStandard();
```

Prelab Activities

Name:

Correct the Code

```
27
28   private:
29      int hour;
30      int minute;
31      int second;
32
33   }; // end class Time
```

(Part 2 of 2.)

Your answer:

36. The following is a definition for class **Time**:

```
1    // class Time definition
2    class Time {
3
4    public:
5       Time( int = 0, int = 0, int = 0 ) const;
6
7       void setTime( int, int, int );
8
9       void setHour( int );
10      int getHour() const;
11
```

(Part 1 of 2.)

Prelab Activities

Name:

Correct the Code

```
12        void setMinute( int );
13        int getMinute() const;
14
15        void setSecond( int );
16        int getSecond() const;
17
18        void printUniversal() const;
19        void printStandard();
20
21  private:
22        int hour;
23        int minute;
24        int second;
25
26  }; // end class Time
```

(Part 2 of 2.)

Your answer:

37. The code that follows is a definition of the **getCount** member function. Variable **count** is a **static int** that stores the number of objects instantiated. Assume that this definition is located within a class definition.

```
1   static int getCount() { return this->count; }
```

Your answer:

Lab Exercises

Lab Exercise 1 — Simple Calculator

Name: _____   **Date:**_____

Section: _____

This problem is intended to be solved in a closed-lab session with a teaching assistant or instructor present. The problem is divided into six parts:

1. Lab Objectives
2. Description of the Problem
3. Sample Output
4. Program Template (Fig. L 7.6 – Fig. L 7.8)
5. Problem-Solving Tips
6. Follow-Up Questions and Activities

The program template represents a complete working C++ program, with one or more key lines of code replaced with comments. Read the problem description and examine the sample output; then study the template code. Using the problem-solving tips as a guide, replace the **/* */** comments with C++ code. Compile and execute the program. Compare your output with the sample output provided. Then answer the follow-up questions. The source code for the template is available at **www.deitel.com** and **www.prenhall.com./deitel**.

Lab Objectives

This lab was designed to reinforce programming concepts from Chapter 7 of *C++ How To Program: Fourth Edition*. In this lab, you will practice:

*   using classes to create a data type **SimpleCalculator** capable of performing arithmetic operations.
*   creating **const** member functions to enforce the principle of least privilege.

The follow-up questions and activities also will give you practice

*   using constructors to specify initial values for data members of a programmer-defined class.

Description of the Problem

Write a **SimpleCalculator** class that has **public** methods for adding, subtracting, multiplying and dividing two **double**s. A sample call is as follows:

```
double answer = sc.add( a, b );
```

Object **sc** is of type **SimpleCalculator**. Member function **add** returns the result of adding its two arguments.

Lab Exercises   Name:

Lab Exercise 1 — Simple Calculator

Sample Output

```
The value of a is: 10
The value of b is: 20

Adding a and b yields 30
Subtracting b from a -10
Multiplying a and b yields 200
Dividing a by b yields 0.5
```

Template

```cpp
1    // Chapter 7 of C++ How to Program
2    // simplecalculator.h
3
4    // class SimpleCalculator definition
5    class SimpleCalculator {
6
7    public:
8       /* write prototype for add method */
9       double subtract( double, double ) const;
10      double multiply( double, double ) const;
11      /* write prototype for divide method */
12
13   }; // end class SimpleCalculator
```

Fig. L 7.6   Contents of **simplecalculator.h**.

```cpp
1    // Chapter 7 of C++ How to Program
2    // simplecalculator.cpp
3    #include "simplecalculator.h"
4
5    /* write definition for add method */
6
7    // function subtract definition
8    double SimpleCalculator::subtract( double a, double b ) const
9    {
10      return a - b;
11
12   } // end function subtract
13
14   // function multiply definition
15   double SimpleCalculator::multiply( double a, double b ) const
16   {
17      return a * b;
18
19   } // end function multiply
20
21   /* Write definition for divide member function */
```

Fig. L 7.7   Contents of **simplecalculator.cpp**.

Lab Exercises   Name:

Lab Exercise 1 — Simple Calculator

```
1   // Chapter 7 of C++ How to Program
2   // calcdriver.cpp
3   #include <iostream>
4   #include "simplecalculator.h"
5
6   using std::cout;
7   using std::endl;
8
9   int main()
10  {
11      double a = 10.0;
12      double b = 20.0;
13      /* Declare any other variables needed here          */
14      /* Instantiate an object of type SimpleCalculator */
15
16      cout << "The value of a is: " << a << "\n"
17          << "The value of b is: " << b << "\n\n";
18
19      /* Write a line that adds a & b through your SimpleCalculator
20          object; assign the result to a variable named "addition" */
21      cout << "Adding a and b yields " << addition << "\n";
22
23      double subtraction = sc.subtract( a, b );
24
25      cout << "Subtracting b from a " << subtraction << "\n";
26
27      double multiplication = sc.multiply( a, b );
28
29      cout << "Multiplying a and b yields " << multiplication
30          << "\n";
31
32      /* Write a line that divides a and b through the
33          SimpleCalculator object; assign the result to a
34          variable named "division" */
35      cout << "Dividing a by b yields " << division << endl;
36
37      return 0;
38
39  } // end main
```

Fig. L 7.8   Contents of **calcdriver.cpp**.

Problem-Solving Tip

1. All member functions have return type **double**.

Follow-Up Questions and Activities

1. Why does the **SimpleCalculator** class have no constructor?

Lab Exercises   Name:

Lab Exercise 1 — Simple Calculator

2. Why are no **private** data members needed for class **SimpleCalculator**?

3. Modify your class so that **SimpleCalculator** has a **private** data member called **answer**. After performing an operation, assign the result to **answer**. Add a member function named **getAnswer** to retrieve the result of the last arithmetic operation performed by the object. Also, add a constructor for class **Simple-Calculator** that initializes the value of **answer** to **0**.

4. Modify the program so that the **SimpleCalculator** class has an **input** member function that allows the user to input two **double**s. The function should then store the values that were input in **private** data members. Create two constructors for this class, one that takes no arguments and initializes **a** and **b** to 0 and another that takes two **double**s and initializes **a** and **b** to those values. Finally, create a member function **printValues** that displays the values of **a** and **b**. A segment of the driver might now look like this:

```
1    SimpleCalculator sc;    // instantiate object
2
3    sc.input();
4    sc.printValues();
5    cout << "Adding a and b yields " << sc.add() << "\n";
```

Lab Exercises   Name:

Lab Exercise 2 — Integer Set

Name: _____   Date:_____

Section: _____

This problem is intended to be solved in a closed-lab session with a teaching assistant or instructor present. The problem is divided into six parts:

1. Lab Objectives
2. Description of the Problem
3. Sample Output
4. Program Template (Fig. L 7.9 – Fig. L 7.11)
5. Problem-Solving Tips
6. Follow-Up Questions and Activities

The program template represents a complete working C++ program, with one or more key lines of code replaced with comments. Read the problem description and examine the sample output; then study the template code. Using the problem-solving tips as a guide, replace the **/* */** comments with C++ code. Compile and execute the program. Compare your output with the sample output provided. Then answer the follow-up questions. The source code for the template is available at **www.deitel.com** and **www.prenhall.com./deitel**.

Lab Objectives
This lab was designed to reinforce programming concepts from Chapter 7 of *C++ How To Program: Fourth Edition*. In this lab, you will practice:

*   using classes to create a data type, **IntegerSet**, capable of storing a set of integers.
*   using dynamic memory allocation with the **new** and **delete** operators.

In the follow-up questions and activities you also will practice:

*   using destructors to deallocate dynamically allocated memory when an object is destroyed.

Description of the Problem
Create a class called **IntegerSet**. A set is represented initially as an array of ones and zeros. Array element **a[i]** is **1** if integer *i* is in the set. Array element **a[j]** is **0** if integer *j* is not in the set. The default constructor initializes a set to the so-called empty-set. (i.e., a set whose array representation contains all zeros).

An object of type **IntegerSet** is instantiated by passing to the constructor an integer representing the range of the set. For example, a set of the integers from 0 to 99 is instantiated as follows:

```
IntegerSet mySet( 100 );
```

An array containing the appropriate number of elements is allocated dynamically and initialized by the constructor.

Provide the member functions for the common set operations. For example, provide a **unionOfInteger-Sets** member function that creates a third set which is the set-theoretic union of two existing sets (i.e., an element of the third array's set is assigned **1** if that element is **1** in either or both of the existing sets).

Provide an **intersectionOfIntegerSets** member function that creates a third set which is the set-theoretic intersection of two existing sets (i.e., an element of the third set's array is set to **0** if that element is **0** in

Lab Exercises   Name:

Lab Exercise 2 — Integer Set

either or both of the existing sets, and an element of the third set's array is set to **1** if that element is **1** in each of the existing sets).

Provide an **insertElement** member function that inserts a new integer **k** into a set (by setting **a[k]** to **1**). Provide a **deleteElement** member function that deletes integer **m** (by setting **a[m]** to **0**).

Provide a **setPrint** member function that prints a set as a list of numbers separated by spaces. Print only those elements which are present in the set (i.e., their position in the array has a value of **1**). Print **- - -** for an empty set.

Provide an **isEqualTo** member function that determines whether two sets are equal.

Provide a copy constructor that takes as a parameter a reference to an **IntegerSet** object.

Sample Output

```
Enter set A:
Enter an element (-1 to end): 1
Enter an element (-1 to end): 2
Enter an element (-1 to end): 3
Enter an element (-1 to end): -1
Entry complete

Enter set B:
Enter an element (-1 to end): 3
Enter an element (-1 to end): 4
Enter an element (-1 to end): 5
Enter an element (-1 to end): 6
Enter an element (-1 to end): 5
Enter an element (-1 to end): -1
Entry complete

Union of A and B is:
{   1   2   3   4   5   6   }
Intersection of A and B is:
{   3   }
Set A is not equal to set B

Inserting 77 into set A...
Set A is now:
{   1   2   3   77   }

Deleting 77 from set A...
Set A is now:
{   1   2   3   }
```

Template

```
1   // Chapter 7 of C++ How to Program
2   // integerset.h
3   #ifndef INTSET_H
4   #define INTSET_H
5
```

Fig. L 7.9   Contents of **integerset.h**. (Part 1 of 2.)

Lab Exercises   Name:

Lab Exercise 2 — Integer Set

```
6    // class IntegerSet definition
7    class IntegerSet {
8
9    public:
10      IntegerSet( int );
11      IntegerSet( const IntegerSet& );
12
13      IntegerSet unionOfIntegerSets( const IntegerSet& );
14      IntegerSet intersectionOfIntegerSets( const IntegerSet& );
15      void emptySet();
16      void inputSet();
17      void insertElement( int );
18      void deleteElement( int );
19      /* write prototype for setPrint */
20      bool isEqualTo( const IntegerSet& ) const;
21
22    private:
23      int *set;   // dynamically allocated set
24      int size;
25
26      // function validEntry definition
27      bool validEntry( int x ) const
28      {
29         return x >= 0 && x < size;
30
31      } // end function validEntry
32
33    }; // end class IntegerSet
34
35    #endif // INTSET_H
```

Fig. L 7.9   Contents of **integerset.h**. (Part 2 of 2.)

```
1    // Chapter 7 of C++ How to Program
2    // integerset.cpp
3    #include <iostream>
4
5    using std::cout;
6    using std::cin;
7
8    #include <iomanip>
9
10   #include <new>
11
12   using std::setw;
13
14   /* Write include directive for integerset.h here */
15
16   // constructor
17   IntegerSet::IntegerSet( int s )
18   {
19      size = s;
20      set = new int[ size ];
21      /* write call to emptySet */
22
23   } // end class IntegerSet constructor
24
```

Fig. L 7.10   Contents of **integerset.cpp**. (Part 1 of 3.)

Lab Exercises

Lab Exercise 2 — Integer Set

```cpp
25   // copy constructor
26   IntegerSet::IntegerSet( const IntegerSet &init )
27   {
28      size = init.size;
29      /* write statement to allocate sufficient memory */
30      emptySet();
31
32      for ( int i = 0; i < size; i++ )
33         /* write statement to copy elements of init */
34
35   } // end copy constructor
36
37   /* write a definition for emptySet */
38
39   // input set
40   void IntegerSet::inputSet()
41   {
42      int number;
43
44      // input set information
45      do {
46         cout << "Enter an element (-1 to end): ";
47         cin >> number;
48
49         // check number first
50         if ( validEntry( number ) )
51            set[ number ] = 1;
52
53         else if ( number != -1 )
54            cout << "Invalid Element\n";
55
56      } while ( number != -1 );
57
58      cout << "Entry complete\n";
59
60   } // end function inputSet
61
62   // print the set
63   void IntegerSet::setPrint() const
64   {
65      int x = 1;
66      bool empty = true;   // assume set is empty
67
68      cout << '{';
69
70      for ( int u = 0; u < size; ++u )
71
72         if ( set[ u ] ) {
73            cout << setw( 4 ) << u << ( x % 10 == 0 ? "\n" : "" );
74            empty = false; // set is not empty
75            ++x;
76
77         } // end if
78
79      if ( empty )
80         cout << setw( 4 ) << "---";   // display an empty set
81
```

Fig. L 7.10   Contents of **integerset.cpp**. (Part 2 of 3.)

Lab Exercises   Name:

Lab Exercise 2 — Integer Set

```
82        cout << setw( 4 ) << "}" << '\n';
83
84   } // end function setPrint
85
86   // finds union of Integer sets
87   IntegerSet IntegerSet::unionOfIntegerSets( const IntegerSet &r )
88   {
89        IntegerSet temp( size > r.size ? size : r.size );
90
91        temp.emptySet();
92
93        int iterations = ( size < r.size ? size : r.size );
94
95        for ( int i = 0; i < iterations; i++ )
96
97           if ( set[ i ] == 1 || r.set[ i ] == 1 )
98              temp.set[ i ] = 1;
99
100       return temp;
101
102   } // end function unionOfIntegerSets
103
104   /* write definition for intersectionOfIntegerSets */
105
106   // insert element into set
107   void IntegerSet::insertElement( int k )
108   {
109       if ( validEntry( k ) )
110          set[ k ] = 1;
111
112       else
113          cout << "Invalid insert attempted!\n";
114
115   } // end function insertElement
116
117   /* write definition for deleteElement */
118
119   /* write definition for isEqualTo */
```

Fig. L 7.10   Contents of **integerset.cpp**. (Part 3 of 3.)

```
1    // Chapter 7 of C++ How to Program
2    // driver for integerSet class
3    #include <iostream>
4
5    using std::cout;
6    using std::endl;
7
8    #include "integerset.h"
9
10   int main()
11   {
12       IntegerSet a( 101 );
13       IntegerSet b( 101 );
```

Fig. L 7.11   Contents of **driver.cpp**. (Part 1 of 2.)

Lab Exercises   Name:

Lab Exercise 2 — Integer Set

```
14        IntegerSet c( 101 );
15        IntegerSet d( 101 );
16
17        cout << "Enter set A:\n";
18        a.inputSet();
19        cout << "\nEnter set B:\n";
20        b.inputSet();
21
22        /* Write call to unionOfIntegerSets for object a
23           passing it b; assign the result to c */
24
25        /* Write call to intersectionOfIntegerSets for
26           object a passing it b; assign the result to d */
27
28        cout << "\nUnion of A and B is:\n";
29        c.setPrint();
30        cout << "Intersection of A and B is:\n";
31        d.setPrint();
32
33        if ( a.isEqualTo( b ) )
34           cout << "Set A is equal to set B\n";
35
36        else
37           cout << "Set A is not equal to set B\n";
38
39        cout << "\nInserting 77 into set A...\n";
40        a.insertElement( 77 );
41        cout << "Set A is now:\n";
42        a.setPrint();
43
44        cout << "\nDeleting 77 from set A...\n";
45        a.deleteElement( 77 );
46        cout << "Set A is now:\n";
47        a.setPrint();
48
49        cout << endl;
50        return 0;
51
52   } // end main
```

Fig. L 7.11   Contents of **driver.cpp**. (Part 2 of 2.)

Problem-Solving Tips

1. Member functions **unionOfIntegerSets** and **intersectionOfIntegerSets** must return an **IntegerSet** object. The object that invokes these functions and the argument set passed to the member functions should not be modified by the operation.

2. When accessing **private** data member **set**, invoke the function **validEntry** to avoid run-time logic errors.

3. Qualify the parameters of **unionOfIntegerSets** and **intersectionOfIntegerSets** as **const**.

4. When **deleteElement** and **insertElement** are invoked with invalid arguments, print an error message to the screen.

Lab Exercises   Name:

Lab Exercise 2 — Integer Set

Follow-Up Questions and Activities

1. Modify the **for** loop in the **setPrint** member function to output **set[u]** rather than **u**. What is output?

2. Why is it advantageous for **set** to be allocated dynamically?

3. Add a destructor to **IntegerSet** that deallocates the dynamically allocated memory.

Lab Exercises

Name:

Lab Exercise 2 — Integer Set

Lab Exercises   Name:

Lab Exercise 3 — Cats

Name: _____   Date:_____

Section: _____

This problem is intended to be solved in a closed-lab session with a teaching assistant or instructor present. The problem is divided into six parts:

1. Lab Objectives

2. Description of the Problem

3. Sample Output

4. Program Template (Fig. L 7.12 – Fig. L 7.14)

5. Problem-Solving Tips

6. Follow-Up Questions and Activities

The program template represents a complete working C++ program, with one or more key lines of code replaced with comments. Read the problem description and examine the sample output; then study the template code. Using the problem-solving tips as a guide, replace the **/* */** comments with C++ code. Compile and execute the program. Compare your output with the sample output provided. Then answer the follow-up questions. The source code for the template is available at **www.deitel.com** and **www.prenhall.com./deitel**.

Lab Objectives

This lab was designed to reinforce programming concepts from Chapter 7 of *C++ How To Program: Fourth Edition*. In this lab, you will practice:

- using **const** member functions.

- using access functions and utility functions so that it is not necessary for non-member functions to access class' data members.

- using dynamic memory allocation.

The follow-up questions and activities will also give you practice:

- using **public** and **private** member access specifiers.

Description of the Problem

Write a program that places a cat into a pen, which can hold up to seven cats, each time a key (e.g., *Enter*) is pressed. Each cat is an object instantiated from class **Cat**—defined in file **cats.h**. Each cat object, when instantiated dynamically, randomly chooses a fur color (i.e., "black," "gray" or "brown"), an eye color (i.e., "green," "blue" or "brown") and a hair length (i.e., "short" or "long"). Provide *get* and *set* methods for these attributes. Carefully consider which *get* and *set* member functions should be **public** and which should be **private**—all member functions are defined in **cats.cpp**.

Certain combinations of cats result in different behaviors. If the number of gray cats exceeds the number of brown cats, the brown cats hide. If at least one black cat with green eyes and at least one black cat with blue eyes are in the pen with exactly one black cat with brown eyes, then the black cat with brown eyes begins meowing. Write a nonmember function named **check** that determines if one of these behaviors has occurred.

Lab Exercises   Name:

Lab Exercise 3 — Cats

Sample Output 1

```
A short-haired gray cat with blue eyes has been added to the pen.
Press a key to add the next cat.

A short-haired gray cat with green eyes has been added to the pen.
Press a key to add the next cat.

A short-haired brown cat with green eyes has been added to the pen.
The brown cat is hiding
Press a key to add the next cat.

A long-haired black cat with brown eyes has been added to the pen.
The brown cat is hiding
Press a key to add the next cat.

A long-haired gray cat with brown eyes has been added to the pen.
The brown cat is hiding
Press a key to add the next cat.

A long-haired gray cat with blue eyes has been added to the pen.
The brown cat is hiding
Press a key to add the next cat.

A long-haired gray cat with blue eyes has been added to the pen.
The brown cat is hiding
Press a key to add the next cat.
```

Lab Exercises

Name:

Lab Exercise 3 — Cats

Sample Output 2

```
A short-haired black cat with blue eyes has been added to the pen.
Press a key to add the next cat.

A short-haired black cat with brown eyes has been added to the pen.
Press a key to add the next cat.

A long-haired black cat with green eyes has been added to the pen.
A black cat with blue eyes is meowing.
Press a key to add the next cat.

A long-haired gray cat with green eyes has been added to the pen.
A black cat with blue eyes is meowing.
Press a key to add the next cat.

A short-haired brown cat with green eyes has been added to the pen.
A black cat with blue eyes is meowing.
Press a key to add the next cat.

A short-haired black cat with green eyes has been added to the pen.
A black cat with blue eyes is meowing.
Press a key to add the next cat.

A short-haired black cat with green eyes has been added to the pen.
A black cat with blue eyes is meowing.
Press a key to add the next cat.
```

Template

```cpp
1   // Chapter 7 of C++ How to Program
2   // cats.h
3   #ifndef CATS_H
4   #define CATS_H
5
6   // class Cat definition
7   class Cat {
8
9   public:
10     Cat();
11     const char *getFurColor() const;
12     const char *getHairLength() const;
13     const char *getEyeColor() const;
14
15   private:
16     void setFurColor();
17     void setHairLength();
18     void setEyeColor();
19     char *furColor;
20     char *hairLength;
21     char *eyeColor;
22
23   }; // end class Cat
24
25   #endif // CATS_H
```

Fig. L 7.12   Contents of `cats.h`.

Lab Exercises   Name:

Lab Exercise 3 — Cats

```
1   // Chapter 7 of C++ How to Program
2   // catsm.cpp
3   #include "cats.h"
4
5   #include <cstdlib>
6
7   #include <ctime>
8
9   // constructor
10  Cat::Cat()
11  {
12     srand( time( 0 ) );
13     setFurColor();
14     setEyeColor();
15     setHairLength();
16
17  } // end class Cat constructor
18
19  // return fur color
20  const char *Cat::getFurColor()
21  {
22     /* Write function implementation here */
23
24  } // end function getFur
25
26  // return hair length
27  const char *Cat::getHairLength()
28  {
29     /* Write function implementation here */
30
31  } // end function getHairLength
32
33  // return eye color
34  const char *Cat::getEyeColor()
35  {
36     /* Write function implementation here */
37
38  } // end function getEyeColor
39
40  // set fur color
41  void Cat::setFurColor()
42  {
43     int x = rand() % 3;
44
45     if ( x == 0 )
46        furColor = "black";
47
48     else if ( x == 1 )
49        furColor = "gray";
50
51     else
52        furColor = "brown";
53
54  } // end function setFurColor
55
```

Fig. L 7.13   Contents of **catsm.cpp**. (Part 1 of 2.)

Lab Exercises   Name:

Lab Exercise 3 — Cats

```
56   // set eye color
57   void Cat::setEyeColor()
58   {
59      int x = rand() % 3;
60
61      if ( x == 0 )
62         eyeColor = "blue";
63
64      else if ( x == 1 )
65         eyeColor = "brown";
66
67      else
68         eyeColor = "green";
69
70   } // end function setEyeColor
71
72   // set hair length
73   void Cat::setHairLength()
74   {
75      int x = rand % 2;
76
77      if ( x == 0 )
78         hairLength = "short";
79
80      else
81         hairLength = "long";
82
83   } // end function setHairLength
```

Fig. L 7.13   Contents of **catsm.cpp**. (Part 2 of 2.)

```
1    // Chapter 7 of C++ How to Program
2    // cats.cpp
3    #include <iostream>
4
5    using std::cout;
6    using std::cin;
7    using std::endl;
8
9    #include <cstring>
10
11   #include "cats.h"
12
13   void check( Cat *pen[], int );
14
15   int main()
16   {
17      const int PEN_SIZE = 7;
18      Cat *pen[ PEN_SIZE ];
19
20      // add cats to pen
21      for ( int c = 0; c < PEN_SIZE; c++ ) {
22         /* Construct a new cat object here          */
23         /* Print the new cat object"s attributes here */
24         /* Write call to function check here        */
```

Fig. L 7.14   Contents of **cats.cpp**. (Part 1 of 2.)

Lab Exercises   Name:

Lab Exercise 3 — Cats

```
25
26          cout << "Press a key to add the next cat." << endl;
27          cin.get();
28
29       } // end for
30
31       /* Write a statement to delete all cat objects */
32
33       return 0;
34
35    } // end main
36
37    // check status of cats
38    void check( Cat *catPen[], int numberOfCats )
39    {
40       int brownCats = 0;
41       int grayCats = 0;
42       int blueEyes = 0;
43       int greenEyes = 0;
44       int brownEyes = 0;
45
46       // determine what cats are in the pen
47       for ( int x = 0; x <= numberOfCats; x++ ) {
48          /* Write a series of statements which sum the total
49             number of each type of cat (i.e., brownCats,
50             grayCats, blueEyes, etc.) currently in the pen */
51
52       } // end for
53
54       if ( /* Write a condition that tests if            */
55             /*    the brown cats need to hide  */ )
56          cout << "The brown cat"
57             << ( brownCats > 1 ? "s are" : " is" ) << " hiding." << endl;
58
59       if ( /* Write a condition that tests if the black cat with
60             blue eyes is meowing */ )
61          cout << "The black cat with blue eyes is meowing."
62             << endl;
63
64    } // end function check
```

Fig. L 7.14   Contents of **cats.cpp**. (Part 2 of 2.)

Problem-Solving Tip

1. Read the problem description carefully. Recall that if the number of gray cats exceeds the number of brown cats, the brown cats hide. The brown cats do not hide if the number of brown cats exceeds the number of gray cats. Also note a black cat with blue eyes meows if other cat combinations include *exactly* one black cat with brown eyes and at least one black cat with green eyes. If the pen contains more than one black cat with brown eyes, the black cat with blue eyes will not meow.

Lab Exercises   Name:

Lab Exercise 3 — Cats

Follow-Up Questions and Activities

1. Why are some **public** member functions declared as **const**?

2. What is the purpose of having the *set* member functions listed as **private**?

3. Change all the **private** member functions to **public**. Rerun the program. Does anything occur different-ly? Try calling **setFurColor** from the **main** function both before and after changing the member-access specifier.

Lab Exercises   Name:

Lab Exercise 3 — Cats

Lab Exercises

Name: _____

Debugging

Name: _____   Date:_____

Section: _____

The following program (Fig. L 7.15–Fig. L 7.17) does not run properly. Fix all the syntax errors so that the program compiles successfully. Once the program compiles, compare the output with that of the sample output and eliminate any logic errors that may exist. The sample output demonstrates what the program output should be once the program's code has been corrected. [*Note:* Make sure any memory allocated dynamically is deleted properly.]

Sample Output

```
There are currently 0 students

A student has been added
Here are the grades for Student 1
   100    75    89

A student has been added
Here are the grades for Student 2
    83    92

A student has been added
Here are the grades for Student 3
    62    91

There are currently 3 students

Student 2 has been deleted
Student 1 has been deleted
Student 3 has been deleted
```

Broken Code

```cpp
1   // Chapter 7 of C++ How to Program
2   // Debugging Problem (student.h)
3
4   #ifndef STUDENT_H
5   #define STUDENT_H
6
7   // class Student definition
8   class Student {
9
10  public:
11     Student( const char * );
12     ~Student();
13     void displayGrades() const;
```

Fig. L 7.15   Contents of **student.h**. (Part 1 of 2.)

Lab Exercises   Name:

Debugging

```
14        Student addGrade( int ) const;
15        static int getNumStudents();
16
17    private:
18        int *grades;
19        char *name;
20        int numGrades;
21        int idNum;
22
23        static int numStudents = 0;
24
25    }; // end class Student
26
27    #endif // STUDENT_H
```

Fig. L 7.15   Contents of **student.h**. (Part 2 of 2.)

```
1    // Chapter 7 of C++ How to Program
2    // Debugging Problem (student.cpp)
3
4    #include <iostream>
5
6    using std::cout;
7    using std::endl;
8
9    #include <iomanip>
10
11   using std::setw;
12
13   #include <cstring>
14
15   #include "student.h"
16
17   #include <new>
18   static int numStudents = 0;
19
20   // constructor
21   Student::Student( const char *nPtr )
22   {
23       grades = new int[ 1 ];
24       grades[ 0 ] = 0;
25       name = new char[ strlen( nPtr ) + 1 ];
26       strcpy( name, nPtr );
27       numGrades = 0;
28       numStudents++;
29
30       cout << "A student has been added\n";
31
32   } // end class Student constructor
33
34   // destructor
35   Student::~Student()
36   {
37       cout << name << " has been deleted\n";
38       delete grades;
```

Fig. L 7.16   Contents of **student.cpp**. (Part 1 of 2.)

Lab Exercises   Name:

Debugging

```
39      delete name;
40      numStudents--;
41
42   } // end class Student destructor
43
44   // function displayGrades definition
45   void Student::displayGrades() const
46   {
47      cout << "Here are the grades for " << name << endl;
48
49      // output each grade
50      for ( int i = 0; i < numGrades; i++ )
51         cout << setw( 5 ) << grades[ i ];
52
53      cout << endl << endl;
54
55   } // end function displayGrades
56
57   // function addGrade definition
58   Student Student::addGrade( int grade ) const
59   {
60      int *temp = new int[ numGrades + 1 ];
61
62      for ( int i = 0; i < numGrades; i++ )
63         temp[ i ] = grades[ i ];
64
65      temp[ numGrades ] = grade;
66      grades = temp;
67      numGrades++;
68
69      return this;
70
71   } // end function addGrade
72
73   // function getNumStudents definition
74   static int Student::getNumStudents()
75   {
76      return numStudents;
77
78   } // end function getNumStudents
```

Fig. L 7.16   Contents of **student.cpp**. (Part 2 of 2.)

```
1    // Chapter 7 of C++ How to Program
2    // Debugging Problem (debugging07.cpp)
3
4    #include <iostream>
5
6    using std::cout;
7    using std::endl;
8
9    #include "student.h"
10
```

Fig. L 7.17   Contents of **debugging07.cpp**. (Part 1 of 2.)

Lab Exercises

Name: _____

Debugging

```
11   int main()
12   {
13      cout << "There are currently " << Student:getNumStudents()
14         << " students\n\n";
15
16      Student s1Ptr = new Student( "Student 1" );
17
18      s1Ptr->addGrade( 100 ).addGrade( 75 ).addGrade( 89 );
19      s1Ptr->displayGrades();
20
21      Student *s2Ptr = new Student( "Student 2" );
22      s2Ptr->addGrade( 83 )->addGrade( 92 );
23      s2Ptr->displayGrades();
24
25      const Student s3( "Student 3" );
26      s3.addGrade( 62 )->addGrade( 91 ).displayGrades();
27
28      cout << "There are currently " << getNumStudents()
29         << " students\n\n";
30
31      delete [] s2Ptr;
32      delete s1Ptr;
33
34      return 0;
35
36   } // end main
```

Fig. L 7.17   Contents of **debugging07.cpp**. (Part 2 of 2.)

Postlab Activities

Coding Exercises

Name: _____   **Date:**_____

Section: _____

These coding exercises reinforce the lessons learned in the lab and provide additional programming experience outside the classroom and laboratory environment. They serve as a review after you have completed the Prelab Activities and Lab Exercises successfully.

For each of the following problems, write a program or a program segment that performs the specified action:

1. Consider the **Polynomial** class from the Coding Exercises in Chapter 6 of this lab manual. Which member functions in your class definition should be declared as **const**?

2. After reading Section 7.6 in *C++ How to Program: Fourth Edition*, rewrite the data members of the class so that an arbitrarily large polynomial can be stored. [*Hint*: A **Polynomial** should be declared with a given **degree**. An array is then allocated to accommodate degree-number of coefficients.]

Postlab Activities   Name:

Coding Exercises

3. Using the **Polynomial** class from the previous Coding Exercises, add a **static** variable to store the number of **Polynomial**s declared.

4. Using class **Polynomial** from Coding Exercise 3, write a definition for a **friend** function to **print** a **Polynomial**.

5. Use the **new** operator to allocate dynamically an integer array of size **300**.

6. Deallocate the array allocated in Coding Exercise 5.

Postlab Activities   Name:

Coding Exercises

7. Write a short program that prompts the user to input an integer between 2 and 500, inclusive. Then allocate an array of **char**s of that size using the **new** operator.

8. Modify your solution to Coding Exercise 7 so that each element in the character array is initialized to the character **'z'**.

9. Modify your solution to Coding Exercise 8 so that is **delete**s the dynamically allocated array before the program terminates.

Postlab Activities   Name:

Coding Exercises

10. Write a proxy class for the **Date** class from Programming Output 30. The class should hide all **private** data and should hide the **Date** constructor and destructor. It should contain a **public** constructor, destructor and **print** function and a **private** pointer to a **Date** object.

Postlab Activities   Name:

Programming Challenges

Name: _____   **Date:** _____

Section: _____

The Programming Challenges are more involved than the Coding Exercises and may require a significant amount of time to complete. Write a C++ program for each of the problems in this section. The answers to these problems are available at **www.deitel.com**, **www.prenhall.com/deitel** and on the *C++ Multimedia Cyber Classroom: Fourth Edition*. Pseudocode, hints and/or sample outputs are provided to aid you in your programming.

11. Create a **Date** class with the following capabilities:

   a) Output the date in multiple formats such as

```
DDD YYYY
MM/DD/YY
June 14, 1992
```

   b) Use overloaded constructors to create **Date** objects initialized with dates of the formats in Part (a).

   c) Create a **Date** constructor that reads the system date, using the standard library functions of the **<ctime>** header, and sets the **Date** members.

Hints:

   • There are four constructors for this class: a default constructor that sets the date to the current date, using **<ctime>**; a constructor that takes a date in the form (*DDD, YYYY*); where *DDD* represents the day of the year, a constructor that takes a date in the form (*MM, DD, YY*), and a constructor which takes the month name, day and year. Use a **char*** and two **int**s for the last constructor.

   • In addition to the four constructors, include functions for setting the **month**, **day** and **year**. No other data members are necessary.

   • Write three different printing member functions. You may find it necessary to implement helper member functions that perform the following tasks:

   • Return the name of a month (as a **char***).

   • Return the number of days in a month.

   • Test for a leap year. A year is a leap year if it is divisible 400 or divisible by four and not by 100.

   • Return the name of a month.

   • Convert *DDD* to *MM DD*.

   • Convert *MM DD* to *DDD*.

   • Convert from month name to *MM*.

12. Create a **SavingsAccount** class. Use a **static** data member to store the **annualInterestRate** for each of the savers. Each member of the class contains a **private** data member **savingsBalance** indicating the amount the saver currently has on deposit. Provide a **calculateMonthlyInterest** member function that calculates the monthly interest by multiplying the **balance** by **annualInterestRate** divided by 12; this interest should be added to **savingsBalance**. Provide a **static** member function **modifyInterestRate** that sets the **static annualInterestRate** to a new value. Write a driver program to test class **SavingsAccount**. Instantiate two different **savingsAccount** objects, **saver1**

Postlab Activities

Name: _____

Programming Challenges

and **saver2**, with balances of $2000.00 and $3000.00, respectively. Set **annualInterestRate** to 3%, then calculate the monthly interest and print the new balances for each of the savers. Then set the **annualInterestRate** to 4%, calculate the next month's interest and print the new balances for each of the savers.

Hints:

- The necessary data members are the account balance (represented as a **double**) and the interest rate (a **static double**) which applies to all **SavingsAccount** objects.

- Write a driver program that iterates through a year's worth of monthly interest calculations at both rates.

Operator Overloading;
String and Array Objects

Objectives

- To understand how to redefine (overload) operators for abstract data types.
- To learn when to, and when not to, overload operators.
- To overload both unary and binary operators.
- To overload operators as member functions and as **friend** functions.
- To overload the stream-insertion and stream-extraction operators.
- To create a class to handle double-subscripted arrays and a class to handle rational numbers.

Assignment Checklist

Name: _____   **Date:** _____

Section: _____

Exercises	Assigned: Circle assignments	Date Due
Prelab Activities		
Matching	YES NO	
Fill in the Blank	11, 12, 13, 14, 15, 16, 17, 18, 19, 20, 21, 22, 23, 24	
Short Answer	25, 26, 27, 28, 29	
Programming Output	30, 31, 32, 33, 34	
Correct the Code	35, 36, 37	
Lab Exercises		
Lab Exercise 1 — Double-Subscripted Array	YES NO	
Follow-Up Questions and Activities	1, 2, 3, 4, 5	
Lab Exercise 2 — Rational Numbers	YES NO	
Follow-Up Questions and Activities	1, 2, 3	
Debugging	YES NO	
Labs Provided by Instructor		
1.		
2.		
3.		
Postlab Activities		
Coding Exercises	1, 2, 3, 4, 5, 6, 7, 8	
Programming Challenges	9, 10	

Assignment Checklist

Name:

Prelab Activities

Matching

Name: _____   **Date:**_____

Section: _____

After reading Chapter 8 of *C++ How to Program: Fourth Edition*, answer the given questions. These questions are intended to test and reinforce your understanding of key concepts and may be done either before the lab or during the lab.

For each term in the column on the left, write the corresponding letter for the description that best matches it from the column on the right.

Term	Description
____ 1. Self-assignment	a) The process of enabling C++'s operators to have class objects as operands.
____ 2. Dangling pointer	b) Constructor that takes as its argument an object of the same class as the current class.
____ 3. Memberwise assignment	c) A C++ operator that cannot be overloaded.
____ 4. Conversion constructor	d) Constructor that transforms objects of one type into objects of a different type.
____ 5. Copy constructor	e) Assigning an object to itself.
____ 6. Operator overloading	f) The default behavior of the = operator.
____ 7. Single-argument constructor	g) Problem that occurs when default memberwise copy is used on objects with dynamically allocated memory.
____ 8. `?:`	h) Any constructor of this type can be thought of as a conversion constructor.
____ 9. `vector`	i) Provides member function `substr`.
____ 10. `string`	j) Does not provide overloaded operators `<<` and `>>`.

Prelab Activities

Matching

Prelab Activities   Name:

Fill in the Blank

Name: _____   Date:_____

Section: _____

Fill in the blank for each of the following statements:

11. **operator** functions can be member functions or non-_____ functions.

12. It is often necessary that non-member **operator** functions be _____ functions.

13. When overloading an operator, the function name must be the keyword _____ followed by the _____ for the operator being overloaded.

14. The _____ and _____ operators may be used by objects of any class without overloading.

15. An operator's precedence, number of operands and _____ cannot be changed by overloading.

16. When overloading any assignment operator (or operators such as **()**, **[]** or **->**) the **operator** function must be defined as a(n) _____.

17. It is not possible to create _____ for new operators; only a subset of the existing operators may be overloaded.

18. The compiler does not know how to convert between _____ types and built-in types—the programmer must specify how such conversions occur explicitly.

19. The _____ operator is the most frequently overloaded operator.

20. To overload the increment operator to allow both _____ and _____, each overloaded **operator** function must have a distinct signature to determine which version of **++** is intended.

21. Copy constructors are invoked whenever a copy of an object is needed, such as call-by-_____.

22. If the left operand must be an object of a different class, the operator function must be implemented as a _____ function.

Prelab Activities

Name: _____

Fill in the Blank

23. **string** member function _____ returns the character at the specified location as an *lvalue* or *rvalue*, depending on the context in which the call appears. This member function is capable of "throwing an exception."

24. To use class **vector**, header file _____ must be included.

Prelab Activities

Name: _____

Short Answer

Name: _____   Date:_____

Section: _____

In the space provided, answer each of the given questions. Your answers should be as concise as possible; aim for two or three sentences.

25. What is operator overloading? How does it contribute to C++'s extensibility?

26. How is operator overloading accomplished?

Prelab Activities

Name:

Short Answer

27. Why is choosing not to overload the assignment operator and using default memberwise copy a potentially dangerous thing to do?

28. Why are some operators overloaded as member functions while others are not?

29. How are the increment and decrement operators overloaded?

Prelab Activities

Name: _____

Programming Output

Name: _____   Date: _____

Section: _____

For each of the given program segments, read the code and write the output in the space provided below each program. [*Note*: Do not execute these programs on a computer.]

30. What is output by the following code? Use class **PhoneNumber** (Fig. L 8.1) and the following numbers as input: (333) 555-7777 and (222) 555-9999

```
1   int main()
2   {
3       PhoneNumber Bill;
4       PhoneNumber Jane;
5
6       cout << "Enter Bill's phone number: ";
7       cin >> Bill;
8
9       cout << endl << "Enter Jane's phone number: ";
10      cin >> Jane;
11
12      cout << "Bill's number is: " << Bill << endl;
13      cout << "Jane's number is: " << Jane << endl;
14
15      return 0;
16
17  } // end main
```

```
1   // class PhoneNumber
2   // Overloading the stream-insertion and stream-extraction operators.
3
4   #include <iostream>
5
6   using std::cout;
7   using std::cin;
8   using std::endl;
9   using std::ostream;
10  using std::istream;
11
12  #include <iomanip>
13
14  using std::setw;
15
16  #include <string>
17
18  using std::string
19
20  // class PhoneNumber definition
21  class PhoneNumber {
22      friend ostream &operator<<( ostream&, const PhoneNumber & );
```

Fig. L 8.1   **PhoneNumber** class. (Part 1 of 2.)

Prelab Activities

Name:

Programming Output

```
23        friend istream &operator>>( istream&, PhoneNumber & );
24
25   private:
26        string areaCode;   // 3-digit area code
27        string exchange;   // 3-digit exchange
28        string line;       // 4-digit line
29
30   }; // end class PhoneNumber
31
32   // overloaded stream-insertion operator; cannot be
33   // a member function if we would like to invoke it with
34   // cout << somePhoneNumber;
35   ostream &operator<<( ostream &output, const PhoneNumber &num )
36   {
37        output << "(" << num.areaCode << ") "
38               << num.exchange << "-" << num.line;
39
40        return output;      // enables cout << a << b << c;
41
42   } // end function operator<<
43
44   // overloaded stream-extraction operator
45   istream &operator>>( istream &input, PhoneNumber &num )
46   {
47        input.ignore();                          // skip (
48        input >> setw( 4 ) >> num.areaCode; // input area code
49        input.ignore( 2 );                       // skip ) and space
50        input >> setw( 4 ) >> num.exchange; // input exchange
51        input.ignore();                          // skip dash (-)
52        input >> setw( 5 ) >> num.line;     // input line
53
54        return input;       // enables cin >> a >> b >> c;
55
56   } // end function operator>>
```

Fig. L 8.1   **PhoneNumber** class. (Part 2 of 2.)

Your answer:

31. What is output by the following program? Use the **PhoneNumber** class shown in Fig. L 8.1 and assume that the following phone number is entered:

    d333qq111w7777

```
1   int main()
2   {
3        PhoneNumber num;
4
```

Prelab Activities   Name:

Programming Output

```
5       cout << "Enter a phone number: ";
6       cin >> num;
7
8       cout << "That number was: " << num << endl;
9
10      return 0;
11
12   } // end main
```

(Part 2 of 2.)

Your answer:

32. What is output by the following code? Use the definition of class **Array** provided in Fig. L 8.2–Fig. L 8.3.

```
1    #include "array1.h"
2
3    int main()
4    {
5       cout << "# of arrays instantiated = "
6            << Array::getArrayCount() << '\n';
7
8       Array integers1( 4 );
9       Array integers2;
10
11      cout << "# of arrays instantiated = "
12           << Array::getArrayCount() << "\n";
13
14      Array integers3( 8 ), *intptr = &integers2;
15
16      cout << "# of arrays instantiated = "
17           << Array::getArrayCount() << "\n\n";
18
19      return 0;
20
21   } // end main
```

```
1    // array1.h
2    // Simple class Array (for integers)
3    #ifndef ARRAY1_H
4    #define ARRAY1_H
5
6    #include <iostream>
7
8    using std::ostream;
9    using std::istream;
```

Fig. L 8.2   Array class. (Part 1 of 2.)

Prelab Activities   Name:

Programming Output

```
10
11   // class Array definition
12   class Array {
13      friend ostream &operator<<( ostream &, const Array & );
14      friend istream &operator>>( istream &, Array & );
15
16   public:
17      Array( int = 10 );                      // default constructor
18      Array( const Array & );                 // copy constructor
19      ~Array();                               // destructor
20      int getSize() const;                    // return size
21      const Array &operator=( const Array & ); // assignment operator
22      bool operator==( const Array & ) const;  // equality operator
23
24      // determine if two arrays are not equal and
25      // return true, otherwise return false (uses operator==)
26      bool operator!=( const Array &right ) const
27      {
28         return ! ( *this == right );
29
30      } // end function operator!=
31
32      int &operator[]( int );                 // subscript operator
33      const int &operator[]( int ) const;     // subscript operator
34      static int getArrayCount();             // return number of
35                                              // arrays instantiated
36   private:
37      int size; // size of array
38      int *ptr; // pointer to first element of array
39      static int arrayCount;   // number of Arrays instantiated
40
41   }; // end class Array
42
43   #endif // ARRAY1_H
```

Fig. L 8.2   **Array** class. (Part 2 of 2.)

```
44   // array1.cpp
45   // Member function definitions for class Array
46   #include <iostream>
47
48   using std::cout;
49   using std::cin;
50   using std::endl;
51
52   #include <iomanip>
53
54   using std::setw;
55
56   #include <cstdlib>
57
58   #include <new>
59
```

Fig. L 8.3   **array1.cpp**. (Part 1 of 4.)

Prelab Activities

Name:

Programming Output

```
60    #include "array1.h"
61
62    // initialize static data member at file scope
63    int Array::arrayCount = 0;    // no objects yet
64
65    // default constructor for class Array (default size 10)
66    Array::Array( int arraySize )
67    {
68       size = ( arraySize > 0 ? arraySize : 10 );
69       ptr = new int[ size ]; // create space for array
70       ++arrayCount;           // count one more object
71
72       for ( int i = 0; i < size; i++ )
73          ptr[ i ] = 0;               // initialize array
74
75    } // end class Array constructor
76
77    // copy constructor for class Array
78    // must receive reference to prevent infinite recursion
79    Array::Array( const Array &arrayToCopy ) : size( arrayToCopy.size )
80    {
81       ptr = new int[ size ]; // create space for array
82       ++arrayCount;           // count one more object
83
84       for ( int i = 0; i < size; i++ )
85          ptr[ i ] = arrayToCopy.ptr[ i ];   // copy arayToCopy into object
86
87    } // end copy constructor
88
89    // destructor for class Array
90    Array::~Array()
91    {
92       delete [] ptr;              // reclaim space for array
93       --arrayCount;               // one fewer object
94
95    } // end class Array destructor
96
97    // get size of array
98    int Array::getSize() const
99    {
100      return size;
101
102   } // end function getSize
103
104   // overloaded assignment operator
105   // const return avoids: ( a1 = a2 ) = a3
106   const Array &Array::operator=( const Array &right )
107   {
108      if ( &right != this ) {   // check for self-assignment
109
110         // for arrays of different sizes, deallocate original
111         // left side array, then allocate new left side array
112         if ( size != right.size ) {
113            delete [] ptr;           // reclaim space
114            size = right.size;       // resize this object
115            ptr = new int[ size ]; // create space for array copy
116
```

Fig. L 8.3   **array1.cpp**. (Part 2 of 4.)

Prelab Activities

Name:

Programming Output

```
117          } // end if
118
119          for ( int i = 0; i < size; i++ )
120             ptr[ i ] = right.ptr[ i ];   // copy array into object
121
122       } // end if
123
124       return *this;    // enables x = y = z;
125
126    } // end function operator=
127
128    // determine if two arrays are equal and
129    // return true, otherwise return false
130    bool Array::operator==( const Array &right ) const
131    {
132       if ( size != right.size )
133          return false;     // arrays of different sizes
134
135       for ( int i = 0; i < size; i++ )
136
137          if ( ptr[ i ] != right.ptr[ i ] )
138             return false; // arrays are not equal
139
140       return true;         // arrays are equal
141
142    } // end function operator==
143
144    // overloaded subscript operator for non-const Arrays
145    // reference return creates an lvalue
146    int &Array::operator[]( int subscript )
147    {
148       // check for subscript out of range error
149       if ( subscript < 0 || subscript >= size ) {
150          cout << "\nError: Subscript " << subscript
151             << " out of range" << endl;
152
153          exit( 1 ); // terminate program; subscript out of range
154
155       } // end if
156
157       return ptr[ subscript ]; // reference return
158
159    } // end function operator[]
160
161    // overloaded subscript operator for const Arrays
162    // const reference return creates an rvalue
163    const int &Array::operator[]( int subscript ) const
164    {
165       // check for subscript out of range error
166       if ( subscript < 0 || subscript >= size ) {
167          cout << "\nError: Subscript " << subscript
168             << " out of range" << endl;
169
170          exit( 1 ); // terminate program; subscript out of range
171
172       } // end if
173
```

Fig. L 8.3   **array1.cpp**. (Part 3 of 4.)

Prelab Activities   Name:

Programming Output

```
174     return ptr[ subscript ]; // const reference return
175
176 } // end function operator[]
177
178 // return number of Array objects instantiated
179 // static functions cannot be const
180 int Array::getArrayCount()
181 {
182    return arrayCount;
183
184 } // end function getArrayCount
185
186 // overloaded input operator for class Array;
187 // inputs values for entire array
188 istream &operator>>( istream &input, Array &a )
189 {
190    for ( int i = 0; i < a.size; i++ )
191       input >> a.ptr[ i ];
192
193    return input;    // enables cin >> x >> y;
194
195 } // end function operator>>
196
197 // overloaded output operator for class Array
198 ostream &operator<<( ostream &output, const Array &a )
199 {
200    int i;
201
202    for ( i = 0; i < a.size; i++ ) {
203       output << setw( 12 ) << a.ptr[ i ];
204
205       if ( ( i + 1 ) % 4 == 0 ) // 4 numbers per row of output
206          output << endl;
207
208    } // end for
209
210    if ( i % 4 != 0 )
211       output << endl;
212
213    return output;
214
215 } // end function operator<<
```

Fig. L 8.3   `array1.cpp`. (Part 4 of 4.)

Your answer:

Prelab Activities

Name:

Programming Output

33. What is the output of the following program? Use the **Array** class shown in Fig. L 8.2–Fig. L 8.3.

```
1   #include "array1.h"
2
3   int main()
4   {
5      Array integers1( 4 );
6      Array integers2( 4 );
7
8      if ( integers1 != integers2 )
9         cout << "Hello";
10
11     else
12        cout << "Goodbye" << endl;
13
14     return 0;
15
16  } // end main
```

Your answer:

34. What is the output of the following program? Use class **Date** (Fig. L 8.4).

```
1   #include "date1.h"
2
3   int main()
4   {
5      Date d1;
6      Date d2( 1, 1, 1984 );
7      Date d3( 8, 12, 1981 );
8
9      cout << "d1 is " << d1
10          << "\nd2 is " << d2
11          << "\nd3 is " << d3 << "\n\n";
12
13     cout << "d2 += 7 is " << ( d2 += 7 ) << "\n\n";
14
15     cout << "d3++ is " << d3++ << "\n\n";
16
17     cout << "d3 now is " << d3 << "\n\n";
18
19     cout << "++d1 is " << ++d1 << "\n";
20
21     return 0;
22
23  } // end main
```

Prelab Activities

Name:

Programming Output

```
1   // date1.h
2   // Definition of class Date
3   #ifndef DATE1_H
4   #define DATE1_H
5   #include <iostream>
6
7   using std::ostream;
8
9   // class Date definition
10  class Date {
11     friend ostream &operator<<( ostream &, const Date & );
12
13  public:
14     Date( int m = 1, int d = 1, int y = 1900 ); // constructor
15     void setDate( int, int, int );  // set date
16     Date &operator++();              // preincrement operator
17     Date operator++( int );          // postincrement operator
18     const Date &operator+=( int );   // add days, modify object
19     bool leapYear( int ) const;      // is this a leap year?
20     bool endOfMonth( int ) const;    // is this end of month?
21
22  private:
23     int month;
24     int day;
25     int year;
26
27     static const int days[];         // array of days per month
28     void helpIncrement();            // utility function
29
30  }; // end class Date
31
32  #endif // DATE1_H
```

Fig. L 8.4   **Date** class.

```
1   // date1.cpp
2   // Member function definitions for Date class
3   #include <iostream>
4
5   #include "date1.h"
6
7   // initialize static member at file scope;
8   // one class-wide copy
9   const int Date::days[] = { 0, 31, 28, 31, 30, 31, 30,
10                             31, 31, 30, 31, 30, 31 };
11
12  // date constructor
13  Date::Date( int m, int d, int y )
14  {
15     setDate( m, d, y );
16
17  } // end class Date constructor
18
```

Fig. L 8.5   **date1.cpp**. (Part 1 of 3.)

Prelab Activities

Name:

Programming Output

```
19    // set date
20    void Date::setDate( int mm, int dd, int yy )
21    {
22       month = ( mm >= 1 && mm <= 12 ) ? mm : 1;
23       year = ( yy >= 1900 && yy <= 2100 ) ? yy : 1900;
24
25       // test for leap year
26       if ( month == 2 && leapYear( year ) )
27          day = ( dd >= 1 && dd <= 29 ) ? dd : 1;
28
29       else
30          day = ( dd >= 1 && dd <= days[ month ] ) ? dd : 1;
31
32    } // end function setDate
33
34    // preincrement operator overloaded as a member function
35    Date &Date::operator++()
36    {
37       helpIncrement();
38       return *this;   // reference return to create lvalue
39
40    } // end function operator++
41
42    // postincrement operator overloaded as a member function
43    // Note that integer parameter does not have
44    // parameter name
45    Date Date::operator++( int )
46    {
47       Date temp = *this;
48       helpIncrement();
49
50       // return non-incremented, temporary object
51       return temp;   // value return; not a reference return
52
53    } // end function operator++
54
55    // add specific number of days to date
56    const Date &Date::operator+=( int additionalDays )
57    {
58       for ( int i = 0; i < additionalDays; i++ )
59          helpIncrement();
60
61       return *this;     // enables cascading
62
63    } // end function operator+=
64
65    // if year is leap year, return true;
66    // otherwise, return false
67    bool Date::leapYear( int y ) const
68    {
69       if ( y % 400 == 0 || ( y % 100 != 0 && y % 4 == 0 ) )
70          return true;   // leap year
71
72       else
73          return false;  // not leap year
74
75    } // end function leapYear
```

Fig. L 8.5   **date1.cpp**. (Part 2 of 3.)

Prelab Activities

Name:

Programming Output

```
76
77   // determine if day is end of month
78   bool Date::endOfMonth( int d ) const
79   {
80      if ( month == 2 && leapYear( year ) )
81         return d == 29; // last day of Feb. in leap year
82
83      else
84         return d == days[ month ];
85
86   } // end function endOfMonth
87
88   // function to help increment date
89   void Date::helpIncrement()
90   {
91      if ( endOfMonth( day ) && month == 12 ) {  // end year
92         day = 1;
93         month = 1;
94         ++year;
95
96      } // end if
97
98      else if ( endOfMonth( day ) ) {            // end month
99         day = 1;
100        ++month;
101
102     } // end if
103
104     else         // not end of month or year; increment day
105        ++day;
106
107  } // end function helpIncrement
108
109  // overloaded output operator
110  ostream &operator<<( ostream &output, const Date &d )
111  {
112     static char *monthName[ 13 ] = { "", "January",
113        "February", "March", "April", "May", "June",
114        "July", "August", "September", "October",
115        "November", "December" };
116
117     output << monthName[ d.month ] << ' '
118           << d.day << ", " << d.year;
119
120     return output;
121
122  } // end function operator<<
```

Fig. L 8.5   **date1.cpp**. (Part 3 of 3.)

Your answer:

Prelab Activities   Name:

Programming Output

Prelab Activities

Name:

Correct the Code

Name: _____   Date:_____

Section: _____

For each of the given program segments, determine if there is an error in the code. If there is an error, specify whether it is a logic error or a syntax error, circle the error in the program, and write the corrected code in the space provided after each problem. If the code does not contain an error, write "no error." [*Note*: It is possible that a program segment may contain multiple errors.]

35. The following code is part of a header file for class **PhoneNumber**. It overloads the **@** operator to perform stream insertion.

```
1   class PhoneNumber {
2       friend ostream &operator@( ostream &, const PhoneNumber & );
```

Your answer:

36. The following code is part of a program that uses the class **Complex**. [*Note*: To view the class definition and member functions for **Complex**, see Fig. L 8.16 and Fig. L 8.17.]

```
1   Complex x, y( 5.2, 9.1 )
2
3   x += y;
4   cout << "x is: ";
5   x.print();
```

Your answer:

Prelab Activities

Name:

Correct the Code

37. The following code is the prototype for the copy constructor for class **Sample**:

```
1    Sample( const Sample );
```

Your answer:

Lab Exercises

Lab Exercise 1 — Double-Subscripted Array

Name: _____   **Date:**_____

Section: _____

This problem is intended to be solved in a closed-lab session with a teaching assistant or instructor present. The problem is divided into six parts:

1. Lab Objectives

2. Description of the Problem

3. Sample Output

4. Program Template (Fig. L 8.6–Fig. L 8.8)

5. Problem-Solving Tips

6. Follow-Up Questions and Activities

The program template represents a complete working C++ program, with one or more key lines of code replaced with comments. Read the problem description and examine the sample output; then study the template code. Using the problem-solving tips as a guide, replace the **/* */** comments with C++ code. Compile and execute the program. Compare your output with the sample output provided. Then answer the follow-up questions. The source code for the template is available at **www.deitel.com** and **www.prenhall.com./deitel**.

Lab Objectives

This lab was designed to reinforce programming concepts from Chapter 8 of *C++ How To Program: Fourth Edition*. In this lab, you will practice:

-   overloading operators to create a two-dimensional array class, **DoubleSubscriptedArray**.

-   writing function prototypes for overloaded operators.

-   function calls to overloaded operators.

-   dynamic memory allocation using the **new** and **delete** operators.

The follow-up questions and activities also will give you practice:

-   ensuring the correct access level of overloaded operators.

-   using the proper return type for an overloaded operator function.

Description of the Problem

Create a class **DoubleSubscriptedArray** that has similar features to class **Array** in Fig. 8.4–Fig 8.5 of *C++ How to Program: Fourth Edition*. The class should be able to create an array containing any number of rows and any number of columns. The class should provide **operator()** to perform double-subscripting operations. For example, in a 3-by-5 **DoubleSubscriptedArray** called **a**, the programmer could write **a(1, 3)** to access the element at row **1** and column **3**. The underlying representation of the double-subscripted array should be a single-subscripted array of integers with *rows * columns* number of elements. Function **operator()** should perform the proper pointer arithmetic to access each element of the array. There should be two versions of **operator()**—one that returns **int &** so an element of a **DoubleSubscriptedArray** can be used as an *lvalue* and one that returns **const int &** so an element of a **const DoubleSubscriptedArray** can be used as an *rvalue*. (See class **String** in Fig. 8.7–Fig. 8.8 of *C++ How to Program: Fourth Edition* for an example of **operator()**.) The class also should provide the following operators: **==**, **!=**, **=**, **<<** (for outputting the array in row and column format) and **>>** (for inputting the entire array contents).

Lab Exercises

Name:

Lab Exercise 1 — Double-Subscripted Array

Sample Output

```
Uninitialized array "a" is:
    0     0     0     0     0     0     0
    0     0     0     0     0     0     0
    0     0     0     0     0     0     0
    0     0     0     0     0     0     0
    0     0     0     0     0     0     0
    0     0     0     0     0     0     0
Uninitialized array "b" is:
    0     0
    0     0
    0     0
    0     0
    0     0
    0     0
    0     0
    0     0

Initialized array "a" is now:
   89    13    54    19    27    30    76
   96    22    21     7    97    26    43
   64    90     4    86     6    66    92
   92    86    19    80    76    60    49
   84    15    56     5    39    97    53
   12    34    49    91    54    98    39
Assigning b = a:
   89    13    54    19    27    30    76
   96    22    21     7    97    26    43
   64    90     4    86     6    66    92
   92    86    19    80    76    60    49
   84    15    56     5    39    97    53
   12    34    49    91    54    98    39
"a" was found to be equal to "b"
The element (2, 1) of array "a" is: 90
Changed element (2, 1) to -1:
   89    13    54    19    27    30    76
   96    22    21     7    97    26    43
   64    -1     4    86     6    66    92
   92    86    19    80    76    60    49
   84    15    56     5    39    97    53
   12    34    49    91    54    98    39
"a" was found to be NOT equal to "b"
```

Lab Exercises   Name:

Lab Exercise 1 — Double-Subscripted Array

Template

```
1   // Chapter 8 of C++ How to Program
2   // doublescriptedarray.h
3   #ifndef DARRAY_H
4   #define DARRAY_H
5
6   #include <iostream>
7
8   using std::ostream;
9   using std::istream;
10
11  // class DoubleScriptedArray definition
12  class DoubleScriptedArray {
13     /* Write declaration for overloaded ostream operator */
14     friend istream &operator>>( istream &, DoubleScriptedArray & );
15
16  public:
17     DoubleScriptedArray( int = 10, int = 10 );
18     DoubleScriptedArray( const DoubleScriptedArray & );
19     ~DoubleScriptedArray();
20     /* Write prototype for overloaded = operator */
21     bool operator==( const DoubleScriptedArray & ) const;
22
23     /* Write header for operator!= */
24     {
25        return ! ( *this == right );
26
27     } // end function operator!=
28
29     int &operator()( int, int );    // lvalue
30     /* Write prototype for overloaded() operator used as
31        an rvalue */
32
33  private:
34     int rows;        // number of rows in array
35     int columns;     // number of columns in array
36     int *ptr;        // pointer to first element of array
37
38  }; // end class DoubleScriptedArray
39
40  #endif // DARRAY_H
```

Fig. L 8.6   Contents of **doublescriptedarray.h**.

```
1   // Chapter 8 of C++ How to Program
2   // doublescriptedarray.cpp
3   #include <iostream>
4
5   using std::cout;
6   using std::cin;
7   using std::endl;
8
9   #include <iomanip>
10
```

Fig. L 8.7   Contents of **doublescriptedarray.cpp**. (Part 1 of 3.)

Lab Exercises   Name:

Lab Exercise 1 — Double-Subscripted Array

```
11   using std::setw;
12
13   #include <cstdlib>
14
15   #include <new>
16
17   #include "doubleScriptedArray.h"
18
19   // constructor
20   DoubleScriptedArray::DoubleScriptedArray( int r, int c )
21   {
22      rows = ( r > 0 ? r : 10 );
23      columns = ( c > 0 ? c : 10 );
24      ptr = new int[ rows * columns ];
25
26      for ( int i = 0; i < rows * columns; i++ )
27         ptr[ i ] = 0;
28
29   } // end class DoubleScriptedArray constructor
30
31   // copy constructor
32   DoubleScriptedArray::DoubleScriptedArray( const DoubleScriptedArray &init )
33   {
34      rows = init.rows;
35      columns = init.columns;
36
37      ptr = new int[ rows * columns ];
38
39      for ( int i = 0; i < rows * columns; i++ )
40         ptr[ i ] = init.ptr[ i ];
41
42   } // end class DoubleScriptedArray copy constructor
43
44   /* Write definition for destructor */
45
46   /* Write definition for operator = */
47
48   // function operator== definition
49   bool DoubleScriptedArray::operator==( const DoubleScriptedArray &right ) const
50   {
51      if ( rows != right.rows || columns != right.columns )
52         return false;
53
54      for ( int i = 0; i < rows * columns; i++ )
55
56         if ( ptr[ i ] != right.ptr[ i ] )
57            return false;
58
59      return true;
60
61   } // end function operator==
62
63   // overloaded subscript operator for non-const Arrays
64   // reference return creates an lvalue
65   int &DoubleScriptedArray::operator()( int s1, int s2 )
66   {
```

Fig. L 8.7   Contents of **doublescriptedarray.cpp**. (Part 2 of 3.)

Lab Exercises   Name:

Lab Exercise 1 — Double-Subscripted Array

```
67    if ( !( s1 > 0 && s1 < rows ) )
68        s1 = 0;
69
70    if ( !( s2 > 0 && s2 < columns ) )
71        s2 = 0;
72
73    return ptr[ ( columns * s1 + s2 ) ];
74
75  } // end function operator()
76
77  // overloaded subscript operator for const Arrays
78  // const reference return creates an rvalue
79  /* Write overloaded subscript operator that returns an rvalue */
80
81  // function operato>> definition
82  istream &operator>>( istream &input, DoubleScriptedArray &a )
83  {
84     for ( int i = 0; i < a.rows * a.columns; i++ )
85        input >> a.ptr[ i ];
86
87     return input;
88
89  } // end function operator>>
90
91  // function operator<< definition
92  /* Write function header for overloaded insertion operator */
93  {
94     for ( int i = 0; i < a.rows * a.columns; i++ ) {
95        output << setw( 6 ) << a.ptr[ i ];
96
97        if ( ( i + 1 ) % a.columns == 0 )
98           output << endl;
99
100   } // end for
101
102   if ( i % a.columns != 0 )
103       output << endl;
104
105    return output;
106
107 } // end function operator<<
```

Fig. L 8.7   Contents of **doublescriptedarray.cpp**. (Part 3 of 3.)

```
1   // Chapter 8 of C++ How to Program
2   // Driver for class DoubleScriptedArray
3   #include <iostream>
4
5   using std::cout;
6   using std::cin;
7   using std::endl;
```

Fig. L 8.8   Contents of **driver.cpp**. (Part 1 of 2.)

Lab Exercises   Name:

Lab Exercise 1 — Double-Subscripted Array

```
8
9   #include <ctime>
10
11  #include "doubleScriptedArray.h"
12
13  int main()
14  {
15     // seed rand function
16     srand( time( 0 ) );
17
18     // create two arrays
19     DoubleScriptedArray a( 6, 7 );
20     DoubleScriptedArray b( 8, 2 );
21
22     cout << "Uninitialized array \"a\" is: \n" << a
23         << "Uninitialized array \"b\" is: \n" << b;
24
25     // initialize array "a" with random values (0-100)
26     for ( int i = 0; i < 6; i++ )
27
28        for ( int j = 0; j < 7; j++ )
29           /* Write statement to insert random values (reduced
30               to a range of 0 - 100) into the array via
31               the overloaded () */
32
33     // use overloaded operator=
34     b = a;
35
36     cout << "\nInitialized array \"a\" is now:\n" << a
37         << "Assigning b = a:\n" << b;
38
39     // check if arrays are equal using overloaded ==
40     if ( a == b )
41        cout << "\"a\" was found to be equal to \"b\"\n";
42     else
43        cout << "\"a\" was found to be not equal to \"b\"\n";
44
45     // retrieve array element using overloaded operator()
46     cout << "The element (2, 1) of array \"a\" is: "
47         << a( 2, 1 ) << endl;
48
49     // change element of array using overloaded operator()
50     a( 2, 1 ) = -1;
51     cout << "Changed element (2, 1) to -1: \n" << a;
52
53     // check if arrays are still equal
54     if ( /* Write condition to check if arrays are equal */ )
55        cout << "\"a\" was found to be equal to \"b\"\n";
56     else
57        cout << "\"a\" was found to be NOT equal to \"b\"\n";
58
59     return 0;
60
61  } // end main
```

Fig. L 8.8   Contents of **driver.cpp**. (Part 2 of 2.)

Lab Exercises   Name:

Lab Exercise 1 — Double-Subscripted Array

Problem-Solving Tips

1. When overloading the = operator, remember that both arrays must be of the same size. If they are not, delete the target array and reallocate an array of the appropriate size.

2. The overloaded **ostream** operator must be declared as a **friend**.

3. The overloaded **operator<<** and **operator>>** functions return a reference to an **ostream** and an **istream** object, respectively. This enables the cascading of function calls.

4. The difference between the *lvalue* **operator()** function and the *rvalue* **operator()** function is that the *rvalue* **operator()** function returns a **const int** and is a constant member function.

Follow-Up Questions and Activities

1. Why must the constructor determine if its parameter values are greater than **0**?

2. What happens if the overloaded **ostream** operator function does not return a reference to an object of type **ostream**? Modify the program so that the function returns **void**. What happens?

3. Why is it necessary for the **>>** and **<<** operators to be **friend**s of **DoubleScriptedArray**?

Lab Exercises   Name:

Lab Exercise 1 — Double-Subscripted Array

4. Modify the program so that the **DoubleScriptedArray** class also can handle single subscripts. Overload the constructor and **operator()** functions. Overload the constructor to take a single integer parameter. To do so, you will need to modify the existing constructor, so that it no longer takes default parameters. [*Hint:* Treat the one-dimensional array as a two-dimensional array with only one row.]

5. Try to overload the **sizeof** operator for class **DoubleScriptedArray**. What happens?

Lab Exercises   Name:

Lab Exercise 2 — Rational Numbers

Name: _____   Date: _____

Section: _____

This problem is intended to be solved in a closed-lab session with a teaching assistant or instructor present. The problem is divided into six parts:

1. Lab Objectives
2. Description of the Problem
3. Sample Output
4. Program Template (Fig. L 8.9–Fig. L 8.11)
5. Problem-Solving Tips
6. Follow-Up Questions and Activities

The program template represents a complete working C++ program, with one or more key lines of code replaced with comments. Read the problem description and examine the sample output; then study the template code. Using the problem-solving tips as a guide, replace the **/* */** comments with C++ code. Compile and execute the program. Compare your output with the sample output provided. Then answer the follow-up questions. The source code for the template is available at **www.deitel.com** and **www.prenhall.com./deitel**.

Lab Objectives

This lab was designed to reinforce programming concepts from Chapter 8 of *C++ How To Program: Fourth Edition*. In this lab, you will practice:

- overloading operators to create a class capable of storing rational numbers and performing rational number arithmetic.
- writing function prototypes for overloaded operators.
- implementing overloaded operator functions.

Description of the Problem

Create a class **RationalNumber** (fractions) with the following capabilities:

a) create a constructor that prevents a **0** denominator in a fraction, reduces or simplifies fractions that are not in reduced form and avoids negative denominators.

b) overload the addition, subtraction, multiplication and division operators for this class.

c) overload the relational and equality operators for this class.

[*Note*: This class is not designed to handle negative numbers.]

The follow-up questions and activities also will give you practice:

- overloading multiple operators.
- overloading the **<<** operator.

Lab Exercises

Name:

Lab Exercise 2 — Rational Numbers

Sample Output

```
7/3 + 1/3 = 8/3
7/3 - 1/3 = 2
7/3 * 1/3 = 7/9
7/3 / 1/3 = 7
7/3 is:
 > 1/3 according to the overloaded > operator
 >= 1/3 according to the overloaded < operator
 >= 1/3 according to the overloaded >= operator
 > 1/3 according to the overloaded <= operator
 != 1/3 according to the overloaded == operator
 != 1/3 according to the overloaded != operator
```

Template

```cpp
1  // Chapter 8 of C++ How to Program
2  // rational.h
3  #ifndef RATIONAL_H
4  #define RATIONAL_H
5
6  // class RationalNumber definition
7  class RationalNumber {
8
9  public:
10    RationalNumber( int = 0, int = 1 ); // default constructor
11
12    const RationalNumber operator+( const RationalNumber& );
13    /* Write prototype for operator- */
14    const RationalNumber operator*( const RationalNumber& );
15    const RationalNumber operator/( const RationalNumber& );
16    bool operator>( const RationalNumber& ) const;
17    bool operator<( const RationalNumber& ) const;
18    bool operator>=( const RationalNumber& ) const;
19    /* Write prototype for operator <= */
20    bool operator==( const RationalNumber& ) const;
21    bool operator!=( const RationalNumber& ) const;
22
23    void printRational() const;
24
25  private:
26    int numerator;
27    int denominator;
28    void reduction();
29
30  }; // end class RationalNumber
31
32  #endif // RATIONAL_H
```

Fig. L 8.9   Contents of `rational.h`.

```cpp
1  // Chapter 8 of C++ How to Program
2  // rational.cpp
```

Fig. L 8.10   Contents of `rational.cpp`. (Part 1 of 4.)

Lab Exercises

Name:

Lab Exercise 2 — Rational Numbers

```cpp
 3   #include <cstdlib>
 4
 5   #include <iostream>
 6
 7   using std::cout;
 8   using std::endl;
 9
10   #include "rational.h"
11
12   // constructor
13   RationalNumber::RationalNumber( int n, int d )
14   {
15      numerator = n;
16      denominator = d;
17      /* Write function call to reduction function */
18
19   } // end class RationalNumber constructor
20
21   /* Write definition for overloaded operator+ */
22
23   // function operator- definition
24   const RationalNumber RationalNumber::operator-(
25      const RationalNumber &s )
26   {
27      RationalNumber sub;
28
29      sub.numerator = numerator * s.denominator - denominator *
30         s.numerator;
31      sub.denominator = denominator * s.denominator;
32      sub.reduction();
33      return sub;
34
35   } // end function operator-
36
37   /* Write definition for overloaded operator * */
38
39   // function operator/ definition
40   const RationalNumber RationalNumber::operator/(
41      const RationalNumber &d )
42   {
43      RationalNumber divide;
44
45      if ( /* Write condition to test for zero numerator */ ) {
46         divide.numerator = numerator * d.denominator;
47         divide.denominator = denominator * d.numerator;
48         divide.reduction();
49
50      } // end if
51
52      else {
53         cout << "Divide by zero error: terminating program\n";
54         exit( 1 );   // cstdlib function
55
56      } // end else
57
58      return divide;
59
```

Fig. L 8.10   Contents of **rational.cpp**. (Part 2 of 4.)

Lab Exercises

Name:

Lab Exercise 2 — Rational Numbers

```
60   } // end function operator/
61
62   // function operator> definition
63   bool RationalNumber::operator>( const RationalNumber &gr ) const
64   {
65      // compare double values of two rational numbers
66      if ( static_cast< double >( numerator ) / denominator >
67           static_cast< double >( gr.numerator ) / gr.denominator )
68         return true;
69
70      else
71         return false;
72
73   } // end function operator>
74
75   // function operator< definition
76   bool RationalNumber::operator<( const RationalNumber &lr ) const
77   {
78      return !( *this > lr );
79
80   } // end function operator<
81
82   // function operator>= definition
83   bool RationalNumber::operator>=( const RationalNumber &rat ) const
84   {
85      return *this == rat || *this > rat;
86
87   } // end function operator>=
88
89   /* Write definition for operator <= */
90
91   /* Write definition for operator == */
92
93   /* Write definition for operator != */
94
95   // function printRational definition
96   void RationalNumber::printRational() const
97   {
98      if ( numerator == 0 )              // print fraction as zero
99         cout << numerator;
100
101     else if ( denominator == 1 )   // print fraction as integer
102        cout << numerator;
103
104     else
105        cout << numerator << '/' << denominator;
106
107  } // end function printRational
108
109  // function reduction definition
110  void RationalNumber::reduction()
111  {
112     int smallest;
113     int gcd = 1;   // greatest common divisor
114
115     smallest = ( numerator < denominator ) ? numerator
116        : denominator;
```

Fig. L 8.10   Contents of **rational.cpp**. (Part 3 of 4.)

Lab Exercises   Name:

Lab Exercise 2 — Rational Numbers

```
117
118     for ( int loop = 2; loop <= smallest; ++loop )
119
120         if ( numerator % loop == 0 && denominator % loop == 0 )
121             gcd = loop;
122
123     numerator /= gcd;
124     denominator /= gcd;
125
126 } // end function reduction
```

Fig. L 8.10   Contents of **rational.cpp**. (Part 4 of 4.)

```
1    // Chapter 8 of C++ How to Program
2    // driver.cpp
3    #include <iostream>
4
5    using std::cout;
6    using std::endl;
7
8    #include "rational.h"
9
10   int main()
11   {
12       RationalNumber c( 7, 3 );
13       RationalNumber d( 3, 9 );
14       RationalNumber x;
15
16       c.printRational();
17       cout << " + " ;
18       d.printRational();
19       cout << " = ";
20       x = c + d;
21       x.printRational();
22
23       cout << '\n';
24       c.printRational();
25       cout << " - " ;
26       d.printRational();
27       cout << " = ";
28       /* Write statement to subtract c from d and assign the result to x */
29       x.printRational();
30
31       cout << '\n';
32       c.printRational();
33       cout << " * " ;
34       d.printRational();
35       cout << " = ";
36       /* Write statement to multiply c and d and assign the result to x */
37       x.printRational();
38
```

Fig. L 8.11   Contents of **driver.cpp**. (Part 1 of 2.)

Lab Exercises

Name:

Lab Exercise 2 — Rational Numbers

```
39        cout << '\n';
40        c.printRational();
41        cout << " / " ;
42        d.printRational();
43        cout << " = ";
44        x = c / d;
45        x.printRational();
46
47        cout << '\n';
48        c.printRational();
49        cout << " is:\n";
50
51        cout << ( ( c > d ) ? "  > " : "  <= " );
52        d.printRational();
53        cout << " according to the overloaded > operator\n";
54
55        cout << ( ( c < d ) ? "  < " : "  >= " );
56        d.printRational();
57        cout << " according to the overloaded < operator\n";
58
59        cout << ( ( c >= d ) ? "  >= " : "  < " );
60        d.printRational();
61        cout << " according to the overloaded >= operator\n";
62
63        cout << ( ( c <= d ) ? "  <= " : "  > " );
64        d.printRational();
65        cout << " according to the overloaded <= operator\n";
66
67        cout << ( ( c == d ) ? "  == " : "  != " );
68        d.printRational();
69        cout << " according to the overloaded == operator\n";
70
71        cout << ( ( c != d ) ? "  != " : "  == " );
72        /* Write statement to print d */
73
74        cout << " according to the overloaded != operator" << endl;
75
76        return 0;
77
78   } // end main
```

Fig. L 8.11   Contents of `driver.cpp`. (Part 2 of 2.)

Problem-Solving Tips

1. The overloaded **ostream** operator must be declared as a **friend**.

2. When overloading the **<=** and **>=** operators, if **<**, **>** or **==** has been defined previously, they can be used in the implementation of **<=** and **>=**.

3. The **this** pointer provides an object with access to its own address.

Follow-Up Questions and Activities

1. Rewrite the **printRational** member function as an overloaded **<< friend** function.

Lab Exercises   Name: _____

Lab Exercise 2 — Rational Numbers

2. Make the **RationalNumber** class more robust by providing additional tests for division by zero.

3. Is it possible to add another overloaded **operator>** function that returns a pointer to the larger of the two rational numbers? Why or why not?

Lab Exercises

Lab Exercise 2 — Rational Numbers

Lab Exercises   Name:

Debugging

Name: _____   Date:_____

Section: _____

The program (Fig. L 8.12–Fig. L 8.14) in this section does not run properly. Fix all the syntax errors so that the program will compile successfully. Once the program compiles, compare the output with the sample output, and eliminate any logic errors that may exist. The sample output demonstrates what the program's output should be once the program's code has been corrected.

Sample Output

[*Note*: There may be rounding errors due to the conversion from a floating-point number to an integer. The numbers may be off by `.01`.]

```
Initial values:
0
0
1.23

Enter a number: 2.345
Enter a number: 3.456
The sum of test1 and test2 is: 5.80

final values:
test1 = 3.34
test2 = 4.45
test3 = 5.69
test1 and test3 are not equal to each other
```

```
Initial values:
0
0
1.23

Enter a number: 0
Enter a number: -2.234
The sum of test1 and test2 is: -2.24

final values:
test1 = 0
test2 = -1.24
test3 = 0
```

Lab Exercises   Name:

Debugging

Broken Code

```
1   // Chapter 8 of C++ How to Program
2   // Debugging Problem (decimal.h)
3
4   #ifndef DECIMAL_H
5   #define DECIMAL_H
6
7   #include <iostream>
8
9   using std::ostream;
10  using std::istream;
11
12  // class Decimal definition
13  class Decimal {
14
15  public:
16     friend istream operator>>( istream &, const Decimal & );
17     Decimal( double = 0.0 );
18
19     void setInteger( double );
20     void setDecimal( double );
21
22     Decimal &operator=( const Decimal );
23     Decimal +( Decimal );
24     Decimal +=( Decimal ) const;
25     Decimal &operator++();
26     Decimal operator++( double );
27     bool operator==( const Decimal );
28
29  private:
30     friend ostream &operator<<( const Decimal & );
31     double integer;
32     double decimal;
33
34  }; // end class Decimal
35
36  #endif // DECIMAL_H
```

Fig. L 8.12   Contents of **decimal.h**.

```
1   // Chapter 8 of C++ How to Program
2   // Debugging Problem (decimal.cpp)
3
4   #include <iostream>
5
6   using std::cout;
7   using std::cin;
8
9   #include <cmath>
10
11  #include "decimal.h"
```

Fig. L 8.13   Contents of **decimal.cpp**. (Part 1 of 4.)

```
12
13   // constructor
14   Decimal::Decimal( double n )
15   {
16      decimal = modf( n, &integer );
17
18   } // end class Decimal constructor
19
20   // function operator<< definition
21   friend ostream & operator<<( const Decimal &d )
22   {
23      double n = 0;
24
25      n = floor( d.decimal * 100 );
26
27      if ( n < 0 )
28         n = 0 - dec;
29
30      if ( d.decimal != 0 ) {
31         output << floor( d.integer ) << ".";
32
33         if ( n > 10 )
34            output << n;
35
36         else
37            output << "0" << n;
38
39      } // end if
40
41      else
42         output << d.integer;
43
44   } // end function operator<<
45
46   // function operator>> definition
47   friend istream operator>>( istream &input, const Decimal &d )
48   {
49      double n;
50
51      cout << "Enter a number: ";
52      istream >> n;
53
54      decimal = modf( n, &integer );
55
56      return input;
57
58   } // end function operator>>
59
60   // function operator= definition
61   Decimal &Decimal::operator=( const Decimal d )
62   {
63      integer = d.integer;
64      decimal = d.decimal;
65
66      return *this;
67
68   } // end function operator=
69
70   // function setDecimal definition
71   void Decimal::setDecimal( double d )
72   {
73      decimal = d;
74
75   } // end function setDecimal
76
```

Fig. L 8.13   Contents of **decimal.cpp**. (Part 2 of 4.)

Lab Exercises

Name:

Debugging

```
77   // function setInteger definition
78   void Decimal::setInteger( double i )
79   {
80      integer = i;
81
82   } // end function setInteger
83
84   // function operator+ definition
85   Decimal Decimal::operator+( Decimal d )
86   {
87      Decimal result;
88
89      result.setDecimal( decimal + d.decimal );
90      result.setInteger( integer + d.integer );
91
92      if ( result.decimal >= 1 ) {
93         result.decimal--;
94         result.integer++;
95
96      } // end if
97
98      else if ( result.decimal <= -1 ) {
99         result.decimal++;
100        result.integer--;
101
102     } // end if
103
104     return result;
105
106  } // end function operator+
107
108  // function operator+= definition
109  Decimal Decimal::operator+=( Decimal d ) const
110  {
111     *this = *this += d;
112     return *this;
113
114  } // end function operator+=
115
116  // function operator++ definition
117  Decimal &Decimal::operator++()
118  {
119     integer++;
120     return integer;
121
122  } // end function operator++
123
124  // function operator++ definition
125  Decimal Decimal::operator++( double )
126  {
127     Decimal temp = *this;
128
129     integer++;
130     return *this;
131
132  } // end function operator++
133
```

Fig. L 8.13   Contents of **decimal.cpp**. (Part 3 of 4.)

Lab Exercises   Name:

Debugging

```
134  // function operator== definition
135  bool Decimal::operator==( const Decimal d )
136  {
137     return ( integer == d.integer && decimal == d.decimal );
138
139  } // end function operator==
```

Fig. L 8.13   Contents of **decimal.cpp**. (Part 4 of 4.)

```
1    // Chapter 8 of C++ How to Program
2    // Debugging Problem (debugging08.cpp)
3
4    #include <iostream>
5
6    using std::cout;
7    using std::endl;
8    using std::cin;
9
10   #include "decimal.h"
11
12   int main()
13   {
14      Decimal test1;
15      Decimal test2;
16      Decimal test3( 1.234 );
17
18      cout << "Initial values:\n"
19           << test1 << endl << test2 << endl << test3
20           << endl << endl;
21
22      cin >> test1 >> test2;
23
24      cout << "The sum of test1 and test2 is: "
25           << test1 + test2 << endl;
26      test3 += ++test2;
27
28      cout << "\nfinal values:\n"
29           << "test1 = " << test1 << endl
30           << "test2 = " << test2 << endl
31           << "test3 = " << test3 << endl;
32
33      if ( test1 != test3 )
34         cout << "test1 and test3 are not equal to each other\n";
35
36      return 0;
37
38   } // end main
```

Fig. L 8.14   Contents of **debugging08.cpp**.

Lab Exercises   Name:

Debugging

Postlab Activities

Coding Exercises

Name: _____   Date:_____

Section: _____

These coding exercises reinforce the lessons learned in the lab and provide additional programming experience outside the classroom and laboratory environment. They serve as a review after you have completed the Prelab Activities and Lab Exercises successfully.

For each of the following problems, write a program or a program segment that performs the specified action. Each problem refers to class **Polygon** (Fig. L 8.15). This class contains a dynamically allocated array of x coordinates and a dynamically allocated array of y coordinates. These coordinates store the polygon's vertices. The **Polygon** constructor takes the initial vertex for the **Polygon**.

```cpp
1   // Chapter 8 of C++ How to Program
2   // Coding Exercises
3   // polygon.cpp
4
5   // class Polygon definition
6   class Polygon {
7
8   public:
9      Polygon( int = 0, int = 0 );
10     ~Polygon();
11
12     void addVertex( int, int );
13     int getNumberOfVertices() const;
14
15   private:
16      int *xPts;
17      int *yPts;
18      int numberOfVertices;
19
20   }; // end class Polygon
21
22   // default constructor
23   Polygon::Polygon( int x, int y )
24   {
25      xPts = new int[ 1 ];
26      yPts = new int[ 1 ];
27
28      xPts[ 0 ] = x;
29      yPts[ 0 ] = y;
30      numberOfVertices = 1;
31
32   } // end class Polygon constructor
33
34   // destructor
35   Polygon::~Polygon()
36   {
37      delete [] xPts;
38      delete [] yPts;
39
40   } // end class Polygon destructor
41
```

Fig. L 8.15   **polygon.cpp**. (Part 1 of 2.)

Postlab Activities

Name: _____

Coding Exercises

```
42   // function addVertex definition
43   void Polygon::addVertex( int x, int y )
44   {
45      int *copyX = new int[ numberOfVertices + 1 ];
46      int *copyY = new int[ numberOfVertices + 1 ];
47
48      for ( int i = 0; i < numberOfVertices; i++ ) {
49         copyX[ i ] = xPts[ i ];
50         copyY[ i ] = yPts[ i ];
51
52      } // end for
53
54      copyX[ numberOfVertices ] = x;
55      copyY[ numberOfVertices ] = y;
56
57      delete [] xPts;
58      delete [] yPts;
59
60      xPts = copyX;
61      yPts = copyY;
62      numberOfVertices++;
63
64   } // end function addVertex
65
66   // function getNumberOfVertices
67   int Polygon::getNumberOfVertices() const
68   {
69      return numberOfVertices;
70
71   } // end function getNumVertices
```

Fig. L 8.15   **polygon.cpp**. (Part 2 of 2.)

1. Overload the stream-insertion operator **<<** to output a **Polygon** object.

2. Create a copy constructor for class **Polygon**.

Postlab Activities   Name:

Coding Exercises

3. Overload the **==** operator to compare two **Polygon**s for equality. This member function should return a **bool**ean value.

4. Overload the **=** operator to assign one **Polygon** object to another. This member function should return a **const** reference to the **Polygon** object invoking the member function. This member function also should test for self assignment.

5. Overload the **+=** operator for the **Polygon** class. Operator **+=** shifts all of a **Polygon**'s vertices upward by a programmer-specified amount (i.e., increase the y coordinate of each vertex).

Postlab Activities   Name:

Coding Exercises

6. Overload the preincrement operator for the **Polygon** class. When a **Polygon** is incremented all of its vertices are shifted up by **1** (i.e., increase the *y* coordinate of each vertex). [Hint: Use the overloaded **+=** operator as part of your solution.]

7. Overload the postincrement operators for the **Polygon** class. [Hint: Use the overloaded **++** preincrement operator as part of your solution.]

8. Overload the tilde (**~**) operator for the **Polygon** class. This member function returns a **Polygon** object containing the calling object's points shifted one position to the right. The last point of the calling object becomes the first point in the object returned. For example, a **Polygon** with coordinates *(1, 1)*, *(2, 2)* and *(3, 3)* would result in a **Polygon** containing coordinates *(3, 3)*, *(1, 1)* and *(2, 2)* being returned.

Postlab Activities   Name:

Programming Challenges

Name: _____   Date:_____

Section: _____

The Programming Challenges are more involved than the Coding Exercises and may require a significant amount of time to complete. Write a C++ program for each of the problems in this section. The answers to these problems are available at **www.deitel.com**, **www.prenhall.com/deitel** and on the *C++ Multimedia Cyber Classroom: Fourth Edition*. Pseudocode, hints and/or sample outputs are provided to aid you in your programming.

9. One nice example of overloading the function call operator **()** is to allow the more common form of double-array subscripting. Instead of saying

    ```
    chessBoard[ row ][ column ]
    ```

    for an array of objects, overload the function call operator to allow the alternate form

    ```
    chessBoard( row, column )
    ```

Hints:

  - Create a class **CallOperator** with an 8-by-8 double-scripted array as its only **private** data member.

  - The only functions needed are the overloaded function call operator and a constructor that provides values for the array.

  - Pseudocode for the driver is as follows:

    Create an object, board, of type CallOperator;
    Print to screen "board[x][y] is: "
    Make a call to the overloaded () operator to reference x, y

  - An output of your program may look like

    ```
    board[ 2 ][ 5 ] is 5
    ```

10. Consider class **Complex** shown inFig. L 8.16–Fig. L 8.17. The class enables operations on *complex numbers*. These are numbers of the form **realPart + imaginaryPart** * *i*, where *i* has the value

    $$\sqrt{-1}$$

    a) Modify the class to enable input and output of complex numbers through the overloaded **>>** and **<<** operators, respectively. (You should remove the **print** member function from the class.)

    b) Overload the multiplication operator to enable multiplication of two complex numbers as in algebra. Complex number multiplication is performed as follows:

        $(a + bi) * (c + di) = (ac - bd) + (ad + bc)i$

    c) Overload the **==** and **!=** operators to allow comparisons of complex numbers.

Postlab Activities   Name:

Programming Challenges

```
1   // complex.h
2   // Definition of class Complex
3   #ifndef COMPLEX_H
4   #define COMPLEX_H
5
6   // class Complex definition
7   class Complex {
8
9   public:
10     Complex( double = 0.0, double = 0.0 );        // constructor
11
12     Complex operator+( const Complex & ) const;   // addition
13     Complex operator-( const Complex & ) const;   // subtraction
14     const Complex &operator=( const Complex & );  // assignment
15
16     void print() const;                           // output
17
18   private:
19     double real;        // real part
20     double imaginary;   // imaginary part
21
22   }; // end class Complex
23
24   #endif // COMPLE1_H
```

Fig. L 8.16   Contents of **complex.h**.

```
1   // complex.cpp
2   // Member function definitions for class Complex
3   #include <iostream>
4
5   using std::cout;
6
7   #include "complex.h"
8
9   // constructor
10  Complex::Complex( double r, double i )
11     : real( r ), imaginary( i )
12  {
13     // empty
14
15  } // end class Complex constructor
16
17  // overloaded addition operator
18  Complex Complex::operator+( const Complex &operand2 ) const
19  {
20     return Complex( real + operand2.real, imaginary + operand2.imaginary );
21
22  } // end function operator+
23
24  // overloaded subtraction operator
25  Complex Complex::operator-( const Complex &operand2 ) const
26  {
27     return Complex( real - operand2.real,
28        imaginary - operand2.imaginary );
```

Fig. L 8.17   Contents of **complex.cpp**. (Part 1 of 2.)

Postlab Activities   Name:

Programming Challenges

```
29
30   } // end function operator-
31
32   // overloaded = operator
33   const Complex& Complex::operator=( const Complex &right )
34   {
35      real = right.real;
36      imaginary = right.imaginary;
37      return *this;
38
39   } // end function operator=
40
41   // display Complex object in form: (a, b)
42   void Complex::print() const
43   {
44      cout << '(' << real << ", " << imaginary << ')';
45
46   } // end function print
```

Fig. L 8.17   Contents of **complex.cpp**. (Part 2 of 2.)

Hints:

* When overloading the stream-extraction operator, use the **ignore** member function of the class **istream**. See Fig. 8.3 of *C++ How to Program: Fourth Edition* for an example.

* When overloading the assignment operator, return the **this** pointer to enable cascading.

* Overloaded **<<** and **>>** should be **friend** functions.

* All other overloaded operator functions should be **const** member functions.

Postlab Activities   Name:

Programming Challenges

Object-Oriented Programming: Inheritance

Objectives

- To understand a form of software reusability called inheritance, in which new classes are created from existing classes by absorbing their attributes and behaviors.
- To create new classes by inheriting from existing classes.
- To understand the notions of base classes and derived classes. A base class is the class from which another class (called the derived class) inherits data members and member functions.
- To understand the different types of inheritance (**public**, **protected** and **private**) and to know when to use each type.
- To use constructors and destructors in derived classes.
- To redefine base-class member functions in a derived class. A derived class can redefine a base-class member function by supplying a new version of that member function with the same signature.

Assignment Checklist

Name: _____   **Date:** _____

Section: _____

Exercises	Assigned: Circle assignments	Date Due
Prelab Activities		
Matching	YES NO	
Fill in the Blank	11, 12, 13, 14, 15, 16, 17, 18, 19, 20, 21, 22	
Short Answer	23, 24, 25, 26, 27, 28, 29	
Programming Output	30, 31	
Correct the Code	32, 33, 34, 35	
Lab Exercises		
Lab Exercise 1 — Cars	YES NO	
Follow-Up Questions and Activities	1, 2, 3, 4	
Lab Exercise 2 — Vehicles	YES NO	
Follow-Up Questions and Activities	1, 2, 3	
Debugging	YES NO	
Labs Provided by Instructor		
1.		
2.		
3.		
Postlab Activities		
Coding Exercises	1, 2, 3, 4, 5	
Programming Challenge	6	

Assignment Checklist

Name:

Prelab Activities

Matching

Name: _____   Date:_____

Section: _____

After reading Chapter 9 of *C++ How to Program: Fourth Edition*, answer the given questions. These questions are intended to test and reinforce your understanding of key concepts and may be done either before the lab or during the lab.

For each term in the column on the left, write the corresponding letter for the description that best matches it from the column on the right.

Term	Description
_____ 1. Inheritance	a) Class from which others are derived.
_____ 2. Abstraction	b) Deriving from more than one base class.
_____ 3. Derived class	c) Class that is created from an existing class.
_____ 4. "Has a" relationship	d) Refers to inheritance.
_____ 5. "Is a" relationship	e) Assigning derived-class pointers to base-class pointers.
_____ 6. Single inheritance	f) Base class that is not listed explicitly in the derived class's definition.
_____ 7. Base class	g) "Seeing the forest through the trees."
_____ 8. Indirect base class	h) Refers to composition.
_____ 9. Upcasting a pointer	i) Deriving from only one base class.
_____ 10. Multiple inheritance	j) A form of software reusability in which new classes are created from existing classes.

Prelab Activities

Name:

Matching

Prelab Activities   Name:

Fill in the Blank

Name: _____   **Date:**_____

Section: _____

Fill in the blank for each of the following statements:

11. Inheritance promotes software _____.

12. The programmer can designate that the new class is to _____ the data members and member functions of a previously defined base class.

13. A base class's **protected** members may be accessed by members and _____ of the base class and by members and **friend**s of the _____ class.

14. With _____ inheritance, a class is derived from only one base class.

15. A derived class cannot access the _____ members of its base class; allowing such access would violate the _____ of the base class.

16. A derived class' constructor always calls the constructor of its _____ first.

17. Destructors are called in _____ order of constructor calls. Therefore, a derived-class destructor is called _____ its base-class destructor.

18. The three forms of inheritance are _____, _____ and _____.

19. With **private** inheritance, **public** and **protected** members of the base class become _____ members of the derived class.

20. A(n) _____ base class is not explicitly listed in the derived-class definition; rather, it is inherited from several levels up the class hierarchy tree.

21. A pointer to a derived-class object can be cast implicitly to a(n) _____ pointer.

22. **friend**s, _____ and _____ are not inherited into derived classes.

Prelab Activities

Name:

Fill in the Blank

Prelab Activities   Name:

Short Answer

Name: _____   Date:_____

Section: _____

In the space provided, answer each of the given questions. Your answers should be as concise as possible; aim for two or three sentences.

23. How does inheritance promote software reusability?

24. What is **protected** access?

25. What is the difference between single and multiple inheritance?

26. What is the difference between direct and indirect base classes?

Prelab Activities

Name:

Short Answer

27. What is the sequence of events that takes place when a derived-class object is destroyed. (That is, in what order are the destructors fired, and why?)

28. What are the primary differences between **public**, **private** and **protected** inheritance?

29. What is meant by redefining a base-class member? How does this process differ from function overloading?

Prelab Activities

Name:

Programming Output

Name: _____ Date: _____

Section: _____

For each of the given program segments, read the code and write the output in the space provided below each program. [*Note*: Do not execute these programs on a computer.]

30. What is output by the given program? Assume the use of the **Point** and **Circle** classes presented in Fig. 9.4, Fig. 9.5, Fig. 9.7 and Fig. 9.8 of C++ *How to Program: Fourth Edition*.

```
1   #include <iostream>
2
3   using std::cout;
4   using std::endl;
5
6   #include "point.h"
7   #include "circle.h"
8
9   int main()
10  {
11      Point p( 8, 14 );
12      p.print();
13      cout << endl;
14
15      Circle circle( 9.9, 10, 22 );
16      circle.print();
17      cout << endl;
18
19      return 0;
20
21  } // end main
```

Your answer:

Prelab Activities

Name:

Programming Output

31. What is output by the given program? Assume the use of **Point3**, **Circle4** and **Cylinder** classes from Section 9.5 of *C++ How to Program: Fourth Edition.*

```
1   #include <iostream>
2
3   using std::cout;
4   using std::endl;
5
6   #include <iomanip>
7
8   #include "point3.h"
9   #include "circle4.h"
10  #include "cylinder.h"
11
12  int main()
13  {
14      Point3 p( 1, 2 );
15      Circle4 c4( -5, -12, 53 );
16      Cylinder c( 44, 98, 6.125, 26 );
17
18      c4.print();
19      cout << endl;
20
21      p.print();
22      cout << endl;
23
24      cout << "Radius = " << c.getRadius()
25           << " "
26           << "Height = " << c.getHeight()
27           << endl;
28
29      return 0;
30
31  } // end main
```

Your answer:

Prelab Activities   Name: _____

Correct the Code

Name: _____   Date:_____

Section: _____

For each of the given program segments, determine if there is an error in the code. If there is an error, specify whether it is a logic error or a syntax error, circle the error in the program, and write the corrected code in the space provided after each problem. If the code does not contain an error, write "no error." [*Note*: It is possible that a program segment may contain multiple errors.]

32. Class **X** inherits from class **Y**.

```
1    #include <iostream>
2
3    using std::cout;
4
5    // class Y definition
6    class Y {
7
8    public:
9
10       // default constructor
11       Y();
12
13       // destructor
14       ~Y();
15
16    private:
17       int data;
18
19    }; // end class Y
20
21    // class X definition
22    class X ; public Y {
23
24    public:
25
26       // function print
27       void print() const
28       {
29          cout << data;
30
31       } // end function print
32
33    }; // end class X
```

Your answer:

Prelab Activities

Name:

Correct the Code

33. The given code should construct a **Derived** object.

```cpp
1   #include <iostream>
2
3   using std::cout;
4
5   // class Base definition
6   class Base {
7
8   private:
9
10     // constructor
11     Base( int b )
12     {
13        cout << b;
14
15     } // end class Base constructor
16
17  }; // end class Base
18
19  // class Derived definition
20  class Derived : public Base {
21
22     // constructor calls base-class constructor
23     Derived( int a ) : Base( a )
24     {
25        // empty
26
27     } // end class Derived constructor
28
29  }; // end class Derived
30
31  int main()
32  {
33     Derived d( 5 );
34
35     return 0;
36
37  } // end main
```

Your answer:

Prelab Activities

Name:

Correct the Code

34. The given code creates an object of type **B**. Class **B** inherits from class **A**.

```cpp
1    #include <iostream>
2
3    using std::cout;
4
5    // class A definition
6    class A {
7
8    public:
9
10       // constructor
11       A( int a )
12       {
13          value = a;
14
15       } // end class A constructor
16
17       // return value
18       int getValue() const
19       {
20          return value;
21
22       } // end function getValue
23
24    private:
25       int value;
26
27    }; // end class A
28
29    // class B definition
30    class B {
31
32    public:
33
34       // constructor
35       B( int b ) : A( b )
36       {
37          // empty
38
39       } // end class B constructor
40
41    }; // end class B
42
43    int main()
44    {
45       B object( 50 );
46       cout << object.getValue();
47
48       return 0;
49
50    } // end main
```

Your answer:

Prelab Activities

Name:

Correct the Code

35. The given code creates an object of type **Y**. Class **Y** inherits from class **X**.

```cpp
1   #include <iostream>
2
3   using std::cout;
4
5   // class X definition
6   class X {
7
8   public:
9
10     // constructor
11     X()
12     {
13        cout << "X constructed!";
14
15     } // end class X constructor
16
17   }; // end class X
18
19   // class Y definition
20   class Y {
21
22   public:
23
24     // redefine inherited constructor
25     X()
26     {
27        cout << "Y created, not X!";
28
29     } // end class Y constructor
30
31   }; // end class Y
32
33   int main()
34   {
35      Y yObject();
36
37      return 0;
38
39   } // end main
```

Your answer:

Lab Exercises

Lab Exercise 1 — Cars

Name: _____   Date:_____

Section: _____

This problem is intended to be solved in a closed-lab session with a teaching assistant or instructor present. The problem is divided into six parts:

1. Lab Objectives

2. Description of the Problem

3. Sample Output

4. Program Template (Fig. L 9.1–Fig. L 9.5)

5. Problem-Solving Tips

6. Follow-Up Questions and Activities

The program template represents a complete working C++ program, with one or more key lines of code replaced with comments. Read the problem description and examine the sample output; then study the template code. Using the problem-solving tips as a guide, replace the **/* */** comments with C++ code. Compile and execute the program. Compare your output with the sample output provided. Then answer the follow-up questions. The source code for the template is available at **www.deitel.com** and **www.prenhall.com./deitel**.

Lab Objectives

This lab was designed to reinforce programming concepts from Chapter 9 of *C++ How To Program: Fourth Edition*. In this lab, you will practice:

- using inheritance to create a vehicle hierarchy that includes a **Car** class and a **Racecar** class.

- using **private** data members to limit access to data members to derived classes and their **friend**s.

- redefining base-class member functions in a derived class.

The follow-up questions and activities also will give you practice:

- differentiating between **public**, **private** and **protected** inheritance.

- calling member functions defined in the base-class and redefined in the derived-class.

- using the scope resolution operator to refer to a data member or to a member function explicitly.

Description of the Problem

Develop a class **Racecar** that inherits **public**ly from class **Car**, which represents a car by its maximum speed, the number of engine valves, its color and its name. A **Racecar** is distinguished by its gearbox (the number of gears it has), its sponsor and the presence of a parachute.

Lab Exercises   Name:

Lab Exercise 1 — Cars

Sample Output

```
chevy:
Car: Chevrolette is black and has a 4-valve engine. MAX SPEED = 95 mph.


f1:
Car: Ferrari is red and has a 40-valve engine. MAX SPEED = 220 mph.
Ferrari also has 7 gears and is sponsored by Bug2Bug.
Ferrari has used its parachute.
```

Template

```cpp
1   // Chapter 9 of C++ How to Program
2   // car.h
3   #ifndef CAR_H
4   #define CAR_H
5
6   #include <iostream>
7
8   #include <string>
9
10  using std::string;
11
12  // class Car definition
13  class Car {
14
15  public:
16     Car( string name, string color );
17
18     void setMaxSpeed( int );
19     int getMaxSpeed() const;
20
21     void setEngineValves( int );
22     int getEngineValves() const
23
24     string getColor() const;
25     string getName() const;
26
27     void print() const;
28
29  private:
30     int maxSpeed;
31     int engineValves;
32     string color;
33     string name;
34
35  }; // end class Car
36
37  #endif // CAR_H
```

Fig. L 9.1   Contents of **car.h**.

Lab Exercises   Name: _____

Lab Exercise 1 — Cars

```cpp
1   // Chapter 9 of C++ How to Program
2   // car.cpp
3   #include <iostream>
4
5   using std::cout;
6   using std::endl;
7
8   #include "car.h"
9
10  /* Write the constructor for Car, which takes the Car's name and
11     color and assigns them to private data members name and
12     color; initialize maxSpeed to 95 and engineValves to 4 */
13
14  // function setMaxSpeed definition
15  void Car::setMaxSpeed( int s )
16  {
17     maxSpeed = ( ( s >= 0 && s < 250 ) ? s : 40 );
18
19  } // end function setMaxSpeed
20
21  // function setEngineValves definition
22  void Car::setEngineValves( int v )
23  {
24     engineValves = ( ( v >= 0 && v < 50 ) ? v : 4 );
25
26  } // end function setEngineValves
27
28  // return maxSpeed
29  int Car::getMaxSpeed() const
30  {
31     return maxSpeed;
32
33  } // end function getMaxSpeed
34
35  // return engineValves
36  int Car::getEngineValves() const
37  {
38     return engineValves;
39
40  } // end function getEngineValves
41
42  // return name
43  string Car::getName() const
44  {
45     return name;
46
47  } // end function getName
48
49  // return color
50  string Car::getColor() const
51  {
52     return color;
53
54  } // end function getColor
55
```

Fig. L 9.2   Contents of `car.cpp`. (Part 1 of 2.)

Lab Exercises   Name:

Lab Exercise 1 — Cars

```
56   // function print definition
57   void Car::print() const
58   {
59      cout << "Car: " << name << " is " << color << " and has a "
60           << engineValves << "-valve engine. MAX SPEED = "
61           << maxSpeed << " mph. " << endl;
62
63   } // end function print
```

Fig. L 9.2   Contents of **car.cpp**. (Part 2 of 2.)

```
1    // Chapter 9 of C++ How to Program
2    // racecar.h
3    #ifndef RACECAR_H
4    #define RACECAR_H
5
6    #include "car.h"
7
8    // class Racecar definition
9    /* Write class header for Racecar, which inherits publicly
10      from Car */
11
12   public:
13      Racecar( string, string, string );
14
15      void setGearbox( int );
16      void useParachute();
17      void print() const;
18
19   private:
20      int gearbox; // number of gears in car (e.g., 5-speed)
21      string sponsor;
22      bool parachuteDeployed;
23
24   }; // end class Racecar
25
26   #endif // RACECAR_H
```

Fig. L 9.3   Contents of **racecar.h**.

```
1    // Chapter 9 of C++ How to Program
2    // racecar.cpp
3    #include <iostream>
4
5    using std::cout;
6    using std::endl;
7
8    #include "racecar.h"
9
```

Fig. L 9.4   Contents of **racecar.cpp**. (Part 1 of 2.)

Lab Exercises

Name:

Lab Exercise 1 — Cars

```
10  // constructor
11  Racecar::Racecar( string n, string c, string s )
12     /* Write code to call base-class constructor */
13  {
14     /* Write code to copy s into private data member sponsor */
15
16     gearbox = 6;
17     parachuteDeployed = false;
18
19  } // end class Racecar constructor
20
21  // function setGearbox definition
22  void Racecar::setGearbox( int gears )
23  {
24     gearbox = ( ( gears <= 10 && gears >= 0 ) ? gears : 6 );
25
26  } // end function setGearbox
27
28  // function useParachute definition
29  void Racecar::useParachute()
30  }
31     parachuteDeployed = true;
32
33  } // end function useParachute
34
35  // function print definition
36  void Racecar::print() const
37  {
38     /* Write statement that calls base-class member function print here */
39     cout << getName() << " also has " << gearbox
40        << " gears and is sponsored by " << sponsor << ". ";
41
42     if ( parachuteDeployed )
43       cout << /* Write statement that accesses base-class version of name here */
44            << " has used its parachute." << endl;
45     else
46       cout << /* Write statement that accesses base-class version of name here */ ;
47            << " has not used its parachute." << endl;
48
49  } // end function print
```

Fig. L 9.4 Contents of `racecar.cpp`. (Part 2 of 2.)

```
1   // Chapter 9 of C++ How to Program
2   // driver for race car and car
3   #include <iostream>
4
5   using std::cout;
6   using std::endl;
7
8   #include "car.h"
9   #include "racecar.h"
10
11  int main()
12  {
```

Fig. L 9.5 Contents of `driver.cpp`. (Part 1 of 2.)

Lab Exercises   Name:

Lab Exercise 1 — Cars

```
13        Car chevy( "Chevrolette", "black" );
14
15        cout << "chevy: \n";
16        /* Write code to print Car object */
17
18        Racecar f1( "Ferrari", "red", "Bug2Bug" );
19
20        f1.setEngineValves( 40 );
21        f1.setMaxSpeed( 220 );
22        f1.setGearbox( 7 );
23        f1.useParachute();
24
25        cout << "\n\nf1: \n";
26        f1.print();
27
28        return 0;
29
30    } // end main
```

Fig. L 9.5   Contents of `driver.cpp`. (Part 2 of 2.)

Problem-Solving Tip

1. The **Racecar** constructor should call the constructor of **Car** explicitly.

Follow-Up Questions and Activities

1. What happens if **Car**'s data members are specified as **protected** instead of **private**?

2. Could **Racecar** have been derived from **Car** using **protected** inheritance? What about **private** inheritance?

Lab Exercises   Name:

Lab Exercise 1 — Cars

3. Is it possible to call class **Car**'s **print** member function via a **Racecar** object? How does the compiler determine which **print** member function to use?

4. Why is it necessary for **Racecar**'s **print** member function to use **getName()** to print the name of the racecar?

Lab Exercises

Name:

Lab Exercise 1 — Cars

Lab Exercises   Name:

Lab Exercise 2 — Vehicles

Name: _____   **Date:**_____

Section: _____

This problem is intended to be solved in a closed-lab session with a teaching assistant or instructor present. The problem is divided into six parts:

1. Lab Objectives
2. Description of the Problem
3. Sample Output
4. Program Template (Fig. L 9.6–Fig. L 9.11)
5. Problem-Solving Tips
6. Follow-Up Questions and Activities

The program template represents a complete working C++ program, with one or more key lines of code replaced with comments. Read the problem description and examine the sample output; then study the template code. Using the problem-solving tips as a guide, replace the **/* */** comments with C++ code. Compile and execute the program. Compare your output with the sample output provided. Then answer the follow-up questions. The source code for the template is available at **www.deitel.com** and **www.prenhall.com/deitel**.

Lab Objectives

This lab was designed to reinforce programming concepts from Chapter 9 of *C++ How To Program: Fourth Edition*. In this lab, you will practice:

- using inheritance to develop a vehicle class hierarchy that contains the classes **Vehicle**, **Taxi** and **Truck**.
- creating classes that **public**ly inherit information from other classes.
- using **friend** functions with inherited classes.
- redefining base-class member functions in a derived class.

The follow-up questions and activities also will give you practice:

- understanding extensibility through inheritance.
- diagramming class hierarchies.

Description of the Problem

Develop a class hierarchy of **Vehicle**s. Create two classes, **Taxi** and **Truck**, that inherit **public**ly from class **Vehicle**. A **Taxi** should contain a data member that indicates whether it is carrying passengers. A **Truck** should contain a data member that indicates whether it is carrying cargo. Add the necessary member functions to manipulate and access class data. Write a driver that prints a **Truck** object and a **Taxi** object to the screen (using an overloaded stream-insertion operator).

Lab Exercises

Name: _____

Lab Exercise 2 — Vehicles

Sample Output

```
Vehicle
        Number of doors: 2
        Number of cylinders: 6
        Transmission type: 3
        Color: blue
        Fuel level: 14.6

Taxi
        Number of doors: 4
        Number of cylinders: 6
        Transmission type: 5
        Color: yellow
        Fuel level: 3.3
        The taxi currently has no customers.

Truck
        Number of doors: 2
        Number of cylinders: 16
        Transmission type: 8
        Color: black
        Fuel level: 7.54
        The truck is currently carrying cargo.

New color is: red
New fuel level is: 4.9
```

Template

```cpp
1   // Chapter 9 of C++ How to Program
2   // vehicle.h
3   #ifndef VEHICLE_H
4   #define VEHICLE_H
5
6   #include <iostream>
7
8   using std::ostream;
9
10  #include <string>
11
12  using std::string;
13
14  // class Vehicle definition
15  class Vehicle {
16      friend ostream& operator<<( ostream &, const Vehicle & );
17
```

Fig. L 9.6   Contents of **vehicle.h**. (Part 1 of 2.)

Lab Exercises　　　　　　　　　　　　　　Name:

Lab Exercise 2 — Vehicles

```
18  public:
19     Vehicle( const int, const int, string, double, const int );
20
21     void setColor( string );
22     string getColor() const;
23
24     void setFuelLevel( double );
25     double getFuelLevel() const;
26
27     void setClassName( string );
28     string getClassName() const;
29
30     int getTransmissionType() const;
31     int getNumberOfDoors() const;
32     int getNumberOfCylinders() const;
33
34  private:
35     const int numberOfDoors;
36     const int numberOfCylinders;
37     string vehicleColor;
38     double fuelLevel;
39     const int transmissionType;
40     string className;
41
42  }; // end class Vehicle
43
44  #endif // VEHICLE_H
```

Fig. L 9.6　　Contents of **vehicle.h**. (Part 2 of 2.)

```
1   // Chapter 9 of C++ How to Program
2   // vehicle.cpp
3   #include <iostream>
4
5   using std::cout;
6   using std::endl;
7
8   #include "vehicle.h"
9
10  // constructor
11  Vehicle::Vehicle( const int doors, const int cylinders,
12     string color, double initialFuel,
13     const int transmission )
14     /* Write the body for Vehicle's constructor */
15
16  } // end class Vehicle constructor
17
18  // function operator<< definition
19  ostream &operator<<( ostream &out, const Vehicle &v )
20  {
```

Fig. L 9.7　　Contents of **vehicle.cpp**. (Part 1 of 3.)

Lab Exercises

Name: _____

Lab Exercise 2 — Vehicles

```
21      out << v.className << "\n"
22          << "\tNumber of doors: " << v.numberOfDoors
23          << "\n\tNumber of cylinders: " << v.numberOfCylinders
24          << "\n\tTransmission type: " << v.transmissionType
25          << "\n\tColor: " << v.vehicleColor
26          << "\n\tFuel level: " << v.fuelLevel << endl;
27
28      return out;
29
30  } // end function operator<<
31
32  /* Write definition for setColor */
33
34  // function setFuelLevel definition
35  void Vehicle::setFuelLevel( double amount )
36  {
37      // assume 20 gallons is full tank
38      if ( amount > 0.0 && amount <= 20.0 )
39          fuelLevel = amount;
40
41      else
42          fuelLevel = 5.0;
43
44  } // end function setFuelLevel
45
46  // return color
47  string Vehicle::getColor() const
48  {
49      return vehicleColor;
50
51  } // end function getColor
52
53  // return fuelLevel
54  double Vehicle::getFuelLevel() const
55  {
56      return fuelLevel;
57
58  } // end function getFuelLevel
59
60  // return transmissionType
61  int Vehicle::getTransmissionType() const
62  {
63      return transmissionType;
64
65  } // end function getTransmissionType
66
67  // return numberOfDoors
68  int Vehicle::getNumberOfDoors() const
69  {
70      return numberOfDoors;
71
72  } // end function getNumberOfDoors
73
74  // return numberOfCylinders
75  int Vehicle::getNumberOfCylinders() const
76  {
```

Fig. L 9.7   Contents of **vehicle.cpp**. (Part 2 of 3.)

Lab Exercises   Name:

Lab Exercise 2 — Vehicles

```
77      return numberOfCylinders;
78
79  } // end function getNumberOfCylinders
80
81  // function setClassName definition
82  void Vehicle::setClassName( string newName )
83  {
84      className = newName;
85
86  } // end function setClassName
87
88  // return className
89  string Vehicle::getClassName() const
90  {
91      return className;
92
93  } // end function getClassName
```

Fig. L 9.7   Contents of **vehicle.cpp**. (Part 3 of 3.)

```
1   // Chapter 9 of C++ How to Program
2   // taxi.h
3   #ifndef TAXI_H
4   #define TAXI_H
5
6   #include <iostream>
7
8   #include "vehicle.h"
9
10  // class Taxi definition
11  class Taxi : public Vehicle {
12      friend ostream& operator<<( ostream &, const Taxi & );
13
14  public:
15      Taxi( double );
16      /* Write prototype for hasCustomers */
17      /* Write prototype for setCustomers */
18
19  private:
20      bool customers;
21
22  }; // end class Taxi
23
24  #endif // TAXI_H
```

Fig. L 9.8   Contents of **taxi.h**.

```
1   // Chapter 9 of C++ How to Program
2   // taxi.cpp
3   #include "taxi.h"
4
```

Contents of **taxi.cpp**. (Part 1 of 2.)

Lab Exercises   Name:

Lab Exercise 2 — Vehicles

```
5   // constructor
6   Taxi::Taxi( double f )
7       : Vehicle( 4, 6, "yellow", f, 5 )
8   {
9       customers = false;
10      setClassName( "Taxi" );
11
12  } // end class Taxi constructor
13
14  /* Write definition for setCustomers */
15
16  /* Write definition for hasCustomers */
17
18  // function operator<< definition
19  ostream &operator<<( ostream &output, const Taxi &t )
20  {
21      output << t.getClassName() << "\n"
22              << "\tNumber of doors: "
23              << t.getNumberOfDoors()
24              << "\n\tNumber of cylinders: "
25              << t.getNumberOfCylinders()
26              << "\n\tTransmission type: "
27              << t.getTransmissionType()
28              << "\n\tColor: " << t.getColor()
29              << "\n\tFuel level: "
30              << t.getFuelLevel() << "\n";
31
32      if ( /* Write statement to check if there are passengers */ )
33          output << "\tThe taxi has passengers.\n";
34
35      else
36          output << "\tThe taxi has no passengers.\n";
37
38      return output;
39
40  } // end function operator
```

Contents of **taxi.cpp**. (Part 2 of 2.)

```
1   // Chapter 9 of C++ How to Program
2   // truck.h
3
4   /* Write contents of truck.h, which defines class Truck */
5
```

Fig. L 9.9   Contents of **truck.h**.

```
1   // Chapter 9 of C++ How to Program
2   // truck.cpp
3   #include "truck.h"
4
5   /* Write definition for class Truck's constructor */
6
```

Fig. L 9.10   Contents of **truck.cpp**. (Part 1 of 2.)

Lab Exercises

Name:

Lab Exercise 2 — Vehicles

```cpp
 7    // function hasCargo definition
 8    bool Truck::hasCargo() const
 9    {
10       return cargo;
11
12    } // end function hasCargo
13
14    // function setCargo definition
15    void Truck::setCargo( bool c )
16    {
17       cargo = c;
18
19    } // end function setCargo
20
21    // function operator<< definition
22    ostream &operator<<( ostream &output, const Truck &t )
23    {
24       output << t.getClassName() << "\n"
25              << "\tNumber of doors: "
26              << t.getNumberOfDoors()
27              << "\n\tNumber of cylinders: "
28              << t.getNumberOfCylinders()
29              << "\n\tTransmission type: "
30              << t.getTransmissionType()
31              << "\n\tColor: " << t.getColor()
32              << "\n\tFuel level: "
33              << t.getFuelLevel() << "\n";
34
35       if ( t.cargo )
36          output << "\tThe truck is carrying cargo.\n";
37
38       else
39          output << "\tThe truck is not carrying cargo.\n";
40
41       return output;
42
43    } // end function operator<<
```

Fig. L 9.10　　Contents of **truck.cpp**. (Part 2 of 2.)

```cpp
 1    // Chapter 9 of C++ How to Program
 2    // driver for inheritance hierarchy
 3    #include <iostream>
 4
 5    using std::cout;
 6    using std::endl;
 7
 8    #include "vehicle.h"
 9    #include "taxi.h"
10    #include "truck.h"
11
12    int main()
13    {
14       Vehicle car( 2, 6, "blue", 14.6, 3 );
15       Taxi cab( 3.3 );
```

Fig. L 9.11　　Contents of **driver.cpp**. (Part 1 of 2.)

Lab Exercises   Name:

Lab Exercise 2 — Vehicles

```
16    Truck mack( 7.54 );
17
18    /* Write code to indicate that mack is carrying cargo */
19
20    /* Write code to print all objects in the Vehicle
21       hierarchy */
22
23    return 0;
24
25  } // end main
```

Fig. L 9.11   Contents of `driver.cpp`. (Part 2 of 2.)

Problem-Solving Tips

1. Use a colon (:) to initialize **const** data members in the constructor for **Vehicle**.

2. Use the member definition file for **Truck** when writing class **Truck**.

Follow-Up Questions and Activities

1. Write the header file for derived-class **MonsterTruck**, which inherits from class **Truck**. Include a **private** data member **truckName** to store the **MonsterTruck**'s show name.

2. Create an additional constructor for the **Truck** class that takes five arguments: number of doors, number of cylinders, transmission type, color and fuel level. Instantiate a blue **Truck** with two doors, 16 cylinders, transmission type 2 and fuel level 20.

Lab Exercises   Name:

Lab Exercise 2 — Vehicles

3. Draw a class hierarchy of all the following modes of transportation: Transportation, Motorcycle, Horse, Car, 747 airplane, Motor boat, Train, Freight train, Harley, Station wagon, Dump truck, Pickup truck, Cruise ship, Jet, Boat, Plane, Speed boat, Passenger train, Animal, Donkey, Bike, Truck and Mountain bike.

Lab Exercises   Name:

Lab Exercise 2 — Vehicles

Lab Exercises   Name:

Debugging

Name: _____   **Date:** _____

Section: _____

The program (Fig. L 9.12–Fig. L 9.18) in this section does not run properly. Fix all the syntax errors so that the program will compile successfully. Once the program compiles, compare the output with the sample output, and eliminate any logic errors that may exist. The sample output demonstrates what the program's output should be once the program's code has been corrected.

Sample Output

```
This animal's height and weight are as follows
Height: 0         Weight: 0

This animal is a dog, its name is: Fido
This animal's height and weight are as follows
Height: 60        Weight: 120

This animal is a dog, its name is: Toto
This animal's height and weight are as follows
Height: 0         Weight: 0

This animal is a lion
This animal's height and weight are as follows
Height: 45        Weight: 300

Animal 1 now has the same height and weight as Dog 1
This animal's height and weight are as follows
Height: 60        Weight: 120

Dog 2 now has the same height and weight as animal 1
This animal is a dog, its name is: Toto
This animal's height and weight are as follows
Height: 60        Weight: 120
```

Broken Code

```cpp
1   // Chapter 9 of C++ How to Program
2   // Debugging Problem (animal.h)
3
4   #ifndef ANIMAL_H
5   #define ANIMAL_H
6
7   #include <string>
8
9   using std::string;
10
```

Fig. L 9.12   Contents of **animal.h**. (Part 1 of 2.)

Lab Exercises   Name:

Debugging

```
11   // class Animal definition
12   class Animal {
13
14   public:
15      Animal( const int = 0, const int = 0 );
16
17      void setHeight( int );
18      int getHeight() const;
19
20      void setWeight( int );
21      int getWeight() const;
22
23      string getName() const;
24      void print() const;
25
26   private:
27      int height;
28      int weight;
29
30   }; // end class Animal
31
32   #endif // ANIMAL_H
```

Fig. L 9.12   Contents of **animal.h**. (Part 2 of 2.)

```
1    // Chapter 9 of C++ How to Program
2    // Debugging Problem (animal.cpp)
3
4    #include <iostream>
5
6    using std::cout;
7    using std::endl;
8
9    #include "animal.h"
10
11   // default constructor
12   Animal::Animal( const int h, const int w )
13   {
14      height = h;
15      weight = w;
16
17   } // end class Animal constructor
18
19   // function print definition
20   void Animal::print() const
21   {
22      cout << "This animal's height and weight are as follows\n"
23           << "Height: " << height << "\tWeight: " << weight
24           << endl << endl;
25
26   } // end function print
27
28   // return height
29   int Animal::getHeight() const
30   {
31      return height;
```

Fig. L 9.13   Contents of **animal.cpp**. (Part 1 of 2.)

Lab Exercises   Name:

Debugging

```
32
33   } // end function getHeight
34
35   // return weight
36   int Animal::getWeight() const
37   {
38      return weight;
39
40   } // end function getWeight
41
42   // function print definition
43   void Animal::setHeight( const int h )
44   {
45      height = h;
46
47   } // end function setHeight
48
49   // function print definition
50   void Animal::setWeight( const int w )
51   {
52      weight = w;
53
54   } // end function setWeight
55
56   // return name
57   string Animal::getName() const
58   {
59      return name;
60
61   } // end function getName
```

Fig. L 9.13   Contents of **animal.cpp**. (Part 2 of 2.)

```
1    // Chapter 9 of C++ How to Program
2    // Debugging Problem (lion.h)
3
4    #ifndef LION_H
5    #define LION_H
6
7    #include "animal.h"
8
9    // class Lion definition
10   class Lion {
11
12   public:
13      Lion( const int = 0, const int = 0 );
14
15      void print() const;
16
17   }; // end class Lion
18
19   #endif // LION_H
```

Fig. L 9.14   Contents of **lion.h**.

Lab Exercises   Name: _____

Debugging

```cpp
1   // Chapter 9 of C++ How to Program
2   // Debugging Problem (lion.cpp)
3
4   #include <iostream>
5
6   using std::cout;
7   using std::endl;
8
9   #include "lion.h"
10
11  // default constructor
12  Lion::Lion( const int h, const int w )
13     : Animal( h, w )
14  {
15     // empty
16
17  } // end class Lion constructor
18
19  // function print definition
20  void Lion::print() const
21  {
22     cout << "This animal is a lion\n";
23     print();
24
25  } // end function print
```

Fig. L 9.15   Contents of `lion.cpp`.

```cpp
1   // Chapter 9 of C++ How to Program
2   // Debugging Problem (dog.h)
3
4   #ifndef DOG_H
5   #define DOG_H
6
7   #include "animal.h"
8
9   // class Dog definition
10  class Dog : public Animal {
11
12  public:
13     Dog( const int, const int, string = "Toto" );
14
15     void Print() const;
16     void setName( string );
17
18  private:
19     string name;
20
21  }; // end class Dog
22
23  #endif // DOG_H
```

Fig. L 9.16   Contents of `dog.h`.

Lab Exercises   Name:

Debugging

```
1   // Chapter 9 of C++ How to Program
2   // Debugging Problem (dog.cpp)
3
4   #include <iostream>
5
6   using std::cout;
7   using std::endl;
8
9   #include "Dog.h"
10
11  // constructor
12  Dog::Dog( const int h, const int w, string n )
13     : Animal( h, w )
14  {
15     setName( n );
16
17  } // end class Dog constructor
18
19  // function setName definition
20  void Dog::setName( const char * n )
21  {
22     n = name;
23
24  } // end function setName
25
26  // function print definition
27  void Dog::Print() const
28  {
29     cout << "This animal is a dog, its name is: " << name << endl;
30
31     print();
32
33  } // end function print
```

Fig. L 9.17   Contents of **dog.cpp**.

```
1   // Chapter 9 of C++ How to Program
2   // Debugging Problem (debugging09.cpp)
3
4   #include <iostream>
5
6   using std::cout;
7   using std::endl;
8
9   #include "animal.h"
10  #include "lion.h"
11
12  int main()
13  {
14     Animal a1( 0, 0 );
15     Dog d1( 60, 120, "Fido" );
16     Dog d2;
17     Lion lion1( 45, 300 );
18
```

Fig. L 9.18   Contents of **debugging09.cpp**. (Part 1 of 2.)

Lab Exercises

Name:

Debugging

```
19      a1.print();
20      d1.print();
21      d2.print();
22      lion1.print();
23
24      a1 = d1;
25      cout << "Animal 1 now has the same height and weight "
26          << "as dog 1\n";
27      a1.print();
28
29      d2 = a1;
30      cout << "Dog 2 now has the same height and weight as animal 1\n"
31      d2.print();
32
33      return 0;
34
35   } // end main
```

Fig. L 9.18   Contents of **debugging09.cpp**. (Part 2 of 2.)

Postlab Activities

Coding Exercises

Name: _____   **Date:** _____

Section: _____

These coding exercises reinforce the lessons learned in the lab and provide additional programming experience outside the classroom and laboratory environment. They serve as a review after you have completed the Prelab Activities and Lab Exercises successfully.

For each of the following problems, write a program or a program segment that performs the specified action:

1. Write the header file for class **Base1**, then, write the header file for class **Derived**, which inherits **publicly** from class **Base1**. Do not provide any class members for either class.

2. Change the class definition so that **protected** inheritance is used.

Postlab Activities   Name:

Coding Exercises

3. Write a **print** member function for **Base1** that prints a string and an integer (values stored in **private** data members), separated by a hyphen (-). Name the **private** data members any way you wish.

4. Redefine the **print** member function in class **Derived**. This member function should print a string and a **double** (values stored in **private** data members), separated by a colon and a space. Name the **private** data members any way you wish.

5. Create a header file for class **Derived2** which inherits from class **Derived publicly**. Do not provide any class members for **Derived2**.

Postlab Activities   Name: _____

Programming Challenges

Name: _____   Date:_____

Section: _____

The Programming Challenges are more involved than the Coding Exercises and may require a significant amount of time to complete. Write a C++ program for each of the problems in this section. The answers to these problems are available at **www.deitel.com**, **www.prenhall.com/deitel** and on the *C++ Multimedia Cyber Classroom: Fourth Edition*. Pseudocode, hints and/or sample outputs are provided to aid you in your programming.

6. Rewrite the **Point**, **Circle**, **Cylinder** program of Section 9.5 of *C++ How to Program: Fourth Edition* as a **Point**, **Square**, **Cube** program. Do this task in two ways—once with inheritance and once with composition.

Hints:

*   Follow Figs. 9.17–9.20 and Figs. 9.22–9.23 of *C++ How to Program: Fourth Edition*.

*   A **Square** is just a **Point** and a **side**. It should include member functions for getting and setting the **side** as well as calculating the area.

*   A **Cube** is a **Square** extended into three dimensions. It requires no additional data members. Redefine the calculation of the area to calculate the surface area and add a member function to calculate the volume. The surface area can be calculated with the formula *side * side * 6*, and the volume may be calculated with the formula *side * side * side*.

*   The output of the program should resemble the following:

```
The point is: [7.90, 12.50, 8.80]

The lower left coordinate of the square is: [0.00, 0.00, 0.00]
The square side is: 5.00
The area of the square is: 25.00

The lower left coordinate of the cube is: [0.50, 8.30, 12.00]
The cube side is: 2.00
The surface area of the cube is: 24.00
The volume of the cube is: 8.00
```

*   When using composition, include a **Point** object member in class **Square** and include a **Square** object member in class **Cube**. Inheritance should not be used.

Postlab Activities

Name:

Programming Challenges

10

Object-Oriented Programming: Polymorphism

Objectives

- To understand the concept of polymorphism, which enables programmers to write programs in a general fashion to handle a wide variety of existing and yet-to-be-specified related classes.
- To understand how to declare and use virtual functions to affect polymorphism.
- To understand the distinction between abstract classes and concrete classes. An abstract class is a base-class for which the programmer never intends to instantiate any objects. Classes from which objects can be instantiated are concrete classes.
- To define pure virtual functions to create abstract classes.
- To appreciate how polymorphism makes systems extensible and maintainable.
- To understand how to use run-time type information.

Assignment Checklist

Name: _____   **Date:** _____

Section: _____

Exercises	Assigned: Circle assignments	Date Due
Prelab Activities		
Matching	YES NO	
Fill in the Blank	11, 12, 13, 14, 15, 16, 17, 18, 19	
Short Answer	20, 21, 22, 23, 24	
Programming Output	25, 26	
Correct the Code	27, 28, 29, 30	
Lab Exercises		
Lab Exercise — **virtual Vehicle** Class	YES NO	
Follow-Up Questions and Activities	1, 2, 3, 4	
Debugging	YES NO	
Labs Provided by Instructor		
1.		
2.		
3.		
Postlab Activities		
Coding Exercises	1, 2, 3, 4, 5, 6	
Programming Challenge	7	

Assignment Checklist

Name:

Prelab Activities

Matching

Name: _____   **Date:** _____

Section: _____

After reading Chapter 10 of *C++ How to Program: Fourth Edition*, answer the given questions. These questions are intended to test and reinforce your understanding of key concepts and may be done either before the lab or during the lab.

For each term in the column on the left, write the corresponding letter for the description that best matches it from the column on the right.

Term	Description
____ 1. **virtual** function	a) Class that is defined, but never intended to be used by the programmer to create objects.
____ 2. **virtual** function table	b) Functions that contain an initializer of **= 0**.
____ 3. Override a **virtual** function	c) Allows objects of different classes related by inheritance to respond differently to the same message.
____ 4. Dynamic binding	d) Part of C++'s run-time type information.
____ 5. **virtual** base-class destructor	e) Process of replacing an inherited base-class member function with a derived-class one.
____ 6. Abstract base class	f) Programming in the general.
____ 7. Pure **virtual** function	g) An executing program uses this to select the proper function implementation each time a virtual function is called.
____ 8. Polymorphism	h) Occurs only off pointer handles.
____ 9. Concrete class	i) Resolves the problem that arises when processing dynamically allocated objects in a class hierarchy, polymorphically.
____ 10. **typeid**	j) Classes from which objects can be instantiated.

Prelab Activities

Name:

Matching

Prelab Activities   Name: _____

Fill in the Blank

Name: _____   Date:_____

Section: _____

Fill in the blank for each of the following statements:

11. _____ functions allow programs to be written to process objects of types that may not exist when the program is under development.

12. _____ is implemented via virtual functions.

13. Classes from which objects can be _____ are called concrete classes.

14. A class is made abstract by declaring one or more of its virtual functions to be _____.

15. _____ classes can provide their own implementations of a base class's virtual function if necessary; but if they do not, the base class's implementation is used.

16. Resolving virtual function references at compile-time is known as _____.

17. Objects of a(n) _____ class cannot be instantiated in a program.

18. The _____ is implemented as an array containing function pointers.

19. A class with **0** pointers in the *vtable* is a(n) _____ class.

Prelab Activities

Name:

Fill in the Blank

Short Answer

Name: _____   **Date:** _____

Section: _____

In the space provided, answer each of the given questions. Your answers should be as concise as possible; aim for two or three sentences.

20. Discuss some of the problems that arise when using **switch** logic to process different objects. How do virtual functions and polymorphic programming eliminate the need for **switch** logic?

21. Briefly discuss what a *vtable* is and how it keeps track of virtual functions.

Prelab Activities   Name:

Short Answer

22. What problem arises when using polymorphism to process dynamically allocated objects of a class hierarchy? How is it resolved?

23. What are some of the program-design advantages of using polymorphism?

24. What is dynamic binding? Give an example of a situation in which dynamic binding might be used.

Prelab Activities   Name:

Programming Output

Name: _____   Date:_____

Section: _____

For each of the given program segments, read the code and write the output in the space provided below each program. [*Note*: Do not execute these programs on a computer.]

25. What is output by the following program? Use class **Oyster** and **VirginiaOyster** (Fig. L 10.1).

```cpp
 1  #include <iostream>
 2
 3  using std::cout;
 4  using std::endl;
 5
 6  #include "oyster.cpp"
 7
 8  int main()
 9  {
10     VirginiaOyster oyster;
11     Oyster *baseClassPtr;
12
13     baseClassPtr = &oyster;
14
15     baseClassPtr->print();
16
17     cout << endl;
18     return 0;
19
20  } // end main
```

```cpp
 1  #include <iostream>
 2
 3  using std::cout;
 4
 5  #include <string>
 6
 7  using std::string
 8
 9  // class Oyster definition
10  class Oyster {
11
12  public:
13
14     // constructor
15     Oyster( string genusString )
16     {
17        genus = genusString;
18
19     } // end class Oyster constructor
20
21     // function getPhylum definition
```

Fig. L 10.1   **oyster.cpp**. (Part 1 of 2.)

Prelab Activities

Name: _____

Programming Output

```cpp
22      string getPhylum() const
23      {
24         return "Mollusca";
25
26      } // end function getPhylum
27
28      // function getName definition
29      virtual string getName() const
30      {
31         return "Oyster class";
32
33      } // end function getName
34
35      // function getGenus definition
36      string getGenus() const
37      {
38         return genus;
39
40      } // end function getGenus
41
42      // print function
43      virtual void print() const = 0;
44
45   private:
46
47      string genus;
48
49   }; // end class Oyster
50
51   // class VirginiaOyster definition
52   class VirginiaOyster : public Oyster {
53
54   public:
55
56      // constructor calls base-class constructor
57      VirginiaOyster() : Oyster( "Crassostrea" )
58      {
59         // empty
60
61      } // end class VirginiaOyster constructor
62
63      // function getName definition
64      virtual string getName() const
65      {
66         return "VirginiaOyster class";
67
68      } // end function getName
69
70      // print function
71      virtual void print() const
72      {
73         cout << "Phylum: " << getPhylum()
74              << "\tGenus: " << getGenus();
75
76      } // end print function
77
78   }; // end class VirginiaOyster
```

Fig. L 10.1   **oyster.cpp**. (Part 2 of 2.)

Prelab Activities   Name:

Programming Output

Your answer:

26. What is output by the following program segment? Assume that the **Oyster** class member function **print** has been changed to that shown below .

```
1  // function print definition
2  virtual void print() const
3  {
4     cout << "Oysters belong to Phylum " << getPhylum() << endl;
5
6  } // end function print
```

```
1  #include <iostream>
2
3  using std::cout;
4  using std::endl;
5
6  #include "oyster.cpp"
7
8  int main()
9  {
10    VirginiaOyster *ptr;
11    VirginiaOyster oyster;
12    Oyster *oysterPtr;
13
14    oysterPtr = &oyster;
15    ptr = &oyster;
16
17    ptr -> print();
18    cout << endl;
19
20    oysterPtr -> print();
21    cout << endl
22         << oysterPtr -> getPhylum();
23
24    cout << endl;
25    return 0;
26
27  } // end main
```

Prelab Activities

Name:

Programming Output

Your answer:

Prelab Activities   Name:

Correct the Code

Name: _____   Date: _____

Section: _____

For each of the given program segments, determine if there is an error in the code. If there is an error, specify whether it is a logic error or a syntax error, circle the error in the program, and write the corrected code in the space provided after each problem. If the code does not contain an error, write "no error." [*Note*: It is possible that a program segment may contain multiple errors.]

27. The following program segment defines an abstract class named **Base**:

```
1   // class Base definition
2   class Base {
3
4   public:
5      void print() const;
6
7   }; // end class Base
```

Your answer:

28. The following is a modified version of the definition of class **VirginiaOyster** from Fig. L 10.1. Assume member function print is defined in another file.

```
1   // class VirginiaOyster definition
2   class VirginiaOyster : public Oyster {
3
4   public:
5
6      // constructor
7      virtual VirginiaOyster( string genusString )
8      {
9         genus = genusString;
10
11     } // end class VirginiaOyster constructor
12
13     // constructor
14     VirginiaOyster( char *genusString )
15     {
16        genus = genusString;
17
18     } // end class VirginiaOyster constructor
19
20     // print function
21     void print() const;
22
23  }; // end class VirginiaOyster
```

Prelab Activities   Name:

Correct the Code

Your answer:

29. The following program defines a class **BaseClass** and instantiates an object of type **BaseClass**. [*Note*: Only the definition for **BaseClass** is shown, assume that another file is provided elsewhere that contains the class's implementation.]

```
1    // class BaseClass definition
2    class BaseClass {
3
4    public:
5       BaseClass( int = 0, int = 0 );
6       virtual void display() = 0;
7
8    private:
9       int x;
10      int y;
11
12   }; // end class BaseClass
13
14   int main()
15   {
16      BaseClass b( 5, 10 );
17
18      b.display();
19      return 0;
20
21   } // end main
```

Your answer:

Prelab Activities   Name:

Correct the Code

30. The following program segments define two classes: **Name** and **NameAndWeight**. **Name** should be an abstract base class and **NameAndWeight** should be a concrete derived class. Function **main** should declare an object of type **NameAndWeight** and print its **name** and **weight**. [*Note*: Only the definitions for **Name** and **NameAndWeight** are shown, assume files containing member function definitions have been provided elsewhere.]

```
1   // class Name definition
2   class Name {
3
4   public:
5       Name( string );
6       virtual void printName() const = 0;
7
8   private:
9       string name
10
11  }; // end class Name
12
13  // class NameAndWeight definition
14  class NameAndWeight : public Name {
15
16  public:
17      NameAndWeight( string, int = 0 );
18      virtual void displayWeight() const;
19
20  private:
21      int weight;
22
23  }; // end class NameAndWeight
```

```
1   #include <iostream>
2
3   using std::cout;
4   using std::endl;
5
6   int main()
7   {
8       NameAndWeight object( "name", 100 );
9
10      cout << "name: " << object.printName() << endl;
11      cout << "weight: " << object.displayWeight() << endl;
12      return 0;
13
14  } // end main
```

Your answer:

Prelab Activities   Name:

Correct the Code

Lab Exercises

Lab Exercise — virtual Vehicle Class

Name: _____   Date:_____

Section: _____

This problem is intended to be solved in a closed-lab session with a teaching assistant or instructor present. The problem is divided into six parts:

1. Lab Objectives

2. Description of the Problem

3. Sample Output

4. Program Template (Fig. L 10.2–Fig. L 10.8)

5. Problem-Solving Tips

6. Follow-Up Questions and Activities

The program template represents a complete working C++ program, with one or more key lines of code replaced with comments. Read the problem description and examine the sample output; then study the template code. Using the problem-solving tips as a guide, replace the **/* */** comments with C++ code. Compile and execute the program. Compare your output with the sample output provided. Then answer the follow-up questions. The source code for the template is available at **www.deitel.com** and **www.prenhall.com./deitel**.

Lab Objectives

This lab was designed to reinforce programming concepts from Chapter 10 of *C++ How To Program: Fourth Edition*. In this lab, you will practice:

- creating a **Vehicle** base class that contains virtual functions and derived classes **Taxi** and **Truck**.

- defining virtual functions.

- calling virtual functions.

The follow-up questions and activities also will give you practice:

- calling derived-class member functions through base-class pointers.

- determining how RTTI might be used to identify object types.

Description of the Problem

Apply the concept of polymorphism to a **Vehicle** hierarchy. Develop an abstract base class **Vehicle** that includes the vehicle's name, color, number of doors, number of cylinders, transmission type and fuel level. Add a member function named **horn** that displays the sound made by the **Vehicle**'s horn. The **print** member function and the **horn** member function should both be virtual functions; **horn** should be a pure virtual function. Class **Taxi** and class **Truck** should both be derived from **Vehicle**.

Write a driver to test the class hierarchy. Instantiate one object of type **Taxi** and one object of type **Truck**. Insert those objects into a "container"—a vector of base-class pointers. For each object in the vector, call virtual functions **horn** and **print**.

Lab Exercises   Name:

Lab Exercise — `virtual Vehicle` Class

Sample Output

```
The vehicles cannot get out of their parking spaces because of traffic,
so they respond:

beep beep
        Number of doors: 4
        Number of cylinders: 6
        Transmission type: 5
        Color: yellow
        Fuel level: 3.3
        The taxi currently has no passengers.
        class name: Taxi

HOOOONK!
        Number of doors: 2
        Number of cylinders: 16
        Transmission type: 8
        Color: black
        Fuel level: 7.54
        The truck is currently carrying cargo.
        class name: Truck
```

Template

```cpp
1   // Chapter 10 of C++ How to Program
2   // vehicle.h
3   #ifndef VEHICLE_H
4   #define VEHICLE_H
5
6   #include <iostream>
7
8   #include <string>
9
10  using std::string;
11
12  // class Vehicle definition
13  class Vehicle {
14
15  public:
16     Vehicle( const int doors, const int cylinders,
17        string color, double initialFuel,
18        const int transmission );
19
20     void setColor( string color );
21     string getColor() const;
22
23     void setFuelLevel( double amount );
24     double getFuelLevel() const;
25
26     int getTransmissionType() const;
27     int getNumberOfDoors() const;
28     int getNumberOfCylinders() const;
```

Fig. L 10.2   Contents of **vehicle.h**. (Part 1 of 2.)

Lab Exercises   Name:

Lab Exercise — virtual Vehicle Class

```
29
30      virtual string getClassName() const;
31
32      /* Write prototype for pure virtual function horn */
33      /* Write prototype for virtual function print      */
34
35   private:
36      const int numberOfDoors;
37      const int numberOfCylinders;
38      string vehicleColor;
39      double fuelLevel;
40      const int transmissionType;
41
42   }; // end class Vehicle
43
44   #endif // VEHICLE_H
```

Fig. L 10.2   Contents of **vehicle.h**. (Part 2 of 2.)

```
1    // Chapter 10 of C++ How to Program
2    // vehicle.cpp
3    #include <iostream>
4
5    using std::cout;
6    using std::endl;
7    using std::ostream;
8
9    #include "vehicle.h"
10
11   // constructor
12   Vehicle::Vehicle( const int doors, const int cylinders,
13      string color, double initialFuel,
14      const int transmission )
15      : numberOfDoors( doors ), numberOfCylinders( cylinders ),
16        transmissionType( transmission )
17   {
18      setFuelLevel( initialFuel );
19
20      setColor( color );
21
22   } // end class Vehicle constructor
23
24   // function print definition
25   void Vehicle::print() const
26   {
27      cout << "\tNumber of doors: " << getNumberOfDoors()
28           << "\n\tNumber of cylinders: " << getNumberOfCylinders()
29           << "\n\tTransmission type: " << getTransmissionType()
30           << "\n\tColor: " << getColor()
31           << "\n\tFuel level: " << getFuelLevel() << endl;
32
33   } // end function print
```

Fig. L 10.3   Contents of **vehicle.cpp**. (Part 1 of 3.)

Lab Exercises

Name:

Lab Exercise — `virtual Vehicle` Class

```
34
35   // function setColor definition
36   void Vehicle::setColor( string color )
37   {
38      vehicleColor = color;
39
40   } // end function setColor
41
42   // function setFuelLevel definition
43   void Vehicle::setFuelLevel( double amount )
44   {
45      // assume 20 gallons is full tank
46      if ( amount > 0.0 && amount <= 20.0 )
47         fuelLevel = amount;
48
49      else
50         fuelLevel = 5.0;
51
52   } // end function setFuelLevel
53
54   // return color
55   string Vehicle::getColor() const
56   {
57      return vehicleColor;
58
59   } // end function getColor
60
61   // return fuelLevel
62   double Vehicle::getFuelLevel() const
63   {
64      return fuelLevel;
65
66   } // end function getFuelLevel
67
68   // return transmissionType
69   int Vehicle::getTransmissionType() const
70   {
71      return transmissionType;
72
73   } // end function getTransmissionType
74
75   // return numberOfDoors
76   int Vehicle::getNumberOfDoors() const
77   {
78      return numberOfDoors;
79
80   } // end function getNumberOfDoors
81
82   // return numberOfCylinders
83   int Vehicle::getNumberOfCylinders() const
84   {
85      return numberOfCylinders;
86
87   } // end function getNumberOfCylinders
88
```

Fig. L 10.3   Contents of **vehicle.cpp**. (Part 2 of 3.)

Lab Exercises   Name:

Lab Exercise — virtual Vehicle Class

```
89   // return class name
90   string Vehicle::getClassName() const
91   {
92      return "Vehicle";
93
94   } // end function getClassName
```

Fig. L 10.3   Contents of **vehicle.cpp**. (Part 3 of 3.)

```
1    // Chapter 10 of C++ How to Program
2    // taxi.h
3    #ifndef TAXI_H
4    #define TAXI_H
5
6    #include <iostream>
7
8    #include "vehicle.h"
9
10   // class Taxi definition
11   class Taxi : public Vehicle {
12
13   public:
14      Taxi( double );
15
16      bool hasCustomers() const;
17      void setCustomers( bool );
18
19      /* Write prototype for virtual function horn */
20
21      virtual void print() const;
22      virtual string getClassName() const;
23
24   private:
25      bool customers;
26
27   }; // end class Taxi
28
29   #endif // TAXI_H
```

Fig. L 10.4   Contents of **taxi.h**.

```
1    // Chapter 10 of C++ How to Program
2    // taxi.cpp
3    #include <iostream>
4
5    using std::cout;
6
7    #include "taxi.h"
8
```

Fig. L 10.5   Contents of **taxi.cpp**. (Part 1 of 2.)

Lab Exercises   Name:

Lab Exercise — virtual Vehicle Class

```
9    // constructor
10   Taxi::Taxi( double fuel )
11      : Vehicle( 4, 6, "yellow", fuel, 5 )
12   {
13      customers = false;
14
15   } // end class Taxi constructor
16
17   // function setCustomers definition
18   void Taxi::setCustomers( bool c )
19   {
20      customers = c;
21
22   } // end function setCustomers
23
24   // function hasCustomers definition
25   bool Taxi::hasCustomers() const
26   {
27      return customers;
28
29   } // end function hasCustomers
30
31   // function print definition
32   void Taxi::print() const
33   {
34      Vehicle::print();
35
36      if ( customers )
37         cout << "\tThe taxi currently has passengers.\n";
38
39      else
40         cout << "\tThe taxi currently has no passengers.\n";
41
42      cout << "class name: " << getClassName() << "\n";
43
44   } // end function print
45
46   // function horn definition
47   void Taxi::horn() const
48   {
49      cout << "beep beep";
50
51   } // end function horn
52
53   // return className
54   string Taxi::getClassName() const
55   {
56      return "Taxi";
57
58   } // end function getClassName
```

Fig. L 10.5   Contents of **taxi.cpp**. (Part 2 of 2.)

Lab Exercises　　　　　　　　　　　　　　　　Name:

Lab Exercise — virtual Vehicle Class

```cpp
1   // Chapter 10 of C++ How to Program
2   // truck.h
3   #ifndef TRUCK_H
4   #define TRUCK_H
5
6   #include <iostream>
7
8   #include "vehicle.h"
9
10  // class Truck definition
11  class Truck : public Vehicle {
12
13  public:
14     Truck( double );
15
16     bool hasCargo() const;
17     void setCargo( bool );
18
19     virtual void horn() const;
20     virtual void print() const;
21     virtual string getClassName() const;
22
23  private:
24     bool cargo;
25
26  }; // end class Truck
27
28  #endif // TRUCK_H
```

Fig. L 10.6　Contents of **truck.h**.

```cpp
1   // Chapter 10 of C++ How to Program
2   // truck.cpp
3   #include <iostream>
4
5   using std::cout;
6
7   #include "truck.h"
8
9   // constructor
10  Truck::Truck( double fuel )
11     : Vehicle( 2, 16, "black", fuel, 8 )
12  {
13     cargo = false;
14
15  } // end class Truck constructor
16
17  // function hasCargo definition
18  bool Truck::hasCargo() const
19  {
20     return cargo;
21
22  } // end function hasCargo
23
```

Fig. L 10.7　Contents of **truck.cpp**. (Part 1 of 2.)

Lab Exercises

Name:

Lab Exercise — virtual Vehicle Class

```
24    // function setCargo definition
25    void Truck::setCargo( bool cargoValue )
26    {
27       cargo = cargoValue;
28
29    } // end function setCargo
30
31    // function print definition
32    void Truck::print() const
33    {
34       Vehicle::print();
35
36       if ( cargo )
37          cout << "\tThe truck is currently carrying cargo.\n";
38
39       else
40          cout << "\tThe truck is currently not carrying cargo.\n";
41
42       cout << "class name: " << getClassName() << "\n";
43
44    } // end function print
45
46    // function horn definition
47    void Truck::horn() const
48    {
49       cout << "HOOOONK!";
50
51    } // end function horn
52
53    // return class name
54    string Truck::getClassName() const
55    {
56       return "Truck";
57
58    } // end function getClassName
```

Fig. L 10.7   Contents of **truck.cpp**. (Part 2 of 2.)

```
1    // Chapter 10 of C++ How to Program
2    // driver for vehicle
3    #include <iostream>
4
5    using std::cout;
6    using std::endl;
7
8    #include <vector>
9
10   using std::vector;
11
12   #include "vehicle.h"
13   #include "taxi.h"
14   #include "truck.h"
15
16   int main()
17   {
```

Fig. L 10.8   Contents of **driver.cpp**. (Part 1 of 2.)

Lab Exercises   Name:

Lab Exercise — virtual Vehicle Class

```
18      Taxi cab( 3.3 );
19      Truck mack( 7.54 );
20
21      /* Write code to indicate that truck is carrying cargo */
22
23      /* Declare a vector, parkingLot, of base-class pointers */
24
25      parkingLot[ 0 ] = &cab;
26      parkingLot[ 1 ] = &mack;
27
28      cout << "\nThe vehicles cannot get out of their parking spaces because of "
29           << "traffic,\nso they respond: \n";
30
31      for ( int i = 0; i < parkingLot.size(); i++ ) {
32
33         /* Write code to call member function horn */
34
35         cout << endl;
36
37         /* Write code to display information about the vehicle honking its horn */
38
39         cout << endl;
40
41      } // end for
42
43      return 0;
44
45   } // end main
```

Fig. L 10.8   Contents of **driver.cpp**. (Part 2 of 2.)

Problem-Solving Tips

1. To indicate a pure virtual function within a class definition, add "= 0"after the function prototype. This should be done only in the base class. Pure virtual functions in a derived class should be preceded by the keyword virtual as a good programming practice.

2. A vector of base-class pointers should be accessed as follows:

   vectorName[i]->_function_**();**

Follow-Up Questions and Activities

1. Rewrite the driver program such that all **Taxi** and **Truck** objects are created dynamically. Do not forget to delete these objects before the program terminates.

Lab Exercises   Name:

Lab Exercise — `virtual Vehicle` Class

2. Modify the program to include a new class **ParkingLot** (Fig. L 10.9). This class should use a vector of **Vehicle**s to store each vehicle parked. Modify the driver program to place **10 Vehicle**s in the parking lot. Modify the **for** loop to honk the horn and to display information about each **Vehicle**.

```
1   // class ParkingLot definition
2   class ParkingLot {
3
4   public:
5      ParkingLot();
6      ~ParkingLot();
7
8      void addVehicle( Vehicle * );
9      void printVehicles() const;
10     int getVehicleCount() const;
11
12  private:
13     vector< Vehicle* > vehicles;
14     int count;
15
16  }; // end class ParkingLot
```

Fig. L 10.9   `ParkingLot.h`.

3. Explain how operator **typeid** could be used to determine an objects class name at run-time.

Lab Exercises

Name:

Lab Exercise — virtual Vehicle Class

4. Explain how **dynamic_cast** could be used to identify **Truck** objects in the **ParkingLot** object.

Lab Exercises

Name: _____

Lab Exercise — virtual Vehicle Class

Lab Exercises

Name: _____

Debugging

Name: _____   Date: _____

Section: _____

The program (Fig. L 10.10–Fig. L 10.16) in this section does not run properly. Fix all the syntax errors so that the program will compile successfully. Once the program compiles, compare the output with the sample output, and eliminate any logic errors that may exist. The sample output demonstrates what the program's output should be once the program's code has been corrected.

Sample Output

```
This animal is a lion
This animal's height and weight are as follows:
Height: 45        Weight: 300

Enter a new height (using standard units): 50
Enter a new weight (using standard units): 400
Here are the new height and weight values
50
400

This animal is a dog, its name is: Fido
This animal's height and weight are as follows:
Height: 60        Weight: 120

Enter a new height (using standard units): 50
Enter a new weight (using standard units): 116
Which units would you like to see the height in? (Enter 1 or 2)
        1. metric
        2. standard
2
Which units would you like to see the weight in? (Enter 1 or 2)
        1. metric
        2. standard
1
Here are the new height and weight values
50
52
```

Broken Code

```
1   // Chapter 10 of C++ How to Program
2   // Debugging Problem (animal.h)
3
4   #ifndef ANIMAL_H
5   #define ANIMAL_H
6
```

Fig. L 10.10 Contents of animal.h. (Part 1 of 2.)

Lab Exercises   Name:

Debugging

```
7   #include <string>
8
9   using std::string;
10
11  // Note: class Animal is an abstract class
12  // class Animal definition
13  class Animal {
14
15  public:
16     Animal( int = 0, int = 0 );
17
18     void setHeight( int );
19     virtual int getHeight() const = 0;
20
21     void setWeight( int );
22     virtual int getWeight() const = 0;
23
24     virtual void print() const = 0;
25
26  private:
27     int height;
28     int weight;
29
30  }; // end class Animal
31
32  #endif // ANIMAL_H
```

Fig. L 10.10   Contents of **animal.h**. (Part 2 of 2.)

```
1   // Chapter 10 of C++ How to Program
2   // Debugging Problem (animal.cpp)
3
4   #include <iostream>
5   using std::cout;
6   using std::endl;
7
8   #include "animal.h"
9
10  // default constructor
11  Animal::Animal( int h, int w )
12  {
13     height = h;
14     weight = w;
15
16  } // end class Animal constructor
17
18  // function print definition
19  virtual void Animal::print() const
20  {
21     cout << "This animal's height and weight are as follows:\n"
22          << "Height: " << height << "\tWeight: " << weight
23          << endl << endl;
24
25  } // end function print
26
```

Fig. L 10.11   Contents of **animal.cpp**. (Part 1 of 2.)

Lab Exercises   Name:

Debugging

```
27   // return height
28   int Animal::getHeight() const
29   {
30      return height;
31
32   } // end function getHeight
33
34   // return weight
35   int Animal::getWeight() const
36   {
37      return weight;
38
39   } // end function getWeight
40
41   // function setHeight definition
42   virtual void Animal::setHeight( int h )
43   {
44      height = h;
45
46   } // end function setHeight
47
48   // function setWeight definition
49   virtual void Animal::setWeight( int w )
50   {
51      weight = w;
52
53   } // end function setWeight
```

Fig. L 10.11   Contents of **animal.cpp**. (Part 2 of 2.)

```
1    // Chapter 10 of C++ How to Program
2    // Debugging Problem (lion.h)
3
4    #ifndef LION_H
5    #define LION_H
6
7    #include "animal.h"
8
9    // class Lion definition
10   class Lion : public Animal {
11
12   public:
13      Lion( int = 0, int = 0 );
14
15      virtual void print() const;
16
17   }; // end class Lion
18
19   #endif // LION_H
```

Fig. L 10.12   Contents of **lion.h**.

```
1    // Chapter 10 of C++ How to Program
2    // Debugging Problem (lion.cpp)
3
```

Fig. L 10.13   Contents of **lion.cpp**. (Part 1 of 2.)

Lab Exercises   Name:

Debugging

```
4   #include <iostream>
5
6   using std::cout;
7   using std::endl;
8
9   #include "lion.h"
10
11  // default constructor
12  Lion::Lion( int h, int w )
13  : Animal( h, w )
14  {
15     // empty
16
17  } // end class Lion constructor
18
19  // function print definition
20  void Lion::print() const
21  {
22     cout << "This animal is a lion\n";
23     Animal::print();
24
25  } // end function print
```

Fig. L 10.13   Contents of **lion.cpp**. (Part 2 of 2.)

```
1   // Chapter 10 of C++ How to Program
2   // Debugging Problem (dog.h)
3
4   #ifndef DOG_H
5   #define DOG_H
6
7   #include "animal.h"
8
9   // class Dog definition
10  class Dog : public Animal {
11
12  public:
13     Dog( int = 0, int = 0, string = "Toto" );
14
15     virtual void print() const = 0;
16     virtual void getHeight() const = 0;
17     virtual void getWeight() const = 0;
18     string getName() const;
19     void setName( string );
20
21  private:
22     bool useMetric( string ) const;
23     string name;
24     int metricHeight;
25     int metricWeight;
26
27  }; // end class Dog
28
29  #endif // DOG_H
```

Fig. L 10.14   Contents of **dog.h**.

Lab Exercises   Name:
_____

Debugging

```cpp
1   // Chapter 10 of C++ How to Program
2   // Debugging Problem (dog.cpp)
3
4   #include <iostream>
5
6   using std::cout;
7   using std::endl;
8   using std::cin;
9
10  #include "dog.h"
11
12  // default constructor
13  Dog::Dog( int h, int w, string n )
14      : Animal( h, w )
15  {
16     setName( n );
17     metricHeight = h * 2.5;
18     metricWeight = w / 2.2;
19
20  } // end class Dog constructor
21
22  // return name
23  string Dog::getName() const
24  {
25     return name;
26
27  } // end function getName
28
29  // function setName definition
30  void Dog::setName( string n )
31  {
32     name = n;
33
34  } // end function setName
35
36  // function print definition
37  void Dog::print() const
38  {
39     cout << "This animal is a dog, its name is: "
40          << name << endl;
41     Animal::print();
42
43  } // end function print
44
45  // return height
46  int Dog::getHeight()
47  {
48     if ( useMetric( "height" ) )
49        return metricHeight;
50
51     else
52        return Animal::getHeight();
53
54  } // end function print
55
```

Fig. L 10.15   Contents of **dog.cpp**. (Part 1 of 2.)

Lab Exercises

Name:

Debugging

```
56   // return weight
57   int Dog::getWeight()
58   {
59      if ( useMetric( "weight" ) )
60         return metricWeight;
61
62      else
63         return Animal::getWeight();
64
65   } // end function getWeight
66
67   // function useMetric definition
68   bool Dog::useMetric( string type ) const
69   {
70      int choice = 0;
71
72      cout << "Which units would you like to see the "
73           << type << " in? (Enter 1 or 2)\n"
74           << "\t1. metric\n"
75           << "\t2. standard\n";
76
77      cin >> choice;
78
79      if ( choice == 1 )
80         return true;
81
82      else
83         return false;
84
85   } // end function useMetric
```

Fig. L 10.15 Contents of **dog.cpp**. (Part 2 of 2.)

```
1    // Chapter 10 of C++ How to Program
2    // Debugging Problem (debugging10.cpp)
3
4    #include <iostream>
5
6    using std::cout;
7    using std::endl;
8    using std::cin;
9
10   #include "animal.h"
11   #include "lion.h"
12   #include "dog.h"
13
14   void setHeightWeight( Animal ) const;
15
16   int main()
17   {
18      Dog dog1( 60, 120, "Fido" );
19      Lion lion1( 45, 300 );
20
21      setHeightWeight( lion1 );
22      setHeightWeight( dog1 );
23
```

Fig. L 10.16 Contents of **debugging10.cpp**. (Part 1 of 2.)

Lab Exercises

Name: _____

Debugging

```
24      return 0;
25
26   } // end main
27
28   // function setHeightWeight definition
29   void setHeightWeight( Animal )
30   {
31      int height;
32      int weight;
33
34      a->print();
35      cout << "Enter a new height (using standard units): ";
36      cin >> height;
37      a->setHeight( height );
38
39      cout << "Enter a new weight (using standard units): ";
40      cin >> weight;
41      a->setWeight( weight );
42
43      height = a->getHeight();
44      weight = a->getWeight();
45
46      cout << "Here are the new height and weight values:\n"
47           << height << endl
48           << weight << endl << endl;
49
50   } // end function setHeightWeight
```

Fig. L 10.16   Contents of **debugging10.cpp**. (Part 2 of 2.)

Lab Exercises   Name:

Debugging

Postlab Activities

Coding Exercises

Name: _____   **Date:** _____

Section: _____

These coding exercises reinforce the lessons learned in the lab and provide additional programming experience outside the classroom and laboratory environment. They serve as a review after you have completed the Prelab Activities and Lab Exercises successfully.

For each of the following problems, write a program or a program segment that performs the specified action:

1. Write the header file for an abstract base class named **Base**. Include a **virtual** destructor and a **virtual print** function.

2. Write the header file for the class **Derived** that inherits **public**ly from class **Base**. Class **Derived** has one integer as its **private** data member and should have a **print** member function.

Postlab Activities   Name:

Coding Exercises

3. Override class **Derived**'s **print** member function to print the value of the class's **private** data member.

4. Create a **Derived** object and assign its address to a **Base** pointer. Explain why this assignment is allowed by the compiler.

5. Assign the **Base** pointer from Coding Exercise 4 to a **Derived** pointer, without using any cast operators. Explain why this assignment is not permitted by the compiler?

Postlab Activities   Name:

Coding Exercises

6. Write a definition for a base-class named **Base2**. Include one virtual function named **function1** and one pure virtual function named **function2**.

Postlab Activities   Name:

Coding Exercises

Postlab Activities   Name:

Programming Challenge

Name: _____   Date:_____

Section: _____

The Programming Challenges are more involved than the Coding Exercises and may require a significant amount of time to complete. Write a C++ program for each of the problems in this section. The answers to these problems are available at **www.deitel.com**, **www.prenhall.com/deitel** and on the *C++ Multimedia Cyber Classroom: Fourth Edition*. Pseudocode, hints and/or sample outputs are provided to aid you in your programming.

7. Modify the payroll system of Fig. 10.23–Fig. 10.33 of *C++ How to Program: Fourth Edition* to include **private** data members **birthDate** (use class **Date** from Fig. 8.10–Fig. 8.11) to class **Employee**. Assume this payroll is processed once per month. Create a **vector** of **Employee** references to store the various **Employee** objects. In a loop, calculate the payroll for each **Employee** (polymorphically), and add a $100.00 bonus to the person's payroll amount if this is the month in which the **Employee**'s birthday occurs.

Hints:

- The **private** data member used to represent the **birthday** is the same for each worker regardless of their occupation. The only class that needs to be modified to add a **birthday** is the base class **Employee**.

- Add an appropriate member function for manipulating the birthday data such as **getBirthDate**.

- Modify the **Employee** class's constructor to handle **birthday**.

Postlab Activities

Name:

Programming Challenge

11

Templates

Objectives

- To use function templates to create a group of related (overloaded) functions. Templates enable programmers to specify, with a single code segment, an entire range of related functions or an entire range of related classes.
- To distinguish between function templates and function-template specializations. Function-template specializations are the range of related functions created from a function template.
- To use class templates to create a group of related types.
- To distinguish between class templates and class-template specializations. Class-template specializations are the range of related classes created from a class template.
- To understand the relationships among templates, friends, inheritance and static members.

Assignment Checklist

Name: _____   **Date:**_____

Section: _____

Exercises	Assigned: Circle assignments	Date Due
Prelab Activities		
Matching	YES NO	
Fill in the Blank	10, 11, 12, 13, 14, 15, 16, 17	
Short Answer	18, 19	
Programming Output	20, 21	
Correct the Code	22, 23, 24	
Lab Exercises		
Lab Exercise — Table	YES NO	
Follow-Up Questions and Activities	1, 2, 3	
Debugging	YES NO	
Labs Provided by Instructor		
1.		
2.		
3.		
Postlab Activities		
Coding Exercises	1, 2	

Assignment Checklist   Name:

Prelab Activities

Matching

Name: _____   **Date:** _____

Section: _____

After reading Chapter 11 of *C++ How to Program: Fourth Edition*, answer the given questions. These questions are intended to test and reinforce your understanding of key concepts and may be done either before the lab or during the lab.

For each term in the column on the left, write the corresponding letter for the description that best matches it from the column on the right.

Term	Description
____ 1. Nontype parameter	a) Class that is a type-specific version of a generic class.
____ 2. Class template	b) Class templates are called this because they require one or more type parameters.
____ 3. `template`	c) Parameter that can have a default argument and is treated as a constant.
____ 4. Type parameter	d) Parameter to a function template that can be any valid identifier and is replaced when the function is invoked.
____ 5. `class/typename`	e) Placed before every formal type parameter of a function template.
____ 6. Function template	f) Performs similar operations on different types of data, assuming the operations are identical for each type.
____ 7. `static` member function	g) Technique provided by class templates.
____ 8. parameterized type	h) All function-template definitions begin with this/these keywords.
____ 9. generic programming	i) Each class-template specialization gets its own copy.

Prelab Activities

Name:

Matching

Prelab Activities   Name:

Fill in the Blank

Name: _____   **Date:**_____

Section: _____

Fill in the blank for each of the following statements:

10. Class templates provide the means for describing a class generically and for instantiating classes that are
    _____ versions of this generic class.

11. Each template class gets a copy of the class template's _____ member functions.

12. Templates allow the programmer to specify a range of related _____ and _____.

13. Formal _____ names among function templates need not be unique.

14. Each class-template specialization has its own copy of each _____ data member of the class template;
    all objects of that template class share that one data member.

15. Class templates are called _____ as they require type parameters to specify how to customize a generic
    class template to form a class-template specialization.

16. A function template itself may be _____ in several ways. We can provide other function templates that
    specify the same function name, but different function parameters. We also can provide other non-template
    functions with the same function name, but different function parameters.

17. A _____ can be derived from a class template or a non-template class.

Prelab Activities   Name:

Fill in the Blank

Prelab Activities   Name:

Short Answer

Name: _____   **Date:** _____

Section: _____

In the space provided, answer each of the given questions. Your answers should be as concise as possible; aim for two or three sentences.

18. What are the advantages of using template functions instead of macros?

Prelab Activities

Name:

Short Answer

19. How does the compiler determine which function to call when a function is invoked? Your answer should include a discussion of how the function invocation is matched with the template function.

Prelab Activities

Name:

Programming Output

Name: _____   Date:_____

Section: _____

For each of the given program segments, read the code and write the output in the space provided below each program. [*Note*: Do not execute these programs on a computer.]

20. What is output by the following program?

```
1   #include <iostream>
2
3   using std::cout;
4   using std::endl;
5
6   // function template mystery definition
7   template< class T >
8   void mystery( const T *a, const int c )
9   {
10      for ( int i = 0; i < c; i++ )
11         cout << a[ i ] << " ** ";
12
13      cout << endl;
14
15  } // end function mystery
16
17  int main()
18  {
19     const int size = 5;
20
21     int i[ size ] = { 22, 33, 44, 55, 66 };
22     char c[ size ] = { 'c', 'd', 'g', 'p', 'q' };
23
24     mystery( i, size );
25     cout << endl;
26     mystery( c, size - 2 );
27     cout << endl;
28     return 0;
29
30  } // end main
```

Your answer:

Prelab Activities

Name:

Programming Output

21. What is output by the following program?

```cpp
1   #include <iostream>
2
3   using std::cout;
4   using std::endl;
5   using std::ios;
6
7   #include <new>
8
9   #include <iomanip>
10
11  using std::setprecision;
12
13  // class template for class Array
14  template< class T >
15  class Array {
16
17  public:
18      Array( int = 5 );
19      ~Array() { delete [] arrayPtr; }
20      T arrayRef( int ) const;
21      int getSize() const;
22
23  private:
24      int size;
25      T *arrayPtr;
26
27  }; // end class Array
28
29  // constructor for class Array
30  template< class T >
31  Array< T >::Array( int x )
32  {
33      size = x;
34      arrayPtr = new T[ size ];
35
36      for ( int i = 0; i < size; i++ )
37          arrayPtr[ i ] = 1.0 * i;
38
39  } // end class Array constructor
40
41  // function arrayRef definition
42  template< class T >
43  T Array< T >::arrayRef( int num ) const
44  {
45      return arrayPtr[ num ];
46
47  } // end function arrayRef
48
49  // return size
50  template< class T >
51  int Array< T >::getSize() const
52  {
53      return size;
54
55  } // end function getSize
```

(Part 1 of 2.)

Prelab Activities

Name:

Programming Output

```
56
57   // non-member function template to print an object of type Array
58   template< class T >
59   void printArray( const Array< T > &a )
60   {
61      for ( int i = 0; i < a.getSize(); i++ )
62         cout << a.arrayRef( i ) << " ";
63
64      cout << endl << endl;
65
66   } // end function printArray
67
68   int main()
69   {
70      Array< int > intArray( 4 );
71      Array< double > doubleArray();
72
73      cout << setprecision( 2 )
74           << fixed;
75      printArray( intArray );
76      printArray( doubleArray );
77
78      return 0;
79
80   } // end main
```

(Part 2 of 2.)

Your answer:

Prelab Activities

Name:

Programming Output

Prelab Activities

Name:

Correct the Code

Name: _____   Date: _____

Section: _____

For each of the given program segments, determine if there is an error in the code. If there is an error, specify whether it is a logic error or a syntax error, circle the error in the program, and write the corrected code in the space provided after each problem. If the code does not contain an error, write "no error." [*Note*: It is possible that a program segment may contain multiple errors.]

22. The following code invokes the function **print**:

```
1    #include <iostream>
2
3    using std::cout;
4    using std::endl;
5
6    // template function print definition
7    template < class T >
8    void print( T left, T right )
9    {
10       cout << "Printing arguments: " << left
11            << "  **  " << right;
12
13   } // end function print
14
15   int main()
16   {
17       cout << endl;
18       print( 3, 5.8 );
19       cout << endl;
20
21       return 0;
22
23   } // end main
```

Your answer:

Prelab Activities

Name:

Correct the Code

23. The following is a class definition for a template class **Stack**:

```
1   #ifndef TSTACK1_H
2   #define TSTACK1_H
3
4   // template class Stack definition
5   template< class T >
6   class Stack {
7
8   public:
9      Stack( int = 10 );
10
11     // destructor
12     ~Stack()
13     {
14        delete [] stackPtr;
15
16     } // end class Stack destructor
17
18     bool push( const T& );
19     bool pop( T& );
20
21  private:
22     int size;
23     int top;
24     T *stackPtr;
25
26     // function isEmpty definition
27     bool isEmpty() const
28     {
29        return top == -1;
30
31     } // end function isEmpty
32
33     // function isFull definition
34     bool isFull() const
35     {
36        return top == size - 1;
37
38     } // end function isFull
39
40  }; // end class Stack
41
42  // constructor
43  Stack< T >::Stack( int s )
44  {
45     size = s > 0 ? s : 10;
46     top = -1;
47     stackPtr = new T[ size ];
48
49  } // end class Stack constructor
50
51  // function push definition
52  bool Stack< T >::push( const T &pushValue )
53  {
```

Prelab Activities

Name:

Correct the Code

```
54      if ( !isFull() ) {
55         stackPtr[ ++top ] = pushValue;
56         return true;
57
58      } // end if
59
60      return false;
61
62   } // end function push
63
64   // function pop definition
65   bool Stack< T >::pop( T &popValue )
66   {
67      if ( !isEmpty() ) {
68         popValue = stackPtr[ top-- ];
69         return true;
70
71      } // end if
72
73      return false;
74
75   } // end function pop
76
77   #endif // TSTACK1_H
```

(Part 2 of 2.)

Your answer:

24. The following code invokes function **print**:

```
1    #include <iostream>
2
3    using std::cout;
4    using std::cin;
5    using std::endl;
6
7    // class MyClass definition
8    class MyClass {
9
10   public:
11      MyClass();
12
13      void set( int );
14      int get() const;
15
```

(Part 1 of 2.)

Lab Exercises   Name:

Lab Exercise — Table

Sample Output

```
Uninitialized array "a" is:
    0     0     0      0      0      0      0
    0     0     0      0      0      0      0
    0     0     0      0      0      0      0
    0     0     0      0      0      0      0
Uninitialized array "b" is:




Initialized array "a" is now:
   54    34    73     34     31     75      7
   99    80    44     30     45     12     36
    0    62    51     43     65     48     58
   75    13    91      1      0     25      9
Initialized array b is now:
    g     g
    g     g
    g     g
    g     g
    g     g

Enter values for b (10 of them):
a b c d e f g h i j

    a     b
    c     d
    e     f
    g     h
    i     j

The element (2, 1) of array "a" is: 62
Changed element (2, 1) to -1:
   54    34    73     34     31     75      7
   99    80    44     30     45     12     36
    0    -1    51     43     65     48     58
   75    13    91      1      0     25      9
```

Template

```cpp
1   // Chapter 11 of C++ How to Program
2   // table.h
3
4   #ifndef TABLE_H
5   #define TABLE_H
6
7   #include <iostream>
```

Fig. L 11.1   Contents of **table.h**. (Part 1 of 4.)

Lab Exercises

Name:

Lab Exercise — Table

```
8
9    using std::ostream;
10   using std::istream;
11
12   #include <new>
13
14   /* Write code that specifies Table as a class template
15      with type parameter elementType */
16   class Table {
17
18   public:
19      Table( int = 10, int = 10 );   // default constructor
20      Table( const Table< elementType > & ); // copy constructor
21      ~Table();
22
23      void print() const;
24      void inputValues();
25      const Table< elementType > &operator=(
26        const Table< elementType > & );
27      bool operator==( const Table< elementType > & ) const;
28
29      // determine if two arrays are not equal and
30      // return true, otherwise return false (uses operator==)
31      bool operator!=( const Table< elementType > &right ) const
32      {
33         return !( *this == right );
34
35      } // end function operator!=
36
37      elementType &operator()( int, int );
38      const elementType &operator()( int, int ) const;
39
40   private:
41      int rows;                 // number of rows in array
42      int columns;              // number of columns in array
43      /* Write declaration for private data member ptr, a pointer to
44         dynamically allocated array */
45
46   }; // end class Table
47
48   // default constructor
49   template < class elementType >
50   Table< elementType >::Table( int r, int c )
51   {
52      rows = ( r > 0 ? r : 10 );
53      columns = ( c > 0 ? c : 10 );
54      /* Write code to allocate dynamically an array with rows *
55         columns elements of type elementType */
56
57      for ( int i = 0; i < rows * columns; i++ )
58         ptr[ i ] = 0; // initialize array
59
60   } // end class Table constructor
61
```

Fig. L 11.1   Contents of **table.h**. (Part 2 of 4.)

Lab Exercises

Name:

Lab Exercise — Table

```
62   // constructor
63   template < class elementType >
64   Table< elementType >::Table(
65      const Table< elementType > &init )
66   {
67      rows = init.rows;
68      columns = init.columns;
69
70      ptr = new elementType[ rows * columns ];
71      for ( int i = 0; i < rows * columns; i++ )
72         ptr[ i ] = init.ptr[ i ];
73
74   } // end class Table constructor
75
76   // destructor
77   template < class elementType >
78   Table< elementType >::~Table()
79   {
80      delete [] ptr;
81
82   } // end class Table destructor
83
84   // template function operator= definition
85   template < class elementType >
86   const Table< elementType > &Table< elementType >
87      ::operator=( const Table< elementType > &right )
88   {
89      if ( &right != this ) {
90
91         if ( rows * columns != right.rows * right.columns ) {
92            delete [] ptr;
93            rows = right.rows;
94            columns = right.columns;
95            ptr = new elementType[ rows * columns ];
96
97         } // end if
98
99         for ( int i = 0; i < rows * columns; i++ )
100           ptr[ i ] = right.ptr[ i ];
101
102     } // end if
103
104     return *this;
105
106  } // end function operator=
107
108  /* Write definition for overloaded operator== */
109
110  /* Write definition for overloaded subscript operator for
111     non-const Tables; reference return creates an lvalue */
112
113  // template function operator() definition
114  template < class elementType >
115  const elementType &Table< elementType >
116     ::operator()( int s1, int s2 ) const
117  {
```

Fig. L 11.1   Contents of **table.h**. (Part 3 of 4.)

Lab Exercises   Name:

Lab Exercise — Table

```
118    if ( !( 0 <= s1 && s1 < rows ) )
119       s1 = 0;
120
121    if ( !( 0 <= s2 && s2 < columns ) )
122       s2 = 0;
123
124    return ptr[ columns * s1 + s2  ]; // rvalue
125
126 } // end function operator()
127
128 // template function inputValues definition
129 template < class elementType >
130 void Table< elementType >
131    ::inputValues()
132 {
133    for ( int i = 0; i < rows * columns; i++ )
134       cin >> ptr[ i ];
135
136 } // end function inputValues
137
138 // template function print definition
139 template < class elementType >
140 void Table< elementType >
141    ::print() const
142 {
143    for ( int i = 0; i < rows * columns; i++ ) {
144       cout << setw( 6 ) << ptr[ i ];
145
146       if ( ( i + 1 ) % columns == 0 )
147          cout << endl;
148
149    } // end for
150
151    if ( i % columns != 0 )
152       cout << endl;
153
154 } // end function print
155
156 #endif // TABLE_H
```

Fig. L 11.1   Contents of `table.h`. (Part 4 of 4.)

```
1  // Chapter 11 of C++ How to Program
2  // Driver for class Table
3
4  #include <iostream>
5
6  using std::cout;
7  using std::cin;
8  using std::endl;
9
10 #include <iomanip>
11
12 using std::setw;
```

Fig. L 11.2   Contents of `driver.cpp`. (Part 1 of 2.)

Lab Exercises

Name:

Lab Exercise — Table

```cpp
13
14   #include <new>
15
16   #include <ctime>
17
18   #include "table.h"
19
20   int main()
21   {
22      srand( time( 0 ) ); // seed random function
23
24      /* Write code to create a Table of ints of size ( 4, 7 );
25         name the Table a */
26      Table< char > b( 5, 2 );
27
28      cout << "Uninitialized array \"a\" is: \n";
29      a.print();
30
31      cout << "Uninitialized array \"b\" is: \n";
32      b.print(); // output null characters
33
34      // initialize array "a" with random values (0-100)
35      for ( int i = 0; i < 4; i++ )
36
37         for ( int j = 0; j < 7; j++ )
38            a( i, j ) = rand() % 101;
39
40      // initialize array "b" with 'g'
41      for ( i = 0; i < 5; i++ )
42
43         for ( int j = 0; j < 2; j++ )
44            b( i, j ) = 'g';
45
46      cout << "\nInitialized array \"a\" is now:\n";
47      a.print();
48
49      cout << "Initialized array b is now: \n";
50      b.print();
51
52      cout << "\nEnter values for b (10 of them): \n";
53      b.inputValues();
54      cout << endl;
55      b.print();
56      cout << endl;
57
58      // retrieve array element using overloaded operator()
59      cout << "The element (2, 1) of array \"a\" is: ";
60      /* Write code that accesses element 2,1 of "b" */
61
62      // change element of array using overloaded operator()
63      a( 2, 1 ) = -1;
64      cout << "Changed element (2, 1) to -1: \n";
65      a.print();
66
67      return 0;
68
69   } // end main
```

Fig. L 11.2   Contents of **driver.cpp**. (Part 2 of 2.)

Lab Exercises   Name:

Lab Exercise — Table

Problem-Solving Tips

1. A **Table** object should be instantiated as follows:

   ```
   Table< int > t1( 5, 5 );
   ```

   This creates a "double-subscripted array" of integers containing **25** elements.

2. The class definition and each member function definition should be preceded by the line

   ```
   template< class elementType >
   ```

3. Overload the following operators: **+, =, ==, !=**, and **()**.

4. There should be two versions of **operator()** — one that returns **elementType &** that element of a **Table** can be used as an *lvalue* and one that returns **const elementType &** so an element of a **const Table** can be used as an *rvalue*.

5. Your class should make it impossible for non-member functions (except for **friend**s) to access the array's data.

Follow-Up Questions and Activities

1. Modify the driver so that it uses the overloaded operators **=**, **==** and **!=**. Create two **Table**s, **table1** and **table2**, of random integers. If the **Table**s do not contain equivalent content, assign **table2** to **table1**, then test for equality. The output for this activity should be as follows:

Lab Exercises   Name:

Lab Exercise — Table

```
Uninitialized array "table1" is:
    0     0     0     0     0     0     0
    0     0     0     0     0     0     0
    0     0     0     0     0     0     0
    0     0     0     0     0     0     0
Uninitialized array "table2" is:
    0     0     0     0     0     0     0
    0     0     0     0     0     0     0
    0     0     0     0     0     0     0
    0     0     0     0     0     0     0
Initialized array "table1" is now:
   68    82    40    33     9     7    74
   10     1    59    31    22    24    47
   23    80    95    85    72    73    27
   13    26     6    72    71    44    34
Initialized array "table2" is now:
   44    59    19    40    90    33    54
   44    75    49    21    83    20    51
   29    63    73    96    32    18    77
   64     2    67    10    34    41    12

Array "table1" and "table2"are not equal.

Array "table1" is now:
   44    59    19    40    90    33    54
   44    75    49    21    83    20    51
   29    63    73    96    32    18    77
   64     2    67    10    34    41    12

Array "table2" is now:
   44    59    19    40    90    33    54
   44    75    49    21    83    20    51
   29    63    73    96    32    18    77
   64     2    67    10    34    41    12

Array "table1" and "table2" are equal.
```

Lab Exercises   Name: _____

Lab Exercise — Table

2. Write a non-member function, **printTable**, that takes a **Table** and prints its contents.

3. Is it possible to create a **DoubleScriptedArray** of **DoubleScriptedArray**s? If yes, write a decla-
    ration. If no, explain why not.

Lab Exercises

Name:

Lab Exercise — Table

Lab Exercises   Name:

Debugging

Name: _____   Date:_____

Section: _____

The program (Fig. L 11.3–Fig. L 11.4) in this section does not run properly. Fix all the syntax errors so that the program will compile successfully. Once the program compiles, compare the output with the sample output, and eliminate any logic errors that may exist. The sample output demonstrates what the program's output should be once the program's code has been corrected.

Sample Output

```
Arithmetic performed on object a:
The result of the operation is: 8
The result of the operation is: 2
The result of the operation is: 15
The result of the operation is: 1

Arithmetic performed on object b:
The result of the operation is: 12.5
The result of the operation is: 2.1
The result of the operation is: 37.96
The result of the operation is: 1.40385
```

Broken Code

```
1   // Chapter 11 of C++ How to Program
2   // Debugging problem (arithmetic.h)
3
4   #ifndef ARITHMETIC_H
5   #define ARITHMETIC_H
6
7   // template class Arithmetic
8   template< T >
9   class Arithmetic {
10
11  public:
12      Arithmetic( T, T );
13      T addition() const;
14      T subtraction() const;
15      T multiplication() const;
16      T division() const;
17
18  private:
19      int value1;
20      int value2;
21
22  }; // end class Arithmetic
23
```

Fig. L 11.3 Contents of **arithmetic.h**. (Part 1 of 2.)

Lab Exercises

Name: _____

Debugging

```
24  // constructor
25  Arithmetic::Arithmetic( T v1, T v2 )
26  {
27     value1 = v1;
28     value2 = v2;
29
30  } // end class Arithmetic constructor
31
32  // template function addition
33  template< class T >
34  T Arithmetic::addition() const
35  {
36     return value1 + value2;
37
38  } // end function addition
39
40  // template function subtraction
41  template< class T >
42  T Arithmetic< T >::subtraction() const
43  {
44     return value1 - value2;
45
46  } // end function subtraction
47
48  // template function multiplication
49  template< class T >
50  T Arithmetic< T >::multiplication() const
51  {
52     return value1 * value2;
53
54  } // end function multiplication
55
56  // template function division
57  template< class X >
58  X Arithmetic< X >::division() const
59  {
60     return val1 / val2;
61
62  } // end function division
63
64  #endif //ARITHMETIC_H
```

Fig. L 11.3   Contents of **arithmetic.h**. (Part 2 of 2.)

```
1  // Chapter 11 of C++ How to Program
2  // Debugging problem (debugging11.cpp)
3
4  #include <iostream>
5
6  using std::cout;
7  using std::endl;
8
```

Fig. L 11.4   Contents of **debugging11.cpp**.

Lab Exercises   Name:

Debugging

```
9   #include "arithmetic.h"
10
11  // template function printResult definition
12  < class T >
13  void printResult( T number )
14  {
15     cout << "The result of the operation is: " << number << endl;
16
17  } // end function printResult
18
19  int main()
20  {
21     Arithmetic a( 5, 3 );
22     Arithmetic< int > b( 7.3, 5.2 );
23
24     cout << "Arithmetic performed on object a:\n";
25     printResult( a< int >.addition() );
26     printResult( a< int >.subtraction() );
27     printResult( a< int >.multiplication() );
28     printResult( a< int >.division() );
29
30     cout << "\nArithmetic performed on object b:\n";
31     printResult( b.addition() );
32     printResult( b.subtraction() );
33     printResult( b.multiplication() );
34     printResult( b.division() );
35
36     return 0;
37
38  } // end main
```

Fig. L 11.4   Contents of **debugging11.cpp**.

Lab Exercises

Name:

Debugging

Postlab Activities

Coding Exercises

Name: _____   **Date:** _____

Section: _____

These coding exercises reinforce the lessons learned in the lab and provide additional programming experience outside the classroom and laboratory environment. They serve as a review after you have completed the Prelab Activities and Lab Exercises successfully.

For each of the following problems, write a program or a program segment that performs the specified action:

1. Write a function template that determines the largest of its four arguments. Assume that all four arguments are of the same type.

Postlab Activities   Name:

Coding Exercises

2. Convert the **linearSearch** program of Fig 4.19 in C++ *How to Program: Fourth Edition* into a template function.

12

C++ Stream Input/ Output

Objectives

- To understand how to use C++ object-oriented stream input/output.
- To format inputs and outputs, using the format flags defined in **<iomanip>**.
- To understand the stream-I/O class hierarchy.
- To understand how to input and output objects of programmer-defined types.
- To create programmer-defined stream manipulators.
- To determine the success or failure of input/output operations by testing the **failbit**, **badbit** and **goodbit** bits in the **ios** class.
- To use the unformatted input/output functions **read**, **gcount** and **write**.

Assignment Checklist

Name: _____　　　　**Date:** _____

Section: _____

Exercises	Assigned: Circle assignments	Date Due
Prelab Activities		
Matching	YES　　NO	
Fill in the Blank	10, 11, 12, 13, 14,	
Short Answer	15, 16, 17	
Programming Output	18, 19, 20	
Correct the Code	21, 22	
Lab Exercises		
Lab Exercise — Formatted Output	YES　　NO	
Follow-Up Questions and Activities	1, 2	
Debugging	YES　　NO	
Labs Provided by Instructor		
1.		
2.		
3.		
Postlab Activities		
Coding Exercises	1, 2, 3	
Programming Challenge	4	

Assignment Checklist

Name: _____

Prelab Activities

Matching

Name: _____   **Date:** _____

Section: _____

After reading Chapter 12 of *C++ How to Program: Fourth Edition*, answer the given questions. These questions are intended to test and reinforce your understanding of key concepts and may be done either before the lab or during the lab.

For each term in the column on the left, write the corresponding letter for the description that best matches it from the column on the right.

Term	Description
_____ 1. Unformatted I/O	a) Overloaded left-shift operator (`<<`).
_____ 2. Formatted I/O	b) Command, such as **endl**.
_____ 3. Parameterized stream manipulator	c) Chaining together a series of calls, such as `cout << a << b << "hi" << endl;`
_____ 4. Stream-insertion operator	d) Performed with the **read** and **write** member functions.
_____ 5. Stream-extraction operator	e) Specify the kinds of formatting to be performed during I/O operations.
_____ 6. Stream	f) Overloaded right-shift operator (`>>`).
_____ 7. Cascaded form	g) Stream manipulator that takes an argument.
_____ 8. Format flag	h) Formatted by functions in the header file `<iomanip>`.
_____ 9. Stream manipulator	i) Sequence of bytes.

Prelab Activities

Name:

Matching

Prelab Activities

Name: _____

Fill in the Blank

Name: _____   Date: _____

Section: _____

Fill in the blank for each of the following statements:

10. In _____ operations, bytes flow from a device (e.g., a keyboard, a disk drive, a network connection) to main memory.

11. In _____ operations, bytes flow from main memory to a device (e.g., a display screen, a printer, a disk drive, a network connection).

12. The _____ header declares services that are important file-processing operations.

13. Stream extraction causes the stream's _____ to be set if data of the wrong type is input and causes the stream's _____ to be set if the operation fails.

14. _____ provides capabilities such as setting field widths, setting precision, setting and unsetting format flags, setting the fill character in fields, flushing streams, inserting a newline in the output stream and flushing the stream, inserting a null character in the output stream and skipping whitespace in the input stream.

Prelab Activities

Name:

Fill in the Blank

Prelab Activities   Name:

Short Answer

Name: _____   Date:_____

Section: _____

In the space provided, answer each of the given questions. Your answers should be as concise as possible; aim for two or three sentences.

15. What is the difference between "low-level" and "high-level" I/O capabilities?

16. Explain how to tie an output stream to an input stream. Why would a programmer want to do this?

17. Explain the concept of type-safe I/O.

Prelab Activities

Name:

Short Answer

Prelab Activities   Name:

Programming Output

Name: _____   Date:_____

Section: _____

For each of the given program segments, read the code and write the output in the space provided below each program. [*Note*: Do not execute these programs on a computer.]

18. What is the output of the given program? Assume that the user enters the sentence "**This is my input sentence.**" when prompted for a sentence.

```cpp
1   #include <iostream>
2
3   using std::cout;
4   using std::cin;
5   using std::endl;
6
7   int main()
8   {
9       const int SIZE = 80;
10      char buffer[ SIZE ];
11
12      cout << "Enter a sentence: \n";
13      cin.read( buffer, 15 );
14      cout << "\nThe sentence entered was:\n";
15      cout.write( buffer, cin.gcount() );
16      cout << endl;
17      return 0;
18
19  } // end main
```

Your answer:

Prelab Activities

Name:

Programming Output

Prelab Activities

Name: _____

Correct the Code

Name: _____   Date:_____

Section: _____

For each of the given program segments, determine if there is an error in the code. If there is an error, specify whether it is a logic error or a syntax error, circle the error in the program, and write the corrected code in the space provided after each problem. If the code does not contain an error, write "no error." [*Note*: It is possible that a program segment may contain multiple errors.]

21. The following program should print a table of numbers:

```
1   #include <iostream>
2
3   using std::cout;
4   using std::endl;
5
6   #include <iomanip>
7
8   using std::setw;
9
10  int main()
11  {
12     int n[ 3 ][ 3 ] = { { 1, 2, 3 }, { 4, 5, 6 }, { 7, 8, 9 } };
13
14     // display each number in a field width of 10
15     cout << setw( 10 );
16
17     for ( int i = 0; i < 3; i++ ){
18          cout << endl;
19        for ( int j = 0; j < 3; j++ )
20           cout << n[i][j];
21
22     } // end for
23
24     return 0;
25
26  } // end main
```

Your Answer:

Prelab Activities   Name:

Correct the Code

22. The given program should output the following results:

```
32 in hexadecimal is: 20
32 in octal is: 40
32 in decimal is: 32
```

```
1    #include <iostream>
2
3    using std::cout;
4    using std::endl;
5
6    #include <iomanip>
7
8    using std::hex;
9    using std::dec;
10   using std::oct;
11
12   int main()
13   {
14      double n = 32;
15
16      cout << n << " in hexadecimal is: "
17           << hex << n << endl
18           << n << " in octal is: "
19           << oct << n << endl
20           << n << " in decimal is: "
21           << dec << n << endl;
22
23      return 0;
24
25   } // end main
```

Your Answer:

Lab Exercises

Lab Exercise — Formatted Output

Name: _____   Date:_____

Section: _____

This problem is intended to be solved in a closed-lab session with a teaching assistant or instructor present. The problem is divided into six parts:

1. Lab Objectives

2. Description of the Problem

3. Sample Output

4. Program Template (Fig. L 12.1)

5. Problem-Solving Tips

6. Follow-Up Questions and Activities

The program template represents a complete working C++ program, with one or more key lines of code replaced with comments. Read the problem description and examine the sample output; then study the template code. Using the problem-solving tips as a guide, replace the /* */ comments with C++ code. Compile and execute the program. Compare your output with the sample output provided. Then answer the follow-up questions. The source code for the template is available at **www.deitel.com** and **www.prenhall.com./deitel**.

Lab Objectives

This lab was designed to reinforce programming concepts from Chapter 12 of *C++ How To Program: Fourth Edition*. In this lab, you will practice:

*   writing programmer-defined stream manipulators

*   varying stream format states

*   controlling stream errors

The follow-up questions and activities also will give you practice:

*   calling unformatted I/O functions

Problem Description

Often, an array's data is displayed in several different formats. While the user inputs integers into an array, use the **ios** state bits to ensure that the user does not enter any nonnumeric values. Once the numbers are input successfully, output a table displaying the numbers in binary, octadecimal, decimal and hexadecimal format. The standard library does not contain a function for converting a number to its binary representation, so you must write the function **convertBinary**. Next, convert the integers to floating-point numbers, and output them in a second table wherein one column is formatted and the other column is not. The numbers in the formatted column should have a precision of **2**, be output in scientific notation and display a sign and decimal point. When spacing the table, create user-defined manipulators that call function **setw**.

Lab Exercises   Name:

Lab Exercise — Formatted Output

Sample Output

```
enter number 1: a
That is invalid input, enter another number: 10
enter number 2: 20
enter number 3: 30
enter number 4: 40
enter number 5: 50

Table with the numbers in various bases
bin        oct        dec        hex
1010       012        10         A
10100      024        20         14
11110      036        30         1E
101000     050        40         28
110010     062        50         32

Table of formatted and unformatted floating points
unformatted formatted
10          +1.00E+001
20          +2.00E+001
30          +3.00E+001
40          +4.00E+001
50          +5.00E+001
```

Template

```cpp
1   // Chapter 12 of C++ How to Program
2   // bases.cpp
3
4   #include <iostream>
5
6   using std::cout;
7   using std::cin;
8   using std::endl;
9   /* Include all necessary using statements from iostream */
10
11  #include <iomanip>
12  /* Include all necessary using statements from iomanip */
13
14  #include <cmath>
15
16  /* Write a programmer-defined manipulator width8 that sets
17     the width to 8 */
18
19  /* Write a programmer-defined manipulator width12 that sets
20     the width to 12 */
21
```

Fig. L 12.1   **bases.cpp**. (Part 1 of 3.)

Lab Exercises   Name:

Lab Exercise — Formatted Output

```cpp
22   // function to convert decimal number to binary number
23   int convertBinary( int x )
24   {
25      int power;
26      int result = 0;
27
28      for ( power = 0; x >= pow( 2, power ); power++ ) ;
29
30      for ( ; power >= 0; power-- ) {
31         result *= 10;
32
33         if ( x / pow( 2, power ) >= 1 ) {
34            result++;
35            x -= pow( 2, power );
36
37         } // end if
38
39      } // end for
40
41      return result;
42
43   } // end function convertBinary
44
45   // function printTable definition
46   void printTable( int a[], const int size )
47   {
48      cout << "\nTable with the numbers in various bases\n";
49
50      /* Write a statement to left justify the following table */
51      /* Write a statement to print the header, use the width8
52         manipulator for spacing */
53
54      for ( int i = 0; i < size; i++ )
55         /* Write a statement to output the table of bases    */
56         /* Octadecimal output should specify the base         */
57         /* Hexadecimal output should include only uppercase */
58
59      cout << "\nTable of formatted and unformatted "
60           << "floating points\n";
61
62      /* Write a statement to print header, use the width12
63         manipulator for spacing */
64
65      for ( int j = 0; j < size; j++ ) {
66         double x = static_cast< double > ( a[ j ] );
67         /* Write a statement to output the formatted vs.
68            unformatted table */
69         /* Formatted output should print in scientific notation,
70            showing the decimal point and the sign, and
71            have a precision of 2 */
72         /* Undo formatting changes */
73
74      } // end for
75
76   } // end function printTable
77
```

Fig. L 12.1   **bases.cpp**. (Part 2 of 3.)

Lab Exercises

Name:

Lab Exercise — Formatted Output

```
78   int main()
79   {
80      int x[ 5 ] = { 0 };
81
82      for ( int counter = 0; counter < 5; counter++ ) {
83         cout << "enter number " << counter + 1 << ": ";
84         cin >> x[ counter ];
85
86         /* Write a statement to test if stream errors occurred */
87         /* If there were stream errors, input another number   */
88
89      } // end for
90
91      printTable( x, 5 );
92
93      return 0;
94
95   } // end main
```

Fig. L 12.1   `bases.cpp`. (Part 3 of 3.)

Problem-Solving Tips

1. To determine whether a user's input is valid, test function **good**. If **cin.good()** returns **false**, the input is invalid. When the input is invalid, restore the stream's state to "good," using **cin.clear**, and ignore the previous input, using **cin.ignore**.

2. Remember to undo formatting changes after outputting a formatted object. Otherwise, the formatting changes will remain in place when the next data set is output.

Follow-Up Questions and Activities

1. Why was **convertBinary** created as a function rather than as a nonparameterized stream manipulator?

2. Modify function **printTable** to display hexadecimal numbers with lowercase letters.

Lab Exercises   Name:

Debugging

Name: _____   Date:_____

Section: _____

The program in this section does not run properly. Fix all the syntax errors so that the program will compile successfully. Once the program compiles, compare the output with the sample output, and eliminate any logic errors that may exist. The sample output demonstrates what the program's output should be once the program's code is corrected.

Sample Output
[*Note*: Be careful when comparing your output with the one shown here. Confirm that your output is formatted identically.]

```
Enter a number: 2.3456
Enter a number: 0.895
The value of x is: +2.346000000
The value of y is:    8.95e-001
```

Broken Code

```cpp
1   // Chapter 12 of C++ How to Program
2   // Debugging problem (debugging12.cpp)
3
4   #include <iostream>
5
6   using std::cout;
7   using std::endl;
8   using std::cin;
9   using std::ios;
10
11  #include <iomanip>
12
13  using std::setw;
14  using std::setprecision;
15  using std::fixed;
16  using std::left;
17  using std::right;
18  using std::scientific;
19
20  double readNumber();
21  void printFormatted( double, double );
22
23  int main()
24  {
25      double x, y;
26
27      x = readNumber();
28      y = readNumber();
29      printFormatted( x, y );
```

Fig. L 12.2   **debugging12.cpp**. (Part 1 of 2.)

Lab Exercises

Name:

Debugging

```
30
31       return 0;
32
33   } // end main
34
35   // function readNumber definition
36   double readNumber()
37   {
38       double number = 0;
39       double place = 10;
40
41       cout << "Enter a number: ";
42       number = cin.getline() - '0';
43
44       while ( cin.peek() != '.' && cin.peek() != '\n' )
45          number *= 10 + atof( cin.get() );
46
47       while ( cin.peek() != '.' ) {
48          number += static_cast< double >( cin.get() ) / place;
49          place *= 10;
50
51       } // end while
52
53       cin.ignore();
54
55       return number;
56
57   } // end function getNumber
58
59   // function printFormatted definition
60   void printFormatted( double x, double y )
61   {
62       char buffer[] = "The value of x is: ";
63
64       for ( int i = 0; buffer[ i ] != '\n'; i++ )
65          cout.put( buffer[ i ] );
66
67       cout << setw( 12 ) << setprecision( 3 ) << setfill( '0' )
68          << ios::fixed
69          << left << x << endl;
70
71       cout.write( "The value of y is: " );
72
73       cout << setprecision( 2 )
74          << ios::scientific << ios::right
75          << y << endl;
76
77   } // end function printFormatted
```

Fig. L 12.2   **debugging12.cpp**. (Part 2 of 2.)

Postlab Activities

Coding Exercises

Name: _____   **Date:**_____

Section: _____

These coding exercises reinforce the lessons learned in the lab and provide additional programming experience outside the classroom and laboratory environment. They serve as a review after you have completed the Prelab Activities and Lab Exercises successfully.

For each of the following problems, write a program or a program segment that performs the specified action.

1. Write a program to test the inputting of integer values in decimal, octal and hexadecimal format. Output each integer read by the program in all three formats. Test the program with the following input data: $10, 010, 0x10$.

Postlab Activities

Name:

Coding Exercises

2. Write a program that prints the value **100.453627** rounded to the nearest digit, tenth position, hundredth position, thousandth position and ten thousandth position.

Postlab Activities   Name:

Coding Exercises

3. Write a program that converts integer Fahrenheit temperatures ranging from **0** to **212** degrees to floating-point Celsius temperatures with three digits of precision. Use the statement

    ```
    celsius = 5.0 / 9.0 * ( fahrenheit - 32 );
    ```

    to perform the calculation. The output should be printed in two right-justified columns, and the Celsius temperature should be preceded by a sign for positive and negative values.

Postlab Activities

Name:

Coding Exercises

Postlab Activities   Name:

Programming Challenges

Name: _____   Date:_____

Section: _____

The Programming Challenges are more involved than the Coding Exercises and may require a significant amount of time to complete. Write a C++ program for each of the problems in this section. The answers to these problems are available at **www.deitel.com**, **www.prenhall.com/deitel** and on the *C++ Multimedia Cyber Classroom: Fourth Edition*. Pseudocode, hints and/or sample outputs are provided to aid you in your programming.

4. Write a program that accomplishes each of the following tasks:

    a) Create a user-defined class **Point** that contains the **private** integer data members **xCoordinate** and **yCoordinate** and declares stream-insertion and stream-extraction overloaded operator functions as **friend**s of the class.

    b) Define the stream-insertion and stream-extraction operator functions. The stream-extraction operator function should determine if the data entered is a point, and, if not, it should set the **ios::failbit** to indicate improper input. The stream-insertion operator should not be able to display the point after an input error occurred.

    Write a **main** function that tests input and output of user-defined class **Point**, using the overloaded stream-extraction and stream-insertion operators.

Hints:

   - Use the **peek** function to determine if the first input is an open-parenthesis character. If it is, then ignore it. Otherwise, use **cin.clear(failbit)** to set the **failbit**, and alert the user of your class that the input is incorrect.

   - The next character should be an integer. The statement **cin >> p.xCoordinate**, where **p** is the **Point** object, sets the **failbit** if the input is not an integer.

   - Similarly, the third character should be a comma. Use **peek** again, and set the **failbit** if necessary.

   - Call the **cin.good** function in your driver to ensure that the **>>** operator works properly. An alternative is to overload the **<<** operator to check if the **failbit** was set.

Postlab Activities   Name:

Programming Challenges

13

Exception Handling

Objectives

- To know when to use and when not to use exception handling.
- To use **try** blocks to detect exceptions.
- To use **throw** statements to communicate information about an error.
- To use **catch** statements to handle exceptions.
- To process caught and uncaught exceptions.

Assignment Checklist

Name: _____   **Date:**_____

Section: _____

Exercises	Assigned: Circle assignments	Date Due
Prelab Activities		
Matching	YES NO	
Fill in the Blank	7, 8, 9, 10, 11, 12, 13	
Short Answer	14, 15	
Programming Output	16, 17	
Correct the Code	18, 19	
Lab Exercises		
Lab Exercise	YES NO	
Follow-Up Questions and Activities	1, 2	
Debugging	YES NO	
Labs Provided by Instructor		
1.		
2.		
3.		
Postlab Activities		
Coding Exercise		

Assignment Checklist   Name:

Prelab Activities

Matching

Name: _____   **Date:** _____

Section: _____

After reading Chapter 13 of *C++ How to Program: Fourth Edition*, answer the given questions. These questions are intended to test and reinforce your understanding of key concepts and may be done either before the lab or during the lab.

For each term in the column on the left, write the corresponding letter for the description that best matches it from the column on the right.

Term	Description
____ 1. **catch** block	a) Helps improve a program's fault tolerance.
____ 2. **auto_ptr**	b) Encloses the code that may generate an exception.
____ 3. Exception handling	c) Exception thrown when **new** fails.
____ 4. **catch(...)**	d) Class template that helps avoid memory leaks.
____ 5. **try** block	e) Encloses the code that is executed when an exception is caught.
____ 6. **bad_alloc**	f) "Catch all" handler that catches any exception.

Prelab Activities   Name:

Matching

Prelab Activities   Name: _____

Fill in the Blank

Name: _____   **Date:** _____

Section: _____

Fill in the blank for each of the following statements:

7. When an exception is not caught in a program, function _____ is called.

8. Exception handling is designed for dealing with _____ errors (i.e., errors that occur as the result of a program's execution).

9. Typically, exception handling deals with errors in a different _____ from that which detected the error.

10. Class _____ is the base class for the exception hierarchy.

11. Once an exception is thrown, control cannot return directly to the _____.

12. _____ catches all exceptions.

13. A derived-class object can be caught either by a handler specifying the derived-class type or by handlers specifying the types of any _____ of that derived class.

Prelab Activities   Name:

Fill in the Blank

Prelab Activities   Name:

Short Answer

Name: _____   **Date:** _____

Section: _____

In the space provided, answer each of the given questions. Your answers should be as concise as possible; aim for two or three sentences.

14. Describe two ways of detecting memory allocation failures.

15. If an exception is thrown, but not caught in a particular scope, to what point does control return? What is the name for this process?

Prelab Activities

Name:

Short Answer

Prelab Activities

Name:

Programming Output

Name: _____   Date:_____

Section: _____

For each of the given program segments, read the code and write the output in the space provided below each program. [*Note*: Do not execute these programs on a computer.]

16. What is output by the following program?

```
1   #include <iostream>
2
3   using std::cout;
4   using std::endl;
5
6   #include <string>
7
8   using std::string;
9
10  // class DivideZero definition
11  class DivideZero {
12
13  public:
14
15     // constructor
16     DivideZero()
17        : out( "EXCEPTION: Division by zero attempted." )
18     {
19        // empty
20
21     } // end class DivideZero exception
22
23     // function display definition
24     string display() const
25     {
26        return out;
27
28     } // end function display
29
30  private:
31     string out;
32
33  }; // end class DivideZero
34
35  // function arithmetic definition
36  double arithmetic( int n, int d )
37  {
38     if ( d == 0 )
39        throw DivideZero();
40
41     return static_cast< double > ( n ) / d;
42
43  } // end function arithmetic
```

Prelab Activities   Name:

Programming Output

```
44
45    int main()
46    {
47       try {
48          cout << arith( 24, 6 ) << endl;
49          cout << arith( 1, 3 ) << endl;
50          cout << arith( 9, 0 ) << endl;
51
52       } // end try
53
54       catch ( DivideZero &e ) {
55          cout << e.display() << endl;
56
57       } // end catch
58
59       return 0;
60
61    } // end main
```

(Part 2 of 2.)

Your answer:

17. What is output by the following program?

```
1     #include <iostream>
2
3     using std::cout;
4     using std::endl;
5
6     #include <stdexcept>
7
8     using std::runtime_error;
9
10    // function function3 definition
11    void function3() throw ( runtime_error )
12    {
13       throw runtime_error( "runtime_error in function3" );
14
15    } // end function function3
16
17    // function function2 definition
18    void function2() throw ( runtime_error )
19    {
20       function3();
21
22    } // end function function2
23
```

(Part 1 of 2.)

Prelab Activities   Name:

Programming Output

```
24   // function function1 definition
25   void function1() throw ( runtime_error )
26   {
27      try {
28         function2();
29
30      } // end try
31
32      catch ( runtime_error e )
33      {
34         cout << "Exception occurred:\n" << e.what()
35            << "; caught in function1\n";
36         throw;
37
38      } // end catch
39
40   } // end function function1
41
42   int main()
43   {
44      try {
45         function1();
46
47      } // end try
48
49      catch ( runtime_error &e )
50      {
51         cout << "Exception occurred:\n" << e.what()
52            << "; caught in main\n";
53
54      } // end catch
55
56      return 0;
57
58   } // end main
```

(Part 2 of 2.)

Your answer:

Prelab Activities

Name:

Programming Output

Prelab Activities   Name:

Correct the Code

Name: _____   Date:_____

Section: _____

For each of the given program segments, determine if there is an error in the code. If there is an error, specify whether it is a logic error or a syntax error, circle the error in the program, and write the corrected code in the space provided after each problem. If the code does not contain an error, write "no error." [*Note*: It is possible that a program segment may contain multiple errors.]

18. The following program segment should **catch** two exception types thrown by **function1**.

```
1      try {
2          function1();
3
4      } // end try
5
6      catch ( runtime_error &r, DivideByZeroException &z ){
7          cout << "Exception( s ) occurred:\n" << r.what() << " and "
8              << z.what() << "; caught in main\n";
9
10     } // end catch
```

Your answer:

Prelab Activities

Name:

Correct the Code

19. The following program segment should **catch runtime_error**s, **DividebyZeroException**s or any other exception thrown by **function2**.

```
1     try {
2         function2();
3     }
4     catch ( ... )
5     catch ( runtime_error &r )
6     {
7         cout << "Exception occurred:\n" << r.what()
8     }
9     catch ( DivideByZeroException &z )
10    {
11        cout << "Exception occurred:\n" << z.what()
12    }
13
```

Your answer:

Lab Exercises

Lab Exercise

Name: _____   **Date:** _____

Section: _____

This problem is intended to be solved in a closed-lab session with a teaching assistant or instructor present. The problem is divided into six parts:

1. Lab Objectives
2. Description of the Problem
3. Sample Output
4. Program Template (Fig. L 13.1)
5. Problem-Solving Tips
6. Follow-Up Questions and Activities

The program template represents a complete working C++ program, with one or more key lines of code replaced with comments. Read the problem description and examine the sample output; then study the template code. Using the problem-solving tips as a guide, replace the /* */ comments with C++ code. Compile and execute the program. Compare your output with the sample output provided. Then answer the follow-up questions. The source code for the template is available at **www.deitel.com** and **www.prenhall.com./deitel**.

Lab Objectives

This lab was designed to reinforce programming concepts from Chapter 13 of *C++ How To Program: Fourth Edition*. In this lab, you will practice:

- writing a class to determine whether a string contains digit characters.

- using exception handling to handle non-numeric inputs.

The follow-up questions and activities also will give you practice:

- using exception handling to handle inputs that are too large.

- contrasting **catch** statements with **catch(...)** statements.

Problem Description

Write a short program that reads a number from the user and stores the number as a string of characters. Convert this string to an integer. Before conversion, test for a **NonNumber** exception, which occurs if one or more of the characters is not a digit. Your program should not **throw** an exception if it detects a – sign before the number.

Lab Exercises   Name:

Lab Exercise

Sample Output

```
Please enter a number (end-of-file to terminate): 4
The number entered was: 4

Please enter a number (end-of-file to terminate): 28
The number entered was: 28

Please enter a number (end-of-file to terminate): -257
The number entered was: -257

Please enter a number (end-of-file to terminate): a23
INVALID INPUT: non-integer detected

Please enter a number (end-of-file to terminate): 34k3
INVALID INPUT: non-integer detected

Please enter a number (end-of-file to terminate): -3413-3
INVALID INPUT: non-integer detected

Please enter a number (end-of-file to terminate): -4-8
INVALID INPUT: non-integer detected

Please enter a number (end-of-file to terminate): ^Z
```

Template

```cpp
1   // Chapter 13 of C++ How to Program
2   // numberverifier.cpp
3   #include <iostream>
4
5   using std::cout;
6   using std::cin;
7   using std::endl;
8
9   #include <cmath>
10
11  #include <string>
12
13  using std::string;
14
15  // class NonNumber definition
16  class NonNumber : public exception {
17  public:
18
19     // constructor
20     NonNumber()
21        : exception( "non-integer detected" )
22     {
23        // empty
24
25     } // end class NonNumber definition
26
27     /* write definition for method what */
```

Fig. L 13.1   **numberverifier.cpp**. (Part 1 of 2.)

Lab Exercises   Name: _____

Lab Exercise

```cpp
28
29  private:
30     string message;
31
32  }; // end class NonNumber
33
34  // function castInput definition
35  int castInput( string input )
36  {
37     int result = 0;
38     int negative = 1;
39
40     if ( !( input.find_first_not_of( "-0123456789" ) == string::npos ) )
41        /* Write code to throw NonNumber exception */
42
43     // check for minus sign
44     if ( input[ 0 ] == '-' )
45       negative = -1;
46
47     for ( int i = input.length() - 1, j = 0; i >= 0; i--, j++ ) {
48
49        if ( negative == -1 && i == 0 )
50           continue;
51
52        if ( input[ i ] != '-' )
53           result += static_cast< int >( input[ i ] - '0' ) * pow( 10, j );
54
55        else
56           /* Write code to throw NonNumber exception */
57
58     } // end for
59
60     return result * negative;
61
62  } // end function castInput
63
64  int main()
65  {
66     string input;
67     int convert;
68
69     cout << "Please enter a number (end-of-file to terminate): ";
70
71     while ( cin >> input ) {
72
73        /* Write try block that calls castInput */
74        /* Write catch handler that catches any exceptions
75           that the call to castInput might have thrown */
76
77        cout << "\n\nPlease enter a number (end-of-file to terminate): ";
78     }
79
80     cout << endl;
81
82     return 0;
83
84  } // end main
```

Fig. L 13.1   **numberverifier.cpp**. (Part 2 of 2.)

Lab Exercises

Name: _____

Lab Exercise

Problem-Solving Tips

1. **try** and **catch** block bodies must be enclosed in curly braces, **{ }**.

2. If the call to **castInput** does not **throw** an exception, execute the line

```
cout << "The number entered was: " << convert;
```

Follow-Up Questions and Activities:

1. Modify the program by creating an exception class **Overflow** for detecting whether the user input "fits" into an **int** variable. Any input longer than 10 digits should generate an overflow error. Modify function **castInput** to check for this error, and add an appropriate **catch** statement in **main** to handle this type of exception if it is thrown. A typical run of your program should look like this:

```
Please enter a number (end-of-file to terminate): 44
The number entered was: 44

Please enter a number (end-of-file to terminate): -44
The number entered was: -44

Please enter a number (end-of-file to terminate): p25
INVALID INPUT: non-integer detected

Please enter a number (end-of-file to terminate): 123456789
The number entered was: 123456789

Please enter a number (end-of-file to terminate): 12345678901
INVALID INPUT: overflow detected

Please enter a number (end-of-file to terminate): ^Z
```

2. In your solution to Follow-Up Question 1, replace the second **catch** with a **catch(...)** statement. What changes occur?

Lab Exercises   Name:

Debugging

Name: _____   Date:_____

Section: _____

The program (Fig. L 13.2) in this section does not run properly. Fix all the syntax errors so that the program will compile successfully. Once the program compiles, compare the output with the sample output, and eliminate any logic errors that may exist. The sample output demonstrates what the program's output should be once the program's code has been corrected.

Sample Output

```
Enter an integer from 1 to 100 (-1 to end): 54
Enter an integer from 1 to 100 (-1 to end): 12
54 / 12 = 4.5

Enter an integer from 1 to 100 (-1 to end): 93
Enter an integer from 1 to 100 (-1 to end): 32
93 / 32 = 2.90625

Enter an integer from 1 to 100 (-1 to end): a
Exception occurred: entered input of the wrong data type
Enter an integer from 1 to 100 (-1 to end): -4
Exception occurred: entered a number not in the range of 1 to 100
Enter an integer from 1 to 100 (-1 to end): 132
Exception occurred: entered a number not in the range of 1 to 100
Enter an integer from 1 to 100 (-1 to end): -1
An unknown exception has occurred, exiting the program
```

Broken Code

```cpp
1   // Chapter 13 of C++ How to Program
2   // Debugging problem (debugging13.cpp)
3
4   #include <iostream>
5
6   using std::cout;
7   using std::cin;
8   using std::endl;
9   using std::ios;
10
11  #include <exception>
12
13  using std::exception;
14
15  // class InvalidInputTypeException definition
16  class InvalidInputTypeException {
17  public:
18
```

Fig. L 13.2   `debugging13.cpp`. (Part 1 of 3.)

Lab Exercises

Name:

Debugging

```
19      // constructor
20      InvalidInputTypeException()
21         : message( "entered input of the wrong data type" )
22      {
23         // empty
24
25      } // end class InvalidInputTypeException
26
27      // function what definition
28      const char *what() const
29      {
30         return message.c_str();
31
32      } // end function what
33
34   private:
35      string message;
36
37   }; // end class InvalidInputTypeException
38
39   // class OutOfRangeException definition
40   class OutOfRangeException {
41   public:
42
43      // constructor
44      exception OutOfRangeException()
45         : message( "entered a number not in the valid range" )
46      {
47         // empty
48
49      } // end class OutOfRangeException constructor
50
51      // function what definition
52      const char *what() const
53      {
54         return message.c_str();
55
56      } // end function what
57
58   private:
59      string message;
60
61   }; // end class OutOfRangeException
62
63   // function inputNumber definition
64   int inputNumber()
65   {
66      int number;
67
68      cout << "Enter an integer from 1 to 100 (-1 to end): ";
69      cin >> number;
70
71      if ( cin.fail() == 1 )
72         throw( InvalidInputTypeException );
73
74      if ( number > 100 || number < 1 )
75         throw exception( OutOfRangeException() );
```

Fig. L 13.2   **debugging13.cpp**. (Part 2 of 3.)

Lab Exercises   Name:

Debugging

```
76
77      if ( num == -1 )
78         throw;
79
80      return number;
81
82   } // end function inputNumber
83
84   int main()
85   {
86      int num1 = 0;
87      int num2 = 0;
88      double result;
89
90      // only way to exit this loop is an exception
91      while ( true ) {
92         number1 = inputNumber();
93         number2 = inputNumber();
94
95         try {
96            result = static_cast< double >( number1 ) / number2;
97            cout << number1 << " / " << number2 << " = " << result
98                 << endl << endl;
99
100        } // end try
101
102        catch ( ... ) {
103           cout << "An unknown exception has occurred, "
104                << "exiting the program\n"
105                << e.what() << endl;
106           exit( 0 );
107
108        }; // end catch
109
110        catch ( InvalidInputTypeException &e ) {
111           cout << "Exception occurred: " << e.what() << '\n';
112           cin.clear();
113           cin.ignore();
114
115        } // end catch
116
117        catch ( OutOfRangeException &&e )
118           cout << "Exception occurred: " << e.what() << '\n';
119
120     } // end while
121
122     return 0;
123
124   } // end main
```

Fig. L 13.2   **debugging13.cpp**. (Part 3 of 3.)

Lab Exercises   Name:

Debugging

Postlab Activities

Coding Exercise

Name: _____   **Date:** _____

Section: _____

These coding exercises reinforce the lessons learned in the lab and provide additional programming experience outside the classroom and laboratory environment. They serve as a review after you have completed the Prelab Activities and Lab Exercises successfully.

For the following problem, write a program or a program segment that performs the specified action:

1. A **try** block contains a function call to **mystery** that could produce any of the following exceptions: **DivideByZeroException**, **InvalidInputException**, **ArithmeticException** or **Invalid CastException**. Class **ArithmeticException** is a base class of **DivideByZeroException**. Write the **try** block and necessary **catch** blocks. Add a **catch** block to handle all other possible exceptions.

Postlab Activities

Name:

Coding Exercise

14

File Processing

Objectives

- To create, read, write and update files.
- To become familiar with sequential-access file processing.
- To use the streams included in the `<fstream>` header.

Assignment Checklist

Name: _____   **Date:** _____

Section: _____

Exercises	Assigned: Circle assignments	Date Due
Prelab Activities		
Matching	YES NO	
Fill in the Blank	7, 8, 9, 10, 11, 12, 13, 14	
Short Answer	15, 16	
Correct the Code	17, 18	
Lab Exercises		
Lab Exercise — **Craps**	YES NO	
Follow-Up Questions and Activities	1, 2, 3	
Labs Provided by Instructor		
1.		
2.		
3.		
Postlab Activities		
Coding Exercises	1, 2	

Assignment Checklist

Name:

Prelab Activities

Matching

Name: _____   **Date:** _____

Section: _____

After reading Chapter 14 of *C++ How to Program: Fourth Edition*, answer the given questions. These questions are intended to test and reinforce your understanding of key concepts and may be done either before the lab or during the lab.

For each term in the column on the left, write the corresponding letter for the description that best matches it from the column on the right.

Term	Description
____ 1. Record	a) Provides rapid access to file-based data.
____ 2. Sequential-access file	b) Group of characters that conveys meaning.
____ 3. Byte	c) Group of bits organized to represent a single data item.
____ 4. Field	d) File that must be read from and written to linearly.
____ 5. Data hierarchy	e) Group of related character fields.
____ 6. Random-access file	f) Data items ranging from bits to databases.

Prelab Activities

Name:

Matching

Prelab Activities

Name:

Fill in the Blank

Name: _____   **Date:** _____

Section: _____

Fill in the blank for each of the following statements:

7. A group of related files is stored in a(n) _____.

8. A collection of programs designed to create and manage databases is called a(n) _____.

9. The header **<fstream>** provides the definitions for stream-class templates _____, _____ and _____.

10. _____ indicates the position in the file from which the next input is to occur.

11. Repositioning the read location in a file requires a call to function _____.

12. Repositioning the write location in a file requires a call to function _____.

13. Unary operator _____ returns a type's size in bytes.

14. Using _____ records only is a convenient way to implement random-access files.

Prelab Activities   Name:

Fill in the Blank

Prelab Activities   Name:

Short Answer

Name: _____   **Date:** _____

Section: _____

In the space provided, answer each of the given questions. Your answers should be as concise as possible; aim for two or three sentences.

15. List the computer data hierarchy from bit to database.

16. Why are random-access files preferable to sequential-access files in performance-oriented situations?

Prelab Activities   Name:

Short Answer

Prelab Activities

Name: _____

Correct the Code

Name: _____   Date:_____

Section: _____

For each of the given program segments, determine if there is an error in the code. If there is an error, specify whether it is a logic error or a syntax error, circle the error in the program, and write the corrected code in the space provided after each problem. If the code does not contain an error, write "no error." [*Note*: It is possible that a program segment may contain multiple errors.]

17. The following code attempts to open **temp.dat** for writing, assume that all the necessary header files and **using** statements have been provided.

```
1   Stream outfile( "temp.dat", ios::out );
2
3   if ( outfile ) {
4      cerr << "operation failed";
5      exit( 1 );
6
7   } // end if
```

Your answer:

18. The program in this section counts the number of Perl keywords in a file. A sample output has been provided.

```
if was used 3 time(s).
else was used 1 time(s).
while was used 1 time(s).
for was used 1 time(s).
sub was used 2 time(s).
foreach was used 1 time(s).
return was used 1 time(s).
print was used 22 time(s).
param was used 5 time(s).
split was used 3 time(s).
```

```
1   #include <fstream>
2   #include <iostream>
3
4   using std::ifstream;
5   using std::ios;
```

(Part 1 of 3.)

Prelab Activities

Name:

Correct the Code

```
 6   using std::cerr;
 7   using std::endl;
 8   using std::cout;
 9
10   #include <new>
11
12   #include <string>
13
14   using std::string;
15
16   int main()
17   {
18      string input;
19      string token;
20      string delims = " \n(";
21      string *keyword[ 10 ];
22      int count[ 10 ] = { 0 };
23
24      // open two file streams
25      ifstream inKeywordStream( "plkeywords.dat", ios::in );
26      ifstream inPerlStream( "cart.pl", ios::app );
27
28      if ( !inPerlStream && !inKeywordStream ) {
29         cerr << "Unable to open file!" << endl;
30         exit( 1 );
31
32      } // end if
33
34      // read all keywords, store values in array
35      for ( int i = 0; inKeywordStream << input && i < 10; i++ ) {
36         keyword[ i ] = input;
37         input.erase();
38
39      } // end for
40
41      // close finished stream
42      inKeywordStream.close();
43
44      // read each word in file, compare against keywords
45      // record the count of each
46      while ( inPerlStream >> input ) {
47         token = strtok( input, delims );
48
49         if ( token != NULL ) {
50            for ( int i = 0; i < 10; i++ )
51               if ( input == keyword[ i ] )
52                  count[ i ]++;
53
54         } // end if
55
56      } // end while
57
58      // display statistics of keyword usage
59      for ( int i = 0; i < 10; i++ )
60         cout << keyword[ i ] << " was used " << count[ i ]
61              << " time(s)." << endl;
62
```

Prelab Activities   Name:

Correct the Code

```
63      return 0;
64
65   } // end main
```

(Part 3 of 3.)

```
1    if
2    else
3    while
4    for
5    sub
6    foreach
7    return
8    print
9    param
10   split
```

Fig. L 14.1   Contents of **p1keywords.dat**.

```
1    #!perl
2    # cart.pl
3    # Add or remove a book from cart and print cart contents
4
5    use CGI qw( :standard );
6
7    @cart = readCookie();
8    $add = param( "REMOVE" );
9
10   if ( $remove )
11   {
12      $number = param( "NUMBER" );
13      @book = splice( @cart, 4 * ($number - 1), 4 );
14
15      writeCookie( @cart );
16      print header;
17      print start_html( "Book removed" );
18
19   print <<End_Remove;
20      <CENTER><P>The book <I>$book[0]</I> has been removed.</P>
21      <A HREF = "cart.pl">Return to cart</A>
22   End_Remove
23
24   }
25   else
26   {
27      @book = param( "NEWBOOK" );
28      push ( @cart, @book );
29
30      if ( ! @cart )
31      {
32         print redirect( "books.pl" );
33         exit;
34      }
```

Fig. L 14.2   **cart.pl**. (Part 1 of 3.)

Prelab Activities   Name:

Correct the Code

```
35
36     writeCookie( @cart );
37     print header;
38     print start_html( "Shopping Cart" );
39
40     print <<End_Add;
41     <CENTER><P>Here is your current order.</P>
42     <TABLE BORDER = "1" CELLPADDING = "7"><TR><TH>Item</TH>
43     <TH>Name</TH><TH>Year</TH><TH>ISBN</TH>
44     <TH>Price</TH><TH></TH></TR>
45   End_Add
46
47     $counter = 1;
48     $total = 0;
49     @cartCopy = @cart;
50     while ( @book = splice( @cartCopy, 0, 4 ) )
51     {
52        print "<TR><FORM METHOD=\"POST\" ACTION=\"cart.pl\">";
53        print "<TD>$counter</TD><TD>$book[ 0 ]</TD><TD>$book[ 1 ]";
54        print "</TD><TD>$book[ 2 ]</TD><TD>$book[ 3 ]</TD>";
55        print "<TD>", submit( "Remove" ), "</TD>";
56
57        param( "ADD", 0 );              # set ADD variable to false
58        param( "NUMBER", $counter );    # book number to remove
59        print hidden( "ADD" );
60        print hidden( "NUMBER" );
61        print "</FORM></TR>";
62
63        $book[ 3 ] =~ s/\$//;            # remove $ sign
64        $total += $book[ 3 ];           # add price
65        $counter++;
66     }
67     print "<TR><TH COLSPAN= \"4\">Total Order</TH><TH>";
68     printf "\$%0.2f", $total;          # print the total
69     print "</TABLE><BR>";
70     print "<A HREF= \"books.pl\">Buy more books</A>";
71   }
72   print end_html;
73
74   sub writeCookie
75   {
76     $expires = "Monday, 14-JUN-10 16:00:00 GMT";
77     print "Set-Cookie: ";
78     print "CART=", join( "\t", @_ ), "; expires=$expires\n";
79   }
80
81   sub readCookie
82   {
83     @cookieValues = split( "; ", $ENV{ 'HTTP_COOKIE' } );
84     foreach ( @cookieValues )
85     {
86        ( $name, $value ) = split ( "=" );
87        if ($name eq "CART")
88        {
89           @data = split ( "\t", $value );
90           last;
91        }
```

Fig. L 14.2   cart.pl. (Part 2 of 3.)

Prelab Activities   Name:

Correct the Code

```
92      }
93      return @data;
94  }
```

Fig. L 14.2   `cart.pl`. (Part 3 of 3.)

Your answer:

Prelab Activities

Name:

Correct the Code

Lab Exercises

Lab Exercise — Craps

Name: _____   Date:_____

Section: _____

This problem is intended to be solved in a closed-lab session with a teaching assistant or instructor present. The problem is divided into six parts:

1. Lab Objectives

2. Description of the Problem

3. Sample Output

4. Program Template (Fig. L 14.4)

5. Problem-Solving Tips

6. Follow-Up Questions and Activities

The program template represents a complete working C++ program, with one or more key lines of code replaced with comments. Read the problem description and examine the sample output; then study the template code. Using the problem-solving tips as a guide, replace the /* */ comments with C++ code. Compile and execute the program. Compare your output with the sample output provided. Then answer the follow-up questions. The source code for the template is available at **www.deitel.com** and **www.prenhall.com./deitel**.

Lab Objectives

This lab was designed to reinforce programming concepts from Chapter 14 of *C++ How To Program: Fourth Edition*. In this lab, you will practice:

- opening both input and output files.

- reading from and writing to a sequential-access file.

- persisting a program's data across multiple executions.

Description of the Problem

Modify the Craps application presented in Chapter 3 of *C++ How to Program: Fourth Edition* to record statistics in a sequential-access file. Allow the user to play a game of craps and record the result (win or lose) and number of die rolls for each game. Allow the user to view the cumulative statistics for the total wins, losses and die rolls for all games.

Lab Exercises   Name:

Lab Exercise — Craps

Sample Output

```
Choose an option
1. Play a game of craps
2. Review cumulative craps statistics
3. Quit program
1
Player rolled 1 + 2 = 3
Player loses

Choose an option
1. Play a game of craps
2. Review cumulative craps statistics
3. Quit program
1
Player rolled 1 + 1 = 2
Player loses

Choose an option
1. Play a game of craps
2. Review cumulative craps statistics
3. Quit program
1
Player rolled 5 + 1 = 6
Point is 6
Player rolled 6 + 2 = 8
Player rolled 4 + 6 = 10
Player rolled 5 + 1 = 6
Player wins

Choose an option
1. Play a game of craps
2. Review cumulative craps statistics
3. Quit program
2
Wins: 1
Losses: 2
Rolls: 6

Choose an option
1. Play a game of craps
2. Review cumulative craps statistics
3. Quit program
3
```

```
1    LOSE 1
2    LOSE 1
3    WIN 4
```

Fig. L 14.3   Contents of **games.dat** corresponding to the sample output.

Lab Exercises   Name:

Lab Exercise — Craps

Template

```
1   // Chapter 14 of C++ How to Program
2   // craps.cpp
3
4   #include <iostream>
5   /* Write statement to include file stream header */
6   #include <cstdlib>
7   #include <ctime>
8
9   using std::cout;
10  using std::cerr;
11  using std::cin;
12  using std::ios;
13  using std::endl;
14  /* Write appropriate using statement(s) */
15
16  void playCraps();
17  void reviewStatistics();
18  int rollDice();
19
20  int main()
21  {
22     int choice;
23
24     // continue game unless user chooses to quit
25     do {
26
27        // offer game options
28        cout << "Choose an option" << endl
29             << "1. Play a game of craps" << endl
30             << "2. Review cumulative craps statistics" << endl
31             << "3. Quit program" << endl;
32
33        cin >> choice;
34
35        if ( choice == 1 )
36           playCraps();
37        else if ( choice == 2 )
38           reviewStatistics();
39
40     } while ( choice != 3 );
41
42     return 0;
43
44  } // end main
45
46  // review cumulative craps statistics
47  void reviewStatistics()
48  {
49     /* Write a body for reviewStatistics which displays
50        the total number of wins, losses and die rolls recorded
51        in craps.dat */
52
53  } // end function reviewStatistics
```

Fig. L 14.4   Contents of **craps.cpp**. (Part 1 of 3.)

Lab Exercises   Name:

Lab Exercise — Craps

```
54
55   // play game
56   void playCraps()
57   {
58      enum Status { CONTINUE, WON, LOST };
59      int sum;
60      int myPoint;
61      int rollCount = 0;
62      Status gameStatus;
63
64      /* Write statement to create an output file stream */
65
66      // seed random number generator and roll dice
67      srand( time( 0 ) );
68      sum = rollDice();
69      rollCount++;
70
71      // check game conditions
72      switch( sum ) {
73         case 7:
74         case 11:
75            gameStatus = WON;
76            break;
77         case 2:
78         case 3:
79         case 12:
80            gameStatus = LOST;
81            break;
82         default:
83            gameStatus = CONTINUE;
84            myPoint = sum;
85            cout << "Point is " << myPoint << endl;
86            break;
87
88      } // end switch
89
90      // keep rolling until player matches point or loses
91      while ( gameStatus == CONTINUE ) {
92         sum = rollDice();
93         rollCount++;
94
95         if ( sum == myPoint )
96            gameStatus = WON;
97
98         else
99            if ( sum == 7 )
100               gameStatus = LOST;
101
102      } // end while
103
104      //  display status message and write results to file
105      if ( gameStatus == WON ) {
106         cout << "Player wins\n" << endl;
107         /* Write player WIN status and the total number of die
108            rolls to a file */
109
110      } // end if
```

Fig. L 14.4   Contents of **craps.cpp**. (Part 2 of 3.)

Lab Exercises

Name:

Lab Exercise — Craps

```
111    else {
112       cout << "Player loses\n" << endl;
113       /* Write player LOSE status and the total number of die
114          rolls to a file */
115
116    } // end else
117
118 } // end function playCraps
119
120 // dice rolling function
121 int rollDice()
122 {
123    int die1;
124    int die2;
125    int workSum;
126
127    // roll two dice
128    die1 = 1 + rand() % 6;
129    die2 = 1 + rand() % 6;
130
131    // total and print results
132    workSum = die1 + die2;
133    cout << "Player rolled " << die1 << " + " << die2
134       << " = " << workSum << endl;
135
136    return workSum;
137
138 } // end function rollDice
```

Fig. L 14.4   Contents of **craps.cpp**. (Part 3 of 3.)

Problem-Solving Tips

1. Remember to check if a file was opened successfully before attempting to use it.

2. Recall that when a file stream object is destroyed its destructor function is invoked, which closes any open files.

3. Be sure to check the output against the data written to the file.

Follow-Up Questions and Activities

1. Modify the program to display the current streak of wins or losses and the record for the most consecutive wins and losses.

Lab Exercises

Name:

Lab Exercise — Craps

2. Modify the program to read from and write to a random-access file. Then allow the user to access the results of any recorded game. Limit the random-access file to 100 records.

3. Allow the user to specify their name, then display statistics by name. Display the results as a top 10 list of names.

Postlab Activities

Coding Exercises

Name: _____   **Date:** _____

Section: _____

These coding exercises reinforce the lessons learned in the lab and provide additional programming experience outside the classroom and laboratory environment. They serve as a review after you have completed the Prelab Activities and Lab Exercises successfully.

For each of the following problems, write a program or a program segment that performs the specified action.

1. Write a program that extracts and displays all vowels in **cart.pl** (Fig. L 14.2). Read through an entire text file character by character and display only the characters that are vowels.

Postlab Activities

Name:

Coding Exercises

2. Write a function that takes an integer array argument and writes the array's data to a text file. Write a second function that retrieves the array data at a specific index from a sequential-access file.

17

Data Structures

Objectives

- To form linked data structures by using pointers, self-referential classes and recursion.
- To understand how to extend and reuse data structures.
- To understand the differences between linked lists, stacks, queues and binary trees.

Assignment Checklist

Name: _____   **Date:** _____

Section: _____

Exercises	Assigned: Circle assignments	Date Due
Prelab Activities		
Matching	YES NO	
Fill in the Blank	8, 9, 10, 11, 12, 13, 14, 15	
Short Answer	16, 17	
Programming Output	YES NO	
Lab Exercises		
Lab Exercise — Character **List**	YES NO	
Follow-Up Questions and Activities	1, 2	
Labs Provided by Instructor		
1.		
2.		
3.		
Postlab Activities		
Coding Exercises	1, 2	
Programming Challenge	YES NO	

Assignment Checklist

Name:

Prelab Activities

Matching

Name: _____   **Date:** _____

Section: _____

After reading Chapter 17 of *C++ How to Program: Fourth Edition*, answer the following questions. These questions are intended to test and reinforce your understanding of key concepts and may be done either before the lab or during the lab.

For each term in the left column, write the corresponding letter for the description that best matches it from the right column.

Term	Description
_____ 1. Self-referential class	a) Contains pointers to objects of the same type.
_____ 2. Queue	b) Traverses the left subtree, processes the root node, then traverses the right tree. The value of each node is not processed until the values in the node's left subtree are processed.
_____ 3. Preorder traversal	c) Last node contains a link to the first node.
_____ 4. Null pointer	d) Nodes are added and removed from the head of the data structure.
_____ 5. Circular linked list	e) Processes the value in the root node, traverses the left subtree then traverses the right subtree. The value of each node is processed as it is encountered.
_____ 6. Inorder traversal	f) Nodes are removed from the head of the data structure and added to the tail.
_____ 7. Stack	g) Normally indicates the end of a data structure.

Prelab Activities

Name:

Matching

Prelab Activities   Name: _____

Fill in the Blank

Name: _____   **Date:**_____

Section: _____

Fill in the blank for each of the following:

8.   A(n) _____ is a linear collection of self-referential class objects.

9.   A tree where the value in the left child of a node is less than the value in its parent node, and the value in the
     right child of a node is greater than or equal to the value in its parent node, is known as a(n) _____.

10. Nodes may be added and removed only from the top of the stack; thus a stack is known as a(n)
     _____ structure.

11. A list usually is terminated by setting the last link to _____.

12. New queue nodes may be added to the head of the queue and removed from the tail. Thus a queue is known
     as a(n) _____ structure.

13. A tree is usually traversed _____, _____ or _____.

14. A data structure that may increase or decrease in size as necessary is known as a(n) _____ data structure.

15. A(n) _____ linked list may be traversed in either direction; the first node contains a pointer to the last
     node, and the last node contains a pointer to the first node. This type of linked list forms a "circle."

Prelab Activities

Name:

Fill in the Blank

Prelab Activities   Name: _____

Short Answer

Name: _____   Date:_____

Section: _____

In the space provided, answer each of the following questions. Answers should be as concise as possible; aim for 2–3 sentences.

16. Compare and contrast linked lists, stacks and queues.

17. What are the differences between fixed-length arrays (e.g., **int a[5]**) and dynamic data structures? What types of situations provide optimal uses for each?

Prelab Activities

Name:

Short Answer

Prelab Activities   Name:

Programming Output

Name: _____   Date:_____

Section: _____

For each of the following program segments, read the code and write the output in the space provided below for each program. [*Note*: Do not execute these programs on a computer.]

18. What is the output for the following program given the input integers of **1**, **2**, **3**, **4**, **5**, **6**, **7**,**8**, **9** and **10**?

```
1   // listnd.h
2   // ListNode template definition
3   #ifndef LISTND_H
4   #define LISTND_H
5
6   template< class NODETYPE > class List;  // forward declaration
7
8   // template class ListNode definition
9   template<class NODETYPE>
10  class ListNode {
11     friend class List< NODETYPE >; // make List a friend
12
13  public:
14     ListNode( const NODETYPE & );  // constructor
15     NODETYPE getData() const;       // return data in the node
16
17  private:
18     NODETYPE data;                  // data
19     ListNode< NODETYPE > *nextPtr; // next node in the list
20
21  }; // end class ListNode
22
23  // constructor
24  template<class NODETYPE>
25  ListNode< NODETYPE >::ListNode( const NODETYPE &info )
26     : data( info ), nextPtr( 0 )
27  {
28     // empty
29
30  } // end class ListNode constructor
31
32  // return a copy of the data in the node
33  template< class NODETYPE >
34  NODETYPE ListNode< NODETYPE >::getData() const
35  {
36     return data;
37
38  } // end function getData
39
40  #endif // LISTND_H
```

Fig. L 17.1   `listnd.h`

Prelab Activities   Name:

Programming Output

```
1    // list.h
2    // Template List class definition
3    #ifndef LIST_H
4    #define LIST_H
5
6    #include <iostream>
7    #include "listnd.h"
8
9    using std::cout;
10
11   #include <new>
12
13   // template class List
14   template< class NODETYPE >
15   class List {
16
17   public:
18      List();        // constructor
19      ~List();       // destructor
20
21      void insertAtFront( const NODETYPE & );
22      void insertAtBack( const NODETYPE & );
23      bool removeFromFront( NODETYPE & );
24      bool removeFromBack( NODETYPE & );
25      bool isEmpty() const;
26      void print() const;
27
28   private:
29      ListNode< NODETYPE > *firstPtr;   // pointer to first node
30      ListNode< NODETYPE > *lastPtr;    // pointer to last node
31
32      // utility function to allocate new node
33      ListNode< NODETYPE > *getNewNode( const NODETYPE & );
34
35   }; // end class List
36
37   // default constructor
38   template< class NODETYPE >
39   List< NODETYPE >::List() : firstPtr( 0 ), lastPtr( 0 )
40   {
41      // empty
42
43   } // end class List constructor
44
45   // destructor
46   template< class NODETYPE >
47   List< NODETYPE >::~List()
48   {
49      if ( !isEmpty() ) {     // List is not empty
50         cout << "Destroying nodes ...\n";
51
52         ListNode< NODETYPE > *currentPtr = firstPtr;
53         ListNode< NODETYPE > *tempPtr;
54
55         while ( currentPtr != 0 ) {  // delete remaining nodes
56            tempPtr = currentPtr;
57            cout << tempPtr->data << '\n';
```

Fig. L 17.2   list.h. (Part 1 of 4.)

Programming Output

```
58              currentPtr = currentPtr->nextPtr;
59              delete tempPtr;
60
61          } // end while
62
63      } // end if
64
65      cout << "All nodes destroyed\n\n";
66
67  } // end class List destructor
68
69  // insert node at front of list
70  template< class NODETYPE >
71  void List< NODETYPE >::insertAtFront( const NODETYPE &value )
72  {
73      ListNode< NODETYPE > *newPtr = getNewNode( value );
74
75      if ( isEmpty() )  // List is empty
76          firstPtr = lastPtr = newPtr;
77
78      else {            // List is not empty
79          newPtr->nextPtr = firstPtr;
80          firstPtr = newPtr;
81
82      } // end else
83
84  } // end function insertAtFront
85
86  // insert node at back of list
87  template< class NODETYPE >
88  void List< NODETYPE >::insertAtBack( const NODETYPE &value )
89  {
90      ListNode< NODETYPE > *newPtr = getNewNode( value );
91
92      if ( isEmpty() )  // List is empty
93          firstPtr = lastPtr = newPtr;
94
95      else {            // List is not empty
96          lastPtr->nextPtr = newPtr;
97          lastPtr = newPtr;
98
99      } // end else
100
101 } // end function insertAtBack
102
103 // delete node from front of list
104 template< class NODETYPE >
105 bool List< NODETYPE >::removeFromFront( NODETYPE &value )
106 {
107     if ( isEmpty() )                // List is empty
108         return false;               // delete unsuccessful
109
110     else {
111         ListNode< NODETYPE > *tempPtr = firstPtr;
112
113         if ( firstPtr == lastPtr )
114             firstPtr = lastPtr = 0;
```

Fig. L 17.2　list.h. (Part 2 of 4.)

Prelab Activities

Name:

Programming Output

```
115
116        else
117           firstPtr = firstPtr->nextPtr;
118
119        value = tempPtr->data;    // data being removed
120        delete tempPtr;
121        return true;              // delete successful
122
123     } // end else
124
125  } // end function removeFromFront
126
127  // delete node from back of list
128  template< class NODETYPE >
129  bool List< NODETYPE >::removeFromBack( NODETYPE &value )
130  {
131     if ( isEmpty() )
132        return false;     // delete unsuccessful
133
134     else {
135        ListNode< NODETYPE > *tempPtr = lastPtr;
136
137        if ( firstPtr == lastPtr )
138           firstPtr = lastPtr = 0;
139
140        else {
141           ListNode< NODETYPE > *currentPtr = firstPtr;
142
143           while ( currentPtr->nextPtr != lastPtr )
144              currentPtr = currentPtr->nextPtr;
145
146           lastPtr = currentPtr;
147           currentPtr->nextPtr = 0;
148
149        } // end else
150
151        value = tempPtr->data;
152        delete tempPtr;
153        return true;    // delete successful
154
155     } // end else
156
157  } // end function removeFromBack
158
159  // is the List empty?
160  template< class NODETYPE >
161  bool List< NODETYPE >::isEmpty() const
162  {
163     return firstPtr == 0;
164
165  } // end function isEmpty
166
167  // return pointer to newly allocated node
168  template< class NODETYPE >
169  ListNode< NODETYPE > *List< NODETYPE >::getNewNode(
170                                      const NODETYPE &value )
171  {
```

Fig. L 17.2   list.h. (Part 3 of 4.)

Prelab Activities   Name:

Programming Output

```
172     ListNode< NODETYPE > *ptr =
173         new ListNode< NODETYPE >( value );
174     return ptr;
175
176 } // end function getNewNode
177
178 // display contents of List
179 template< class NODETYPE >
180 void List< NODETYPE >::print() const
181 {
182     if ( isEmpty() ) {
183         cout << "The list is empty\n\n";
184         return;
185
186     } // end if
187
188     ListNode< NODETYPE > *currentPtr = firstPtr;
189
190     cout << "The list is: ";
191
192     while ( currentPtr != 0 ) {
193         cout << currentPtr->data << ' ';
194         currentPtr = currentPtr->nextPtr;
195
196     } // end while
197
198     cout << "\n\n";
199
200 } // end function print
201
202 #endif // LIST_H
```

Fig. L 17.2   **list.h**. (Part 4 of 4.)

```
 1  #include <iostream>
 2  #include "list.h"
 3
 4  using std::cin;
 5  using std::endl;
 6
 7  // function to test integer List
 8  template< class T >
 9  void testList( List< T > &listObject, string type )
10  {
11      cout << "Testing a List of " << type << " values\n";
12      int value;
13
14      for ( int i = 0; i < 10; i++ ) {
15          cout << "Enter " << type << ": ";
16          cin >> value;
17
```

(Part 1 of 2.)

Prelab Activities

Name: _____

Programming Output

```
18          if ( static_cast< int >( value ) % 2 == 1 ) {
19              listObject.insertAtFront( value );
20              listObject.print();
21
22          } // end if
23
24      } // end for
25
26      cout << "End list test\n\n";
27
28  } // end function testList
29
30  int main()
31  {
32      List< int > integerList;
33      testList( integerList, "integer" ); // test integerList
34
35      return 0;
36
37  } // end main
```

(Part 2 of 2.)

Your answer:

Lab Exercises

Lab Exercise — Character List

Name: _____   **Date:** _____

Section: _____

This problem is intended to be solved in a closed-lab session with a teaching assistant or instructor present. The problem is divided into six parts:

1. Lab Objectives

2. Description of the Problem

3. Sample Output

4. Program Template (Fig. L 17.3–Fig. L 17.5)

5. Problem-Solving Tips

6. Follow-Up Questions and Activities

The program template represents a complete working C++ program, with one or more key lines of code replaced with comments. Read the problem description and examine the sample output; then study the template code. Using the problem-solving tips as a guide, replace the **/* */** comments with C++ code. Compile and execute the program. Compare your output with the sample output provided. Then answer the follow-up questions. The source code for the template is available at **www.deitel.com** and **www.prenhall.com./deitel**.

Lab Objectives

This lab was designed to reinforce programming concepts from Chapter 17 of *C++ How To Program: Fourth Edition*. In this lab, you will practice:

- using and manipulating dynamic data structures.

- duplicating an existing linked list.

- reversing the order of linked list values.

The follow-up questions and activities also will give you practice:

- using operator overloading with data structures.

Description of the Problem

Write a program that creates a linked list object of 10 characters then creates a second list object containing a copy of the first list, but in reverse order.

Lab Exercises   Name:

Lab Exercise — Character List

Sample Output

```
The list is: a b c d e f g


All nodes destroyed

After reversing:
The list is: g f e d c b a

Destroying nodes ...
g f e d c b a
All nodes destroyed

Destroying nodes ...
a b c d e f g
All nodes destroyed
```

Template

```cpp
1   // reverseCharacter.cpp
2   #include <iostream>
3
4   using std::cout;
5
6   #include "list.h"
7
8   /* Write a function that reverses the values of a list
9      and stores them in another list */
10
11  int main()
12  {
13     List< char > list1, list2;
14
15     for ( char c = 'a'; c <= 'g'; ++c )
16        list1.insertAtBack( c );
17
18     list1.print();
19
20     /* Write call function to reverse list */
21     cout << "After reversing:\n";
22     list2.print();
23
24     return 0;
25
26  } // end main
```

Fig. L 17.3   Contents of **reverseCharacter.cpp**.

Lab Exercises   Name:

Lab Exercise — Character List

```
1    // LIST.H
2    // Template list class definition
3
4    #ifndef LIST_H
5    #define LIST_H
6
7    #include <iostream>
8
9    using std::cout;
10
11   #include <new>
12   #include "listnd.h"
13
14   // template class List definition
15   template< class NODETYPE >
16   class List {
17
18   public:
19      List();                           // default constructor
20
21      /* Write the prototype for a constructor which creates
22         a copy of another List */
23      ~List();                          // destructor
24
25      void insertAtFront( const NODETYPE & );
26      void insertAtBack( const NODETYPE & );
27      bool removeFromFront( NODETYPE & );
28      bool removeFromBack( NODETYPE & );
29      bool isEmpty() const;
30      void print() const;
31
32   private:
33      ListNode< NODETYPE > *firstPtr;   // pointer to first node
34      ListNode< NODETYPE > *lastPtr;    // pointer to last node
35
36      // utility function to allocate new node
37      ListNode< NODETYPE > *getNewNode( const NODETYPE & );
38
39   }; // end class List
40
41   // default constructor
42   template< class NODETYPE >
43   List< NODETYPE >::List()
44   {
45      firstPtr = lastPtr = 0;
46
47   } // end class List constructor
48
49   /* Write the definition for the constructor which creates
50      a copy of another List */
51
52   // destructor
53   template< class NODETYPE >
54   List< NODETYPE >::~List()
55   {
56      if ( !isEmpty() ) {    // List is not empty
57         cout << "Destroying nodes ...\n";
```

Fig. L 17.4   Contents of `list.h`. (Part 1 of 4.)

Lab Exercises   Name:

Lab Exercise — Character List

```
58
59          ListNode< NODETYPE > *currentPtr = firstPtr;
60          ListNode< NODETYPE > *tempPtr;
61
62          while ( currentPtr != 0 ) {   // delete remaining nodes
63             tempPtr = currentPtr;
64             cout << tempPtr -> data << ' ';
65             currentPtr = currentPtr -> nextPtr;
66             delete tempPtr;
67
68          } // end while
69
70       } // end if
71
72       cout << "\nAll nodes destroyed\n\n";
73
74    } // end class List destructor
75
76    // insert node at front of list
77    template< class NODETYPE >
78    void List< NODETYPE >::insertAtFront( const NODETYPE &value )
79    {
80       ListNode<NODETYPE> *newPtr = getNewNode( value );
81
82       if ( isEmpty() )   // List is empty
83          firstPtr = lastPtr = newPtr;
84
85       else {            // List is not empty
86          newPtr -> nextPtr = firstPtr;
87          firstPtr = newPtr;
88
89       } // end else
90
91    } // end function insertAtFront
92
93    // insert node at back of list
94    template< class NODETYPE >
95    void List< NODETYPE >::insertAtBack( const NODETYPE &value )
96    {
97       ListNode< NODETYPE > *newPtr = getNewNode( value );
98
99       if ( isEmpty() )   // List is empty
100          firstPtr = lastPtr = newPtr;
101
102       else {            // List is not empty
103          lastPtr -> nextPtr = newPtr;
104          lastPtr = newPtr;
105
106       } // end else
107
108    } // end function insertAtBack
109
110    // delete node from front of list
111    template< class NODETYPE >
112    bool List< NODETYPE >::removeFromFront( NODETYPE &value )
113    {
```

Fig. L 17.4   Contents of `list.h`. (Part 2 of 4.)

Lab Exercises   Name:

Lab Exercise — Character List

```
114      if ( isEmpty() )                // List is empty
115         return false;                // delete unsuccessful
116
117      else {
118         ListNode< NODETYPE > *tempPtr = firstPtr;
119
120         if ( firstPtr == lastPtr )
121            firstPtr = lastPtr = 0;
122
123         else
124            firstPtr = firstPtr -> nextPtr;
125
126         value = tempPtr -> data;   // data being removed
127         delete tempPtr;
128         return true;                // delete successful
129
130      } // end else
131
132 } // end function removeFromFront
133
134 // delete node from back of list
135 template< class NODETYPE >
136 bool List< NODETYPE >::removeFromBack( NODETYPE &value )
137 {
138      if ( isEmpty() )
139         return false;    // delete unsuccessful
140
141      else {
142         ListNode< NODETYPE > *tempPtr = lastPtr;
143
144         if ( firstPtr == lastPtr )
145            firstPtr = lastPtr = 0;
146
147         else {
148            ListNode< NODETYPE > *currentPtr = firstPtr;
149
150            while ( currentPtr -> nextPtr != lastPtr )
151               currentPtr = currentPtr -> nextPtr;
152
153            lastPtr = currentPtr;
154            currentPtr -> nextPtr = 0;
155
156         } // end else
157
158         value = tempPtr -> data;
159         delete tempPtr;
160         return true;    // delete successful
161
162      } // end else
163
164 } // end function removeFromBack
165
166 // is List empty?
167 template< class NODETYPE >
168 bool List< NODETYPE >::isEmpty() const
169 {
```

Fig. L 17.4   Contents of `list.h`. (Part 3 of 4.)

Lab Exercises   Name:

Lab Exercise — Character List

```
170      return firstPtr == 0;
171
172  } // end function isEmpty
173
174  // Return a pointer to a newly allocated node
175  template< class NODETYPE >
176  ListNode< NODETYPE > *List< NODETYPE >::getNewNode(
177      const NODETYPE &value )
178  {
179      ListNode< NODETYPE > *ptr = new ListNode< NODETYPE >( value );
180
181      return ptr;
182
183  } // end function getNewNode
184
185  // display contents of List
186  template< class NODETYPE >
187  void List< NODETYPE >::print() const
188  {
189      if ( isEmpty() ) {
190         cout << "The list is empty\n\n";
191         return;
192
193      } // end if
194
195      ListNode< NODETYPE > *currentPtr = firstPtr;
196
197      cout << "The list is: ";
198
199      while ( currentPtr != 0 ) {
200         cout << currentPtr -> data << ' ';
201         currentPtr = currentPtr -> nextPtr;
202
203      } // end while
204
205      cout << "\n\n";
206
207  } // end function print
208
209  #endif // LIST_H
```

Fig. L 17.4   Contents of `list.h`. (Part 4 of 4.)

```
1   // LISTND.H
2   // ListNode template definition
3   #ifndef LISTND_H
4   #define LISTND_H
5
6   template< class T > class List;   // forward declaration
7
8   // template class ListNode definition
9   template< class NODETYPE >
10  class ListNode {
11     friend class List< NODETYPE >; // make List a friend
```

Fig. L 17.5   Contents of `listnd.cpp`. (Part 1 of 2.)

Lab Exercises   Name:

Lab Exercise — Character List

```
12
13   public:
14      ListNode( const NODETYPE & );   // constructor
15
16      NODETYPE getData() const;      // return data in node
17      void setNextPtr( ListNode *nPtr ) { nextPtr = nPtr; }
18      ListNode *getNextPtr() const { return nextPtr; }
19
20   private:
21      NODETYPE data;                 // data
22      ListNode *nextPtr;             // next node in list
23
24   }; // end class ListNode
25
26   // constructor
27   template< class NODETYPE >
28   ListNode< NODETYPE >::ListNode( const NODETYPE &info )
29   {
30      data = info;
31      nextPtr = 0;
32
33   } // end class ListNode constructor
34
35   // return copy of data in node
36   template< class NODETYPE >
37   NODETYPE ListNode< NODETYPE >::getData() const
38   {
39      return data;
40
41   } // end function getData
42
43   #endif // LISTND_H
```

Fig. L 17.5   Contents of `listnd.cpp`. (Part 2 of 2.)

Problem-Solving Tips

1. Write a copy constructor.

2. Use both **removeFromFront** and **insertAtFront** in **reverseList**.

Lab Exercises   Name:

Lab Exercise — Character List

Follow-Up Questions and Activities

1. Write a program that populates a **List** with random integers from 0 to 19, then calls a function that divides the **List** into two **List**s. The function should remove all values greater than **9** from the **List** and store them in a new **List**.

Lab Exercises   Name:

Lab Exercise — Character List

2. Extend the lab exercise to use a stack structure (Fig. 17.10 of *C++ How to Program: Fourth Edition*) to reverse the order of the characters.

Lab Exercises

Name:

Lab Exercise — Character List

Postlab Activities

Coding Exercises

Name: _____   **Date:** _____

Section: _____

These exercises reinforce the lessons learned in the lab and provide additional programming experience outside the classroom and laboratory environment. The answers to selected problems are provided at the end of the lab manual. The following "Coding Exercises" serve as a review after having completed the "Prelab Activities" and "Lab Exercises" successfully.

For each of the following problems, write a program or a program segment that performs the specified action.

1. Write a function that stores a tree's data in a linked list.

2. Modify the binary search tree example in Fig. 17.18 of *C++ How to Program: Fourth Edition* by adding a constructor that creates a binary tree from a **List** of integers.

Lab Exercises

Coding Exercises

Lab Exercises   Name:

Programming Challenges

Name: _____   **Date:** _____

Section: _____

The following "Programming Challenges" are more involved than the "Coding Exercises" and may require a significant amount of time to complete. Write a C++ program for each of the problems in this section. The answers to these problems are available at **www.deitel.com** and **www.prenhall.com/deitel** and on the *C++ Multimedia Cyber Classroom: Fourth Edition.* Pseudocode, hints and/or sample outputs are provided to aid you in your programming.

3. Write a program that concatenates two linked list objects of characters. The program should include function **concatenate**, which takes references to both list objects as arguments and concatenates the second list to the first list.

Lab Exercises

Programming Challenges

Index

The DEITEL™ Suite of Products...

HOW TO PROGRAM BOOKS

C++ How to Program Fourth Edition
BOOK / CD-ROM

©2003, 1400 pp., paper (0-13-038474-7)

The world's best selling C++ textbook is now even better! Designed for beginning through intermediate courses, this comprehensive, practical introduction to C++ includes hundreds of hands-on exercises, and uses 267 LIVE-CODE™ programs to demonstrate C++'s powerful capabilities. This edition includes a new chapter—Web Programming with CGI—that provides everything readers need to begin developing their own Web-based applications that will run on the Internet! Readers will learn how to build so-called n-tier applications, in which the functionality provided by each tier can be distributed to separate computers across the Internet or executed on the same computer. This edition uses a new code-highlighting style with a yellow background to focus the reader on the C++ features introduced in each program. The book provides a carefully designed sequence of examples that introduces inheritance and polymorphism and helps students understand the motivation and implementation of these key object-oriented programming concepts. In addition, the OOD/UML case study has been upgraded to UML 1.4 and all flow-charts and inheritance diagrams in the text have been converted to their UML counterparts. The book presents an early introduction to strings and arrays as objects using standard C++ classes string and vector. The book also covers key concepts and techniques standard C++ developers need to master, including control structures, functions, arrays, pointers and strings, classes and data abstraction, operator overloading, inheritance, virtual functions, polymorphism, I/O, templates, exception handling, file processing, data structures and more. The book includes a detailed introduction to Standard Template Library (STL) containers, container adapters, algorithms and iterators. It also features insight into good programming practices, maximizing performance, avoiding errors, debugging and testing.

Java™ How to Program Fourth Edition
BOOK / CD-ROM

©2002, 1546 pp., paper (0-13-034151-7)

The world's best-selling Java text is now even better! The Fourth Edition of *Java How to Program* includes a new focus on object-oriented design with the UML, design patterns, full-color program listings and figures and the most up-to-date Java coverage available.

Readers will discover key topics in Java programming, such as graphical user interface components, exception handling, multithreading, multimedia, files and streams, networking, data structures and more. In addition, a new chapter on design patterns explains frequently recurring architectural patterns—information that can help save designers considerable time when building large systems.

The highly detailed optional case study focuses on object-oriented design with the UML and presents fully implemented working Java code.

Updated throughout, the text includes new and revised discussions on topics such as Swing, graphics and socket- and packet-based networking. Three introductory chapters heavily emphasize problem solving and programming skills. The chapters on RMI, JDBC™, servlets and JavaBeans have been moved to *Advanced Java 2 Platform How to Program*, where they are now covered in much greater depth. (See *Advanced Java 2 Platform How to Program* below.)

Advanced Java™ 2 Platform How to Program
BOOK / CD-ROM

©2002, 1811 pp., paper (0-13-089560-1)

Expanding on the world's best-selling Java textbook—*Java How to Program—Advanced Java 2 Platform How To Program* presents advanced Java topics for developing sophisticated, user-friendly GUIs; significant, scalable enterprise applications; wireless applications and distributed systems. Primarily based on Java 2 Enterprise Edition (J2EE), this textbook integrates technologies such as XML, JavaBeans, security, Java Database Connectivity (JDBC), JavaServer Pages (JSP), servlets, Remote Method Invocation (RMI), Enterprise JavaBeans™ (EJB) and design patterns into a production-quality system that allows developers to

Sign up now for the new *DEITEL™ Buzz Online* newsletter at:

benefit from the leverage and platform independence Java 2 Enterprise Edition provides. The book also features the development of a complete, end-to-end e-business solution using advanced Java technologies. Additional topics include Swing, Java 2D and 3D, XML, design patterns, CORBA, Jini™, JavaSpaces™, Jiro™, Java Management Extensions (JMX) and Peer-to-Peer networking with an introduction to JXTA. This textbook also introduces the Java 2 Micro Edition (J2ME™) for building applications for handheld and wireless devices using MIDP and MIDlets. Wireless technologies covered include WAP, WML and i-mode.

Visual C++ .NET How to Program

BOOK / CD-ROM

©2003, 1600 pp., paper (0-13-437377-4)

Visual C++® .NET How to Program provides a comprehensive introduction to building Visual C++ applications for Microsoft's new .NET Framework. The book begins with a strong foundation in introductory and intermediate programming principles, including control structures, functions, arrays, pointers, strings, classes and data abstraction, inheritance, virtual methods, polymorphism, I/O, exception handling, file processing, data structures and more. The book discusses program development with the Microsoft® Visual Studio® .NET integrated development environment (IDE) and shows how to edit, compile and debug applications with the IDE. The book then explores more sophisticated .NET application-development topics in detail. Key topics include: creating reusable software components with assemblies, modules and dynamic link libraries; using classes from the Framework Class Library (FCL); building graphical user interfaces (GUIs) with the FCL; implementing multithreaded applications; building networked applications; manipulating databases with ADO .NET and creating XML Web services. The first 75% of the book covers programming with Microsoft's new managed-code approach. The five chapters in the last quarter of the book focus on programming with unmanaged code in Visual C++ .NET. These chapters demonstrate how to use "attributed programming" to simplify common tasks (such as connecting to databases) and to improve code readability; how to integrate managed- and unmanaged-code software components; and how to use ATL Server to create Web-based applications and Web services with unmanaged code. The book features LIVE-CODE ™ examples that highlight crucial .NET-programming concepts and demonstrate Web services at work. Substantial introductions to XML and XHTML also are included.

C# How to Program

BOOK / CD-ROM

©2002, 1568 pp., paper (0-13-062221-4)

An exciting new addition to the How to Program series, *C# How to Program* provides a comprehensive introduction to Microsoft's new object-oriented language. C# builds on the skills already mastered by countless C++ and Java programmers, enabling them to create powerful Web applications and components—ranging from XML-based Web services on Microsoft's .NET platform to middle-tier business objects and system-level applications. *C# How to Program* begins with a strong foundation in the introductory and intermediate programming principles students will need in industry. It then explores such essential topics as object-oriented programming and exception handling. Graphical user interfaces are extensively covered, giving readers the tools to build compelling and fully interactive programs. Internet technologies such as XML, ADO .NET and Web services are also covered as well as topics including regular expressions, multithreading, networking, databases, files and data structures.

Visual Basic .NET How to Program Second Edition

BOOK / CD-ROM

©2002, 1400 pp., paper (0-13-029363-6)

Teach Visual Basic .NET programming from the ground up! This introduction of Microsoft's .NET Framework marks the beginning of major revisions to all of Microsoft's programming languages. This book provides a comprehensive introduction to the next version of Visual Basic—Visual Basic .NET—featuring extensive updates and increased functionality. *Visual Basic .NET How to Program, Second Edition* covers introductory programming techniques as well as more advanced topics, featuring enhanced treatment of developing Web-based applications. Other topics discussed include an extensive treatment of XML and wireless applications, databases, SQL and ADO .NET, Web forms, Web services and ASP .NET.

C How to Program Third Edition

BOOK / CD-ROM

©2001, 1253 pp., paper (0-13-089572-5)

Highly practical in approach, the Third Edition of the world's best-selling C text introduces the fundamentals of structured programming and software engineering and gets up to speed quickly. This comprehensive book not only covers the full C language, but also reviews library functions and introduces object-based and object-oriented programming in C++ and Java. The Third Edition includes a new 346-page introduction to Java 2 and the basics of GUIs, and the 298-page introduction to C++ has been updated to be consistent with the most current ANSI/ISO C++ standards. Plus, icons throughout the book point out valuable programming tips such as Common Programming Errors, Portability Tips and Testing and Debugging Tips.

www·deitel·com/newsletter/subscribe·html

Getting Started with Microsoft® Visual C++™ 6 with an Introduction to MFC

`BOOK / CD-ROM`

©2000, 163 pp., paper (0-13-016147-0)

Internet & World Wide Web How to Program, Second Edition

`BOOK / CD-ROM`

©2002, 1428 pp., paper (0-13-030897-8)

The revision of this ground-breaking book in the Deitels' *How to Program Series* offers a thorough treatment of programming concepts that yield visible or audible results in Web pages and Web-based applications. This book discusses effective Web-based design, server- and client-side scripting, multitier Web-based applications development, ActiveX® controls and electronic commerce essentials. This book offers an alternative to traditional programming courses using markup languages (such as XHTML, Dynamic HTML and XML) and scripting languages (such as JavaScript, VBScript, Perl/CGI, Python and PHP) to teach the fundamentals of programming "wrapped in the metaphor of the Web."

Updated material on **www.deitel.com** and **www.prenhall.com/deitel** provides additional resources for instructors who want to cover Microsoft® or non-Microsoft technologies. The Web site includes an extensive treatment of Netscape® 6 and alternate versions of the code from the Dynamic HTML chapters that will work with non-Microsoft environments as well.

Wireless Internet & Mobile Business How to Program

© 2002, 1292 pp., paper (0-13-062226-5)

While the rapid expansion of wireless technologies, such as cell phones, pagers and personal digital assistants (PDAs), offers many new opportunities for businesses and programmers, it also presents numerous challenges related to issues such as security and standardization. This book offers a thorough treatment of both the management and technical aspects of this growing area, including coverage of current practices and future trends. The first half explores the business issues surrounding wireless technology and mobile business, including an overview of existing and developing communication technologies and the application of business principles to wireless devices. It also discusses location-based services and location-identifying technologies, a topic that is revisited throughout the book. Wireless payment, security, legal and social issues, international communications and more are also discussed. The book then turns to programming for the wireless Internet, exploring topics such as WAP (including 2.0), WML, WMLScript, XML, XHTML™, wireless Java programming (J2ME)™, Web Clipping and more. Other topics covered include career resources, wireless marketing, accessibility, Palm™, PocketPC, Windows CE, i-mode, Bluetooth, MIDP, MIDlets, ASP, Microsoft .NET Mobile Framework, BREW™, multimedia, Flash™ and VBScript.

Python How to Program

`BOOK / CD-ROM`

©2002, 1376 pp., paper (0-13-092361-3)

This exciting new book provides a comprehensive introduction to Python—a powerful object-oriented programming language with clear syntax and the ability to bring together various technologies quickly and easily. This book covers introductory-programming techniques and more advanced topics such as graphical user interfaces, databases, wireless Internet programming, networking, security, process management, multithreading, XHTML, CSS, PSP and multimedia. Readers will learn principles that are applicable to both systems development and Web programming. The book features the consistent and applied pedagogy that the *How to Program Series* is known for, including the Deitels' signature LIVE-CODE™ Approach, with thousands of lines of code in hundreds of working programs; hundreds of valuable programming tips identified with icons throughout the text; an extensive set of exercises, projects and case studies; two-color four-way syntax coloring and much more.

e-Business & e-Commerce for Managers

©2001, 794 pp., cloth (0-13-032364-0)

This comprehensive overview of building and managing e-businesses explores topics such as the decision to bring a business online, choosing a business model, accepting payments, marketing strategies and security, as well as many other important issues (such as career resources). The book features Web resources and online demonstrations that supplement the text and direct readers to additional materials. The book also includes an appendix that develops a complete

Sign up now for the new DEITEL™ Buzz Online newsletter at:

Web-based shopping-cart application using HTML, JavaScript, VBScript, Active Server Pages, ADO, SQL, HTTP, XML and XSL. Plus, company-specific sections provide "real-world" examples of the concepts presented in the book.

XML How to Program

BOOK / CD-ROM

©2001, 934 pp., paper (0-13-028417-3)

This book is a comprehensive guide to programming in XML. It teaches how to use XML to create customized tags and includes chapters that address standard custom-markup languages for science and technology, multimedia, commerce and many other fields. Concise introductions to Java, JavaServer Pages, VBScript, Active Server Pages and Perl/CGI provide readers with the essentials of these programming languages and server-side development technologies to enable them to work effectively with XML. The book also covers cutting-edge topics such as XSL, DOM™ and SAX, plus a real-world e-commerce case study and a complete chapter on Web accessibility that addresses Voice XML. It includes tips such as Common Programming Errors, Software Engineering Observations, Portability Tips and Debugging Hints. Other topics covered include XHTML, CSS, DTD, schema, parsers, XPath, XLink, namespaces, XBase, XInclude, XPointer, XSLT, XSL Formatting Objects, JavaServer Pages, XForms, topic maps, X3D, MathML, OpenMath, CML, BML, CDF, RDF, SVG, Cocoon, WML, XBRL and BizTalk™ and SOAP™ Web resources.

Perl How to Program

BOOK / CD-ROM

©2001, 1057 pp., paper (0-13-028418-1)

This comprehensive guide to Perl programming emphasizes the use of the Common Gateway Interface (CGI) with Perl to create powerful, dynamic multi-tier Web-based client/server applications. The book begins with a clear and careful introduction to programming concepts at a level suitable for beginners, and proceeds through advanced topics such as references and complex data structures. Key Perl topics such as regular expressions and string manipulation are covered in detail. The authors address important and topical issues such as object-oriented programming, the Perl database interface (DBI), graphics and security. Also included is a treatment of XML, a bonus chapter introducing the Python programming language, supplemental material on career resources and a complete chapter on Web accessibility. The text includes tips such as Common Programming Errors, Software Engineering Observations, Portability Tips and Debugging Hints.

e-Business & e-Commerce How to Program

BOOK / CD-ROM

©2001, 1254 pp., paper (0-13-028419-X)

This innovative book explores programming technologies for developing Web-based e-business and e-commerce solutions, and covers e-business and e-commerce models and business issues. Readers learn a full range of options, from "build-your-own" to turnkey solutions. The book examines scores of the top e-businesses (examples include Amazon, eBay, Priceline, Travelocity, etc.), explaining the technical details of building successful e-business and e-commerce sites and their underlying business premises. Learn how to implement the dominant e-commerce models—shopping carts, auctions, name-your-own-price, comparison shopping and bots/ intelligent agents—by using markup languages (HTML, Dynamic HTML and XML), scripting languages (JavaScript, VBScript and Perl), server-side technologies (Active Server Pages and Perl/CGI) and database (SQL and ADO), security and online payment technologies. Updates are regularly posted to **www.deitel.com** and the book includes a CD-ROM with software tools, source code and live links.

ORDER INFORMATION

SINGLE COPY SALES:
Visa, Master Card, American Express, Checks, or Money Orders only
Toll-Free: 800-643-5506; Fax: 800-835-5327

GOVERNMENT AGENCIES:
Prentice Hall Customer Service (#GS-02F-8023A)
Phone: 201-767-5994; Fax: 800-445-6991

COLLEGE PROFESSORS:
For desk or review copies, please visit us on the World Wide Web at www.prenhall.com

CORPORATE ACCOUNTS:
Quantity, Bulk Orders totaling 10 or more books. Purchase orders only — No credit cards.
Tel: 201-236-7156; Fax: 201-236-7141
Toll-Free: 800-382-3419

CANADA:
Pearson Technology Group Canada
10 Alcorn Avenue, suite #300
Toronto, Ontario, Canada M4V 3B2
Tel.: 416-925-2249; Fax: 416-925-0068
E-mail: phcinfo.pubcanada@pearsoned.com

UK/IRELAND:
Pearson Education
Edinburgh Gate
Harlow, Essex CM20 2JE UK
Tel: 01279 623928; Fax: 01279 414130
E-mail: enq.orders@pearsoned-ema.com

EUROPE, MIDDLE EAST & AFRICA:
Pearson Education
P.O. Box 75598
1070 AN Amsterdam, The Netherlands
Tel: 31 20 5755 800; Fax: 31 20 664 5334
E-mail: amsterdam@pearsoned-ema.com

ASIA:
Pearson Education Asia
317 Alexandra Road #04-01
IKEA Building
Singapore 159965
Tel: 65 476 4688; Fax: 65 378 0370

JAPAN:
Pearson Education
Nishi-Shinjuku, KF Building 101
8-14-24 Nishi-Shinjuku, Shinjuku-ku
Tokyo, Japan 160-0023
Tel: 81 3 3365 9001; Fax: 81 3 3365 9009

INDIA:
Pearson Education Indian Liaison Office
90 New Raidhani Enclave, Ground Floor
Delhi 110 092, India
Tel: 91 11 2059850 & 2059851
Fax: 91 11 2059852

AUSTRALIA:
Pearson Education Australia
Unit 4, Level 2
14 Aquatic Drive
Frenchs Forest, NSW 2086, Australia
Tel: 61 2 9454 2200; Fax: 61 2 9453 0089
E-mail: marketing@pearsoned.com.au

NEW ZEALAND/FIJI:
Pearson Education
46 Hillside Road
Auckland 10, New Zealand
Tel: 649 444 4968; Fax: 649 444 4957
E-mail: sales@pearsoned.co.nz

SOUTH AFRICA:
Pearson Education
P.O. Box 12122
Mill Street
Cape Town 8010 South Africa
Tel: 27 21 686 6356; Fax: 27 21 686 4590

LATIN AMERICA:
Pearson Education Latinoamerica
815 NW 57th Street Suite 484
Miami, FL 33158
Tel: 305 264 8344; Fax: 305 264 7933

Complete Training Courses

Each complete package includes the corresponding *How to Program Series* book and interactive multimedia CD-ROM Cyber Classroom. *Complete Training Courses* are perfect for anyone interested Web and e-commerce programming. They are affordable resources for college students and professionals learning programming for the first time or reinforcing their knowledge.

Each *Complete Training Course* is compatible with Windows 95, Windows 98, Windows NT and Windows 2000 and includes the following features:

Intuitive Browser-Based Interface

You'll love the *Complete Training Courses'* new browser-based interface, designed to be easy and accessible to anyone who's ever used a Web browser. Every *Complete Training Course* features the full text, illustrations and program listings of its corresponding *How to Program* book—all in full color—with full-text searching and hyperlinking.

Further Enhancements to the Deitels' Signature LIVE-CODE™ Approach

Every code sample from the main text can be found in the interactive, multimedia, CD-ROM-based *Cyber Classrooms* included in the *Complete Training Courses*. Syntax coloring of code is included for the *How to Program* books that are published in full color. Even the recent two-color and one-color books use effective multi-way syntax shading. The *Cyber Classroom* products always are in full color.

Audio Annotations

Hours of detailed, expert audio descriptions of thousands of lines of code help reinforce concepts.

Easily Executable Code

With one click of the mouse, you can execute the code or save it to your hard drive to manipulate using the programming environment of your choice. With selected *Complete Training Courses*, you can also load all of the code into a development environment such as Microsoft® Visual C++™, enabling you to modify and execute the programs with ease.

Abundant Self-Assessment Material

Practice exams test your understanding with hundreds of test questions and answers in addition to those found in the main text. Hundreds of self-review questions, all with answers, are drawn from the text; as are hundreds of programming exercises, half with answers.

www.phptr.com/phptrinteractive

Sign up now for the new *DEITEL™ Buzz Online* newsletter at:

BOOK/MULTIMEDIA PACKAGES

The Complete C++ Training Course, Fourth Edition
(0-13-100252-X)

The Complete C# Training Course
(0-13-064584-2)

The Complete e-Business & e-Commerce Programming Training Course
(0-13-089549-0)

The Complete Internet & World Wide Web Programming Training Course, Second Edition
(0-13-089550-4)

The Complete Java™ 2 Training Course, Fourth Edition
(0-13-064931-7)

The Complete Perl Training Course
(0-13-089552-0)

The Complete Python Training Course
(0-13-067374-9)

The Complete Visual Basic 6 Training Course
(0-13-082929-3)

You can run the hundreds of Visual Basic programs with the click of a mouse and automatically load them into Microsoft®'s Visual Basic® 6 Working Model edition software, allowing you to modify and execute the programs with ease.

The Complete Visual Basic .NET Training Course, Second Edition
(0-13-042530-3)

The Complete Wireless Internet & Mobile Business Programming Training Course
(0-13-062335-0)

The Complete XML Programming Training Course
(0-13-089557-1)

All of these ISBNs are retail ISBNs. College and university instructors should contact your local Prentice Hall representative or write to `cs@prenhall.com` *for the corresponding student edition ISBNs.*

If you would like to purchase the Cyber Classrooms separately...

Prentice Hall offers Multimedia Cyber Classroom CD-ROMs to accompany the *How to Program* series texts for the topics listed at right. If you have already purchased one of these books and would like to purchase a stand-alone copy of the corresponding *Multimedia Cyber Classroom*, you can make your purchase at the following Web site:

www.informit.com/cyberclassrooms

For **C++ Multimedia Cyber Classroom, 4/E**, ask for product number 0-13-100253-8

For **C# Multimedia Cyber Classroom**, ask for product number 0-13-064587-7

For **e-Business & e-Commerce Cyber Classroom**, ask for product number 0-13-089540-7

For **Internet & World Wide Web Cyber Classroom, 2/E**, ask for product number 0-13-089559-8

For **Java Multimedia Cyber Classroom, 4/E**, ask for product number 0-13-064935-X

For **Perl Multimedia Cyber Classroom**, ask for product number 0-13-089553-9

For **Python Multimedia Cyber Classroom**, ask for product number 0-13-067375-7

For **Visual Basic 6 Multimedia Cyber Classroom**, ask for product number 0-13-083116-6

For **Visual Basic .NET Multimedia Cyber Classroom, 2/E**, ask for product number 0-13-065193-1

For **XML Multimedia Cyber Classroom**, ask for product number 0-13-089555-5

For **Wireless Internet & m-Business Programming Multimedia Cyber Classroom**, ask for product number 0-13-062337-7

e-LEARNING • www.InformIT.com/deitel

Deitel & Associates, Inc. has partnered with Prentice Hall's parent company, Pearson PLC, and its information technology Web site, `InformIT.com`, to launch the Deitel InformIT kiosk at `www.InformIT.com/deitel`. The Deitel InformIT kiosk contains information on the continuum of Deitel products, including:

- **Free informational articles**
- **Deitel e-Matter**
- **Books and e-Books**
- **Web-based training**

- **Instructor-led training by Deitel & Associates**
- *Complete Training Courses/Cyber Classrooms*

Deitel & Associates is also contributing to two separate weekly InformIT e-mail newsletters.

The first is the InformIT promotional newsletter, which features weekly specials and discounts on Pearson publications. Each week a new Deitel™ product is featured along with information about our corporate instructor-led training courses and the opportunity to read about upcoming issues of our own e-mail newsletter, the DEITEL™ BUZZ ONLINE.

The second newsletter is the InformIT editorial newsletter, which contains approximately 50 new articles per week on various IT topics, including programming, advanced computing, networking, security, databases, creative media, business, Web development, software engineering, operating systems and more. Deitel & Associates contributes 2-3 articles per week pulled from our extensive existing content base or material being created during our research and development process.

Both of these publications are sent to over 750,000 registered users worldwide (for opt-in registration, visit `www.InformIT.com`).

e-LEARNING • from Deitel & Associates, Inc.

Cyber Classrooms, Web-Based Training and Course Management Systems

DEITEL is committed to continuous research and development in e-Learning.

We are pleased to announce that we have incorporated examples of Web-based training, including a five-way Macromedia® Flash™ animation of a `for` loop in Java™, into the *Java 2 Multimedia Cyber Classroom, 4/e* (which is included in *The Complete Java 2 Training Course, 4/e*). Our instructional designers and Flash animation team are developing additional simulations that demonstrate key programming concepts.

We are enhancing the Multimedia Cyber Classroom products to include more audio, pre- and post-assessment questions and Web-based labs with solutions for the benefit of professors and students alike. In addition, our Multimedia Cyber Classroom products, currently available in CD-ROM format, are being ported to Pearson's CourseCompass course-management system—*a powerful e-platform for teaching and learning.* Many Deitel materials are available in WebCT, Blackboard and CourseCompass formats for colleges, and will soon be available for various corporate learning management systems.

Sign up now for the new *DEITEL™ Buzz Online* **newsletter at:**

Future Publications

Here are some new titles we are considering for 2002/2003 release:

Computer Science Series: *Operating Systems 3/e, Data Structures in C++, Data Structures in Java, Theory and Principles of Database Systems.*

Database Series: *Oracle, SQL Server, MySQL.*

Internet and Web Programming Series: *Open Source Software Development: Apache, Linux, MySQL and PHP.*

Programming Series: *Flash™.*

.NET Programming Series: *ADO .NET with Visual Basic .NET, ASP .NET with Visual Basic .NET, ADO .NET with C#, ASP .NET with C#.*

Object Technology Series: *OOAD with the UML, Design Patterns, Java™ and XML.*

Advanced Java™ Series: *JDBC, Java 2 Enterprise Edition, Java Media Framework (JMF), Java Security and Java Cryptography (JCE), Java Servlets, Java2D and Java3D, JavaServer Pages™ (JSP), JINI and Java 2 Micro Edition™ (J2ME).*

DEITEL™ BUZZ ONLINE Newsletter

The Deitel and Associates, Inc. free opt-in newsletter includes:

- Updates and commentary on industry trends and developments
- Resources and links to articles from our published books and upcoming publications.
- Information on the Deitel publishing plans, including future publications and product-release schedules
- Support for instructors
- Resources for students
- Information on Deitel Corporate Training

To sign up for the Deitel™ Buzz Online newsletter, visit www.deitel.com /newsletter/subscribe.html.

E-Books

We are committed to providing our content in traditional print formats and in emerging electronic formats, such as e-books, to fulfill our customers' needs. Our R&D teams are currently exploring many leading-edge solutions.

Visit www.deitel.com and read the DEITEL™ BUZZ ONLINE for periodic updates.

Turn the page to find out more about Deitel & Associates!

The Deitels are the authors of best-selling Java™, C++, C#, C, Visual Basic® and Internet and World Wide Web Books and Multimedia Packages

Corporate Training Delivered Worldwide

Deitel & Associates, Inc. provides intensive, lecture-and-laboratory courses to organizations worldwide. The programming courses use our signature LIVE-CODE™ approach, presenting complete working programs.

Deitel & Associates, Inc. has trained hundreds of thousands of students and professionals worldwide through corporate training courses, public seminars, university teaching, *How to Program Series* books, *Deitel™ Developer Series* books, *Cyber Classroom Series* multimedia packages, *Complete Training Course Series* book and multimedia packages, broadcast-satellite courses and Web-based training.

Educational Consulting

Deitel & Associates, Inc. offers complete educational consulting services for corporate training programs and professional schools including:

- Curriculum design and development
- Preparation of Instructor Guides
- Customized courses and course materials
- Design and implementation of professional training certificate programs
- Instructor certification
- Train-the-trainers programs
- Delivery of software-related corporate training programs

Visit our Web site for more information on our corporate training curriculum and to purchase our training products.
www.deitel.com

Would you like to review upcoming publications?

If you are a professor or senior industry professional interested in being a reviewer of our forthcoming publications, please contact us by email at **deitel@deitel.com**. Insert "Content Reviewer" in the Subject heading.

Are you interested in a career in computer education, publishing, and training?

We are growing rapidly and have a limited number of full-time competitive opportunities available for college graduates in computer science, information systems, information technology, management information systems, English and communications, marketing, multimedia technology and other areas. Please contact us by email at **deitel@deitel.com**. Insert "Full-time Job" in the subject heading.

Are you a Boston-area college student looking for an internship?

We have a limited number of competitive summer positions and 20-hr./week school-year opportunities for computer science, English and business majors. Students work at our worldwide headquarters about 35 minutes west of Boston. We also offer full-time internships for students taking a semester off from school. This is an excellent opportunity for students looking to gain industry experience or for students who want to earn money to pay for school. Please contact us by email at **deitel@deitel.com**. Insert "Internship" in the Subject heading.

Would you like to explore contract training opportunities with us?

Deitel & Associates, Inc. is growing rapidly and is looking for contract instructors to teach software-related topics at our clients' sites in the United States and worldwide. Applicants should be experienced professional trainers or college professors. For more information, please visit **www.deitel.com** and send your resume to Abbey Deitel, President at **abbey.deitel@deitel.com**

Are you a training company in need of quality course materials?

Corporate training companies worldwide use our *Complete Training Course Series* book and multimedia packages, and our *Web-Based Training Series* courses in their classes. We have extensive ancillary instructor materials for each of our products. For more details, please visit **www.deitel.com** or contact Abbey Deitel, President at **abbey.deitel@deitel.com**

Sign up now for the new *DEITEL™ Buzz Online* newsletter at:

PROGRAMMING LANGUAGE TEXTBOOK AUTHORS

DEITEL & Associates Inc.

Check out our Corporate On-site Seminars...

Java
- Java for Nonprogrammers
- Java for VB/COBOL Programmers
- Java for C/C++ Programmers

Advanced Java
- Java™ Web Services
- J2ME™
- Graphics (2D & 3D)
- JavaServer Pages (JSP)
- Servlets
- Enterprise JavaBeans (EJB™)
- Jiro™
- Jini
- Advanced Swing GUI
- RMI
- Web Services
- JDBC
- Messaging with JMS
- CORBA
- JavaBeans™

Internet & World Wide Web Programming
- Client-Side Internet & World Wide Web Programming
- Server-Side Internet & World Wide Web Programming
- JavaScript™
- VBScript®
- XHTML
- Dynamic HTML
- Active Server Pages (ASP)
- XML, XSLT™
- Perl/CGI, Python, PHP

C/C++
- C and C++ Programming: Part 1 (for Nonprogrammers)
- C and C++ Programming: Part 2 (for Non-C Programmers)
- C++ and Object-Oriented Programming
- Advanced C++ and Object-Oriented Programming

XML
- XML Programming for programmers with Java, Web or other programming experience

.NET Programming
- C# Programming
- Advanced C# Programming
- Visual Basic .NET Programming
- Advanced Visual Basic .NET Programming
- Visual C++ .NET Programming
- Advanced Visual C++ .NET Programming

Wireless Programming
- Wireless Programming
- WAP/WML/WMLScript
- J2ME
- i-mode and cHTML
- XHTML Basic

Other Topics
- Object-Oriented Analysis and Design with the UML
- SQL Server

Deitel & Associates has delivered training for the following organizations:

3Com
Argonne National Laboratories
Art Technology
Arthur Andersen
Avid Technology
Bank of America
BEA Systems
Boeing
Bristol-Myers Squibb
Cambridge Technology Partners
Cap Gemini
Compaq
Concord Communications
Dell
Dunn & Bradstreet
Eastman Kodak
EMC²
Federal Reserve Bank of Chicago
Fidelity
GE
General Dynamics Electric Boat Corporation
Gillette
GTE
Hitachi
IBM
JPL Laboratories
Lockheed Martin
Lucent
Motorola
NASA's Kennedy Space Center
NASDAQ
National Oceanographic and Atmospheric Administration
Nortel Networks
Omnipoint
One Wave
Open Market
Oracle
Progress Software
Rogue Wave Software
Schlumberger
Stratus
Sun Microsystems
Symmetrix
The Foxboro Company
Thompson Technology
Tivoli Systems
Toys "R" Us
U.S. Army at Ft. Leavenworth
Visa International
Washington Post Newsweek Interactive
White Sands Missile Range
and many others...

For Detailed Course Descriptions, Visit Our Web Site: www.deitel.com

Through our worldwide network of trainers, we would be happy to attempt to arrange corporate on-site seminars for you in virtually any software-related field.

For Additional Information about Our Corporate On-Site and Public Seminars, contact:

Abbey Deitel, President
Email: abbey.deitel@deitel.com
Phone: (978) 461-5880/Fax: (978) 461-5884

www.deitel.com/newsletter/subscribe.html

Announcing the *new* DEITEL™ DEVELOPER SERIES!

Deitel & Associates is recognized worldwide for its best-selling *How to Program* series of books for college and university students and its signature LIVE-CODE™ approach to teaching programming languages. Now, for the first time, Deitel & Associates brings its proven teaching methods to a new series of books specifically designed for professionals.

THREE TYPES OF BOOKS FOR THREE DISTINCT AUDIENCES:

A Technical Introduction	**A Technical Introduction** books provide programmers, technical managers, project managers and other technical professionals with introductions to broad new technology areas.
A Programmer's Introduction	**A Programmer's Introduction** books offer focused treatments of programming fundamentals for practicing programmers. These books are also appropriate for novices.
For Experienced Programmers	**For Experienced Programmers** books are for experienced programmers who want a detailed treatment of a programming language or technology. These books contain condensed introductions to programming language fundamentals and provide extensive intermediate level coverage of high-end topics.

Sign up now for the new *DEITEL™ Buzz Online* newsletter at:

Java™ Web Services for Experienced Programmers

© 2003, 700 pp., paper (0-13-046134-2)

Java™ Web Services for Experienced Programmers from the DEITEL™ Developer Series provides the experienced Java programmer with 103 LIVE-CODE™ examples and covers industry standards including XML, SOAP, WSDL and UDDI. Learn how to build and integrate Web services using the Java API for XML RPC, the Java API for XML Messaging, Apache Axis and the Java Web Services Developer Pack. Develop and deploy Web services on several major Web services platforms. Register and discover Web services through public registries and the Java API for XML Registries. Build Web Services clients for several platforms, including J2ME. Significant Web Services case studies also are included.

Web Services: A Technical Introduction

© 2003, 400 pp., paper (0-13-046135-0)

Web Services: A Technical Introduction from the DEITEL™ Developer Series familiarizes programmers, technical managers and project managers with key Web services concepts, including what Web services are and why they are revolutionary. The book covers the business case for Web services—the underlying technologies, ways in which Web services can provide competitive advantages and opportunities for Web services-related lines of business. Readers learn the latest Web-services standards, including XML, SOAP, WSDL and UDDI; learn about Web services implementations in .NET and Java; benefit from an extensive comparison of Web services products and vendors; and read about Web services security options. Although this is not a programming book, the appendices show .NET and Java code examples to demonstrate the structure of Web services applications and documents. In addition, the book includes numerous case studies describing ways in which organizations are implementing Web services to increase efficiency, simplify business processes, create new revenue streams and interact better with partners and customers.